TEACHING METHOD FOR SIXTH GRADE

My Music Journal

FLORENTINA ALEXANDRU

APOLLO
PUBLISHING

www.mymusicjournal.org

PREFACE

Audio and video files can be found on our website **MyMusicJournal.org** and are publicly available examples intended for music education. All audio and video recordings are labeled per grade level. To access the recordings, go to MyMusicJournal.org, hover over the Courses tab, and then select the grade level. Please click the audio or video recording as it is labeled inside the music textbook. This website contains audio/video recordings created by Florentina Alexandru and external weblinks to audition classical pieces from famous composers. These recordings are intended to help students, teachers, and parents to follow along with the material in My Music Journal textbooks, such as practicing a rhythm, solfege, or learning to sing a song. For this reason, a parent or teacher must be present when a child accesses this material.

Standard Disclaimer for External Links

All external links are provided for convenience and informational purposes only. No external links found within the My Music Journal website constitute an endorsement or approval of any of the products, services, or content owned by the corporation, organization, or individual owners of these websites. My Music Journal is not responsible for the accuracy, legality, or content found at these external websites or subsequent links from these sites.

My Music Journal makes no guarantee that any material provided for download, viewing, or streaming on any external website is within the public domain in any specific country. Therefore, My Music Journal assumes no legal responsibility or liability for the copyright status of such materials.

Music Teachers

Please email us at mmj@mymusicjournal.org and request **Curriculum Outline and Assessments.**

Music Education - My Music Journal
Teaching Method for Sixth Grade

Published in the United States by Apollo Publishing
5415 Lake Howell Rd. No 114
Winter Park, Florida 32789
United States of America
www.mymusicjournal.org
©2020 Florentina Alexandru
All rights reserved.

ISBN# 978-1-7339987-6-5
Printed in China

Warning! Copyright law protects the contents of this publication. Copying or reproducing the contents of this publication by any method is a violation of copyright law. For each violation, anyone who reproduces copyrighted material faces serious fines and assessments. Without the author's written permission, no part of this book may be copied, adapted, organized, stored in a retrieval system, or transmitted by any means.

Table of Contents

The Star-Spangled Banner..4

Vocal Development (2 Lessons)
Vocal Development - Singing Posture - Aura Lea.....................................5
Singing Skills - Vocal Warm-ups..6
Singing Skills - Vocal Warm-ups..7
All Quiet Along the Potomac..8

Rhythm (11 Lessons)
The Treble Clef and Staff..9
Brennan on the Moor...10
Measures & Bar Lines..11
Rhythm Activity..12
Note Values..13
Solfege - Jingle Bells..14
How to Count and Sing in Cut Time Signature.......................................15
How to Count and Sing in Cut Time Signature.......................................16
America, the Beautiful...17
How to Count and Sing in Common Time Signature..............................18
Common Time and Cut Time (Alla Breve)..19
Hildegard von Bingen..20
Coloring Time...Fun...Fun...21
Hildegard von Bingen Quiz...22
Botany Bay...23
Time Signature 2/4 and 3/4...24
Time Signature 2/4 and 3/4...25
Henry Martin..26
Eighth Note & Eighth Rest Sixteenth Note and Sixteenth Rest............27
Eighth Note & Eighth Rest Sixteenth Note and Sixteenth Rest............28
Rosebud in June..29
Let's compose a little song...30
Elements of Music-Rhythm..31
Tie, Fermata, Slur, Phrase Mark..32
Syncopation, Upbeat...33
The Battle of New Orleans..34
Eighth Note Triplets..35
Francesca Caccini...36
Coloring Time...Fun...Fun...37
Francesca Caccini Quiz..38
3/8 and 6/8 Time Signature..39
Solfege...40
Ostinato Solfege..41
Snare Drum Exercise/Rhythm Composition...42
Fennario...43
Bolero...44
Sol - Mi Duet..45
Let's Practice More Fun Rhythm...46
Music Theory Crossword..47
Note Values..48
Time Signature..49

Assessment	50
Poor Old Crow	51
Let's Learn Piano	52
Happy, Scary, Halloween!	53
Henry Purcell	54
Coloring Time...Fun...Fun	55
Henry Purcell Quiz	56
The Origins of Blues Music	57
Backwater Blues	58
Brown's Ferry Blues	59
Song Composition	60

Melody (5 Lessons)

Melody	61
Musical Intervals	62
Musical Intervals	63
Musical Intervals	64
Wait for the Wagon	65
Piano Lesson	66
C Major and A minor Chord	67
Major & Minor Third Interval	68
Thanksgiving Day	69
Swing Low, Sweet Chariot	70
Slurs, Ties and Phrases	71
Treble Clef (G Clef)	72
Bass Clef (F Clef)	73
Treble Clef and Bass Clef Notes	74
Grand Staff	75
Grand Staff	76
Key Signatures	77
Accidentals - Sharps, Flat and Natural	78
Enharmonic Notes	79
Major and Minor Pentatonic Scale	80
Deck The Halls	81
Twelve Days Of Christmas	82

Tone Color (2 Lessons)

Orchestral Instruments	83
Orchestral Instruments	84
Keyboard Instruments	85
Making Music	86
Vocal Types and Ranges	87
Vocal Types and Ranges	88
Reading Treble Clef and Bass Clef Notes	89
Beats Counting Exercise	90

Tempo (3 Lessons)

Watkins Ale	91
Brennan on the Moor	92
Fanny Mendelssohn	93
Coloring Time...Fun...Fun	94
Fanny Mendelssohn Quiz	95
Step and Leap Piano Exercise	96

What is tempo in music?......97
Tempo Crossword Puzzle......98
Song Composition......99
Happy Birthday......100
Tempo Markings and Articulation Symbols......101

Dynamics (2 Lessons)
Dynamic Markings......102
Darcy Farrow......103
Raindrops-Piano Lesson......104
Solfege......105
Repeat Signs - D.C. al Coda - D.S. al Fine - D.S. al Coda......106
Repeat Signs - D.C. al Coda - D.S. al Fine - D.S. al Coda......107
Major and Minor Scale......108
Intervals Assignment......109
Danny Boy (Londonderry Air)......110
Danny Boy (Londonderry Air)......111

Form (2 Lessons)
Theme And Variations......112
Theme And Variations......113
Elephant Song......114
Rondo Form......115
Rondo Form......116
Rondo Form......117
Opera, Operetta, Musical Theater, Concerto, and Oratorio......118
Opera, Operetta, Musical Theater, Concerto, and Oratorio......119
Opera, Operetta, Musical Theater, Concerto, and Oratorio......120
Opera, Operetta, Musical Theater, Concerto, and Oratorio......121
Ear Training Exercises......122

Harmony/Texture (5 Lessons)
Major Chords and Major Triads......123
Minor Chords and Minor Triads......124
Scale Degree Names......125
Chord Progression......126
Harmonizing A Melody & Composing A Melody......127
Santa Lucia......128
Down by the Sally Gardens......129
Compose a melody over the existing harmony......130
What is Ostinato?......131
What is a Round?......132
What are Partner Songs?......133
Descant/Counter-melody......134
What is a two-part harmony?......135
Old Folks At Home......136

Style (4 Lessons)
Popular music styles......137
Research Project-music styles......138
Oregon My Oregon......139
Brazilian Music Styles......140
Brazilian Music Styles......141
I Love You California......142

Word Search	143
The Yellow Rose Of Texas	144
Japanese Music Styles	145
Alabama	146
Here We Have Idaho	147
Go, Mississippi/Carolina	148
O, Fair New Mexico	149
My Oklahoma Home, It Blowed Away	150
Tennessee/The West Virginia Hills	151
Going to Kentucky/The Old North State	152
Old Folks at Home	153
Meet Me in St. Louis	154
Home Means Nevada	155
Utah, We Love Thee	156
Glossary of Musical Terms	157

I am excited for the year ahead and can't wait to start writing

My Music Journal!

I look forward to learning how to play a musical instrument and even write my music. I want to explore the meaning of tempo, harmony, and pitch; learn about music composers, rhythm, dynamics, forms, genres, and texture to become a well-rounded musician. I have a feeling this year is going to be extra fun thanks to

My Music Journal!

Student Name: _____

Dear students, parents, and teachers,

Music education is a continuous, systematic, and complex activity that begins in childhood and continues throughout your entire life. Did you ever ask what a life without music would be? Have you ever wondered how strange it would be to rock a baby without the famous "Lullaby," composed by Johannes Brahms?

What would it be like to dance without music—without body movement, without the accompaniment of musical instruments (drums, shakers, triangle, bells, recorder, etc.)?

Each piece of music—heard or read—brings new ideas and facts, which increase children's spiritual heritage and their ability to see, understand, feel, and appreciate. Children at very young ages demonstrate instinctual impulses to sing, regardless of their cultural environment.

Rhythm, for instance, is naturally expressed through breathing, walking, and most importantly, through our heartbeat. Human vocal cords are uniquely designed for a wide range of sounds, which helps express musical melody.

Music education is a necessary means through which students can discover and express their own emotions. Music classes provide students the opportunity to grow emotionally, mentally, and physically, as well as helping them with necessary life skills such as self-discipline, self-expression, responsibility, patience, and teamwork. Music education is a way to instill the love of music that will remain with students for the rest of their lives.

Pythagoras is widely known as the "Father of Mathematics" and the "Father of Geometry," but few know that he is also credited as "Father of Music" and the "Father of Harmonics." He discovered that musical intervals could be used for healing purposes and eventually became the first person to prescribe music as medicine. He applied the principles of harmonics to creative work—such as art and architecture—and extended them to multiple facets of life such as running a government, raising a family, friendship, and personal development.

Pythagoras taught that music could never be approached purely for the sake of entertainment. Rather, he saw music as an expression of "Harmonia," the divine concept that brings harmony to disorder and discord. Thus, music has a dual value, similar to mathematics, as it enables people to witness and comprehend various nature structures. Furthermore, he taught that if utilized properly, music can:

a) Bring harmony to faculties of the soul.
b) Compose and purify the mind.
c) Heal the physical body, thus restoring and maintaining perfect health.

Everyone, you included, has talent. All you need to do is allow it to shine.
Best of luck!

Florentina Alexandru

The Star-Spangled Banner

Lyrics by Francis Scott Key
Music by John Stafford Smith

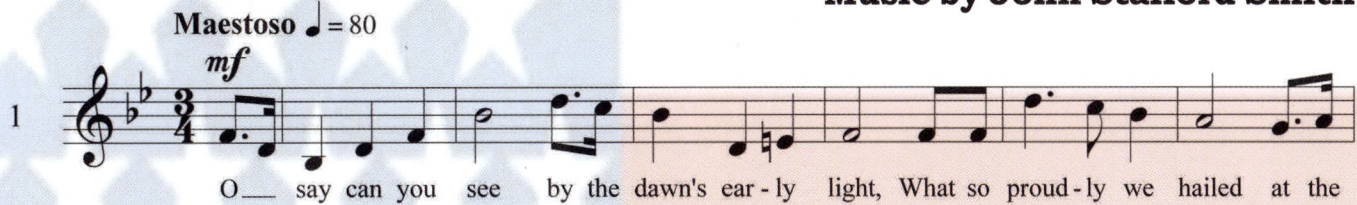

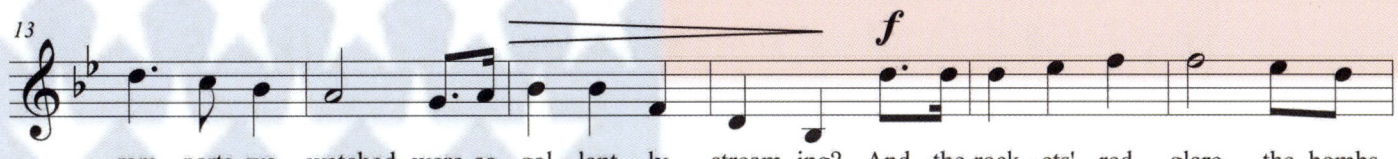

Oh, say can you see by the dawn's early light
What so proudly we hailed at the twilight's last gleaming?
Whose broad stripes and bright stars thru the perilous fight,
O'er the ramparts we watched were so gallantly streaming?
And the rocket's red glare, the bombs bursting in air,
Gave proof through the night that our flag was still there.
Oh, say does that star-spangled banner yet wave
O'er the land of the free and the home of the brave?

🔊 **Audio G01**

Listen quietly to "The Star-Spangled Banner."
Learn and sing the national anthem of the United States.

Vocal Development
Singing Posture

🔊 Audio G02

Aura Lea

Andante ♩ = c. 80

Traditional Song

When the black-bird in the Spring, 'On the wil-low tree, Sat and rocked, I heard him sing, Sing-ing Au-ra Lea.

In thy blush the rose was born, Mu-sic, when you spake, Through thine a-zure eye the morn, Spark-ling seemed to break.

Au-ra Lea, Au-ra Lea, with gol-den hair; Sun-shine came a-long with thee, And swal-lows in the air.

Au-ra Lea, Au-ra Lea, Birds of crim-son wing, Ne-ver song have sung to me, As in that sweet spring.

- The general rule is, to begin with, the 'head voice' and bring it down into the 'chest voice.' Finally, have patience! Most of the students whom you think will never get it' will find their voice when they are ready. Continue to work for that breakthrough.
  - The key elements of good posture are:
    - a) Extended spine
    - b) Shoulders back and down
    - c) Relaxed body
    - d) Slightly lifted sternum (or rib cage)
    - e) Keep your head level
- Learn to sing the song with proper interpretation and pronunciation.
- Clap the beats out loud while singing the song.

Singing Skills

Singing can be music's most physically demanding skill. Use these basic daily exercises with your students to help build their vocal muscles for better tone, pitch, and power. Since singing uses the entire body, the first part of the warm-up is not a musical exercise. Instead, it involves some basic, slow stretches of the neck, arms, legs, and back. Lead your class in doing this first. Next, have them take some breaths and work on using their diaphragm to support the air.

Let us work on our first exercise to produce this "ssss, mmm, rrr" sound, but focusing on making the sound stable and keeping the volume constant. Without breath, we can not sing! To vocalize even the slightest sustained word or note, we need breath, and breath support is vital in helping us produce a well-supported and stable sound.

Vowel Warm-Ups

The warm-up starts on middle C and is sung on one-octave arpeggios, ascending and descending chromatically. Have students work through the entire range singing on 'Ah,' then repeat the exercise on 'Eh,' and continue in this way through all the vowel sounds (Ah, Eh, Ee, Oh, Ooh).

There are many variations on this warm-up, including consonants such as Maw, Meh, Mi, Moh, Moo; Kaw, Keh, Ki, Koh, Koo; Law, Leh, Lee, Loh, Loo; Naw, Neh, Nee, Noh, and Noo.

Physical activity is crucial to a complete choral warm-up. It engages and energizes the body. Middle school students should feel and experience the level to which their bodies must be engaged to support a healthy sound. A verbal explanation of this concept is not enough. An example of physical warm-ups includes the following:

- Shakeout: shaking each limb and counting to 8, then 7, then 6, and so on.
- Echo clapping and movement: tapping your shoulders or nose, patting your knees, funny dance moves, and more.
- Stretching
- Four behind me: exactly like echo clapping and movement, but the pace is much faster. The leader moves to the next four-count pattern demonstration while the choir is starting the echo.

Follow the physical warm-up with breathing exercises. Breathing is the foundation of a beautiful choral tone, and it must be practiced regularly.

Teach the look and feel of a deep and full breath in as many ways as possible—with demonstration, description, and metaphor.

Every student must understand the different parts of their voice. Our voices are split primarily into head voice, chest voice, and a mixture of the two (mixed voice).

Young girls should be singing almost exclusively in their head voices, only occasionally mixing in a chest voice sound. For boys, the divide between voices is much more obvious and trickier to maneuver.

- Lips are closed, but teeth slightly open. All in one breath, slide gently down-up-down-up, then down by steps.
- Repeat one step higher, five or six times.

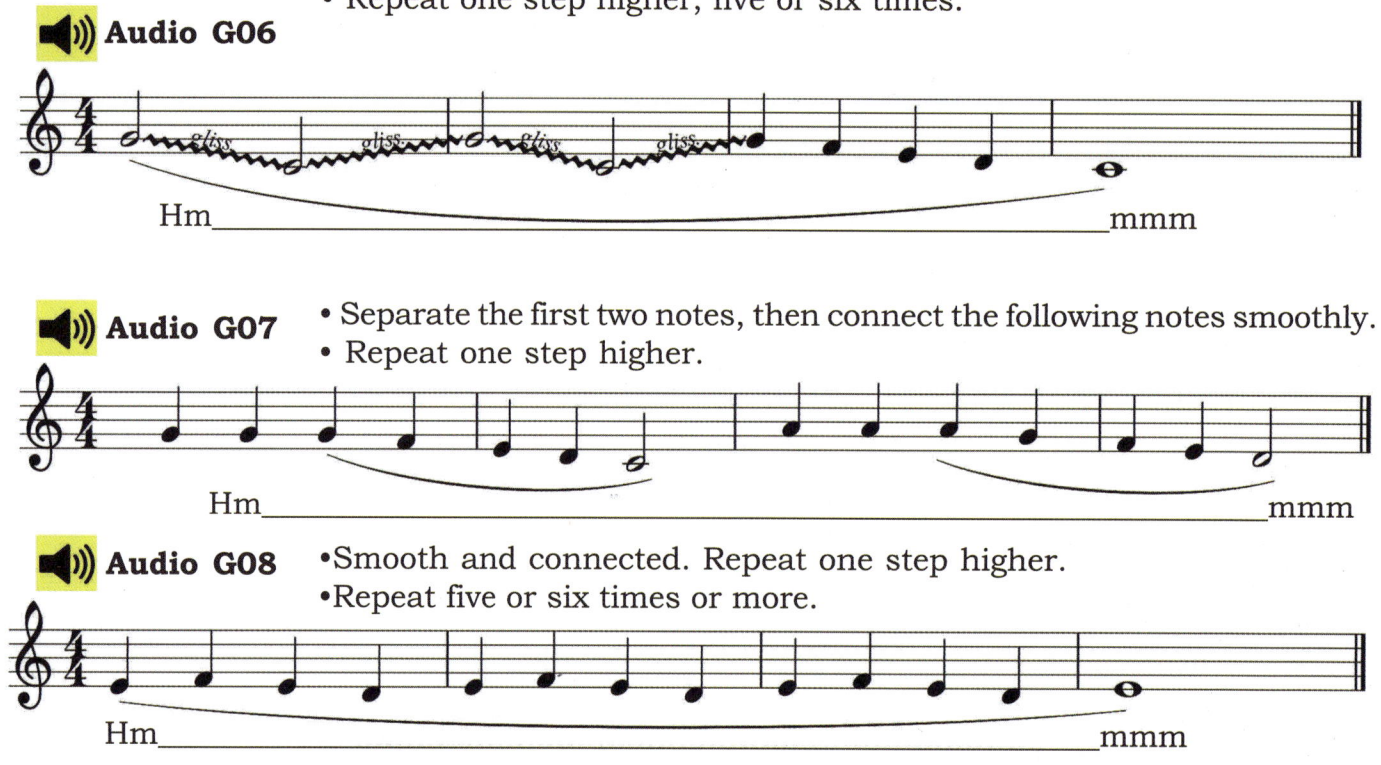

- Separate the first two notes, then connect the following notes smoothly.
- Repeat one step higher.

- Smooth and connected. Repeat one step higher.
- Repeat five or six times or more.

Yawn-Sigh Technique

Just yawn (take in the air) with your mouth closed for this quick vocal exercise. Exhale through the nose, then, as if you were sighing. This will help your voice relax and enhance its range.

Humming Warm-ups

Humming is one of the best vocal warm-ups because it does not put much strain on your vocal cords. Place the tip of your tongue behind your front teeth at the bottom and hum each musical note up and down while keeping your mouth closed. Each note should sound like "hmmm" — including the "h" sound is less taxing on your voice.

All Quiet Along the Potomac

Audio G09

Traditional Song

"All qui- et a- long the Po- to- mac," they say, Ex- cept now and then a stray

pic- ket Is shot as he walks on his beat to and fro by a ri- fle- man hid in the

thic- ket. 'Tis no- thing! A pri- vate or two now and then Will not count in the news of the

bat- tle, Not an of- fi- cer lost! on- ly one of the men, Moa- ning out, all a- lone, the death

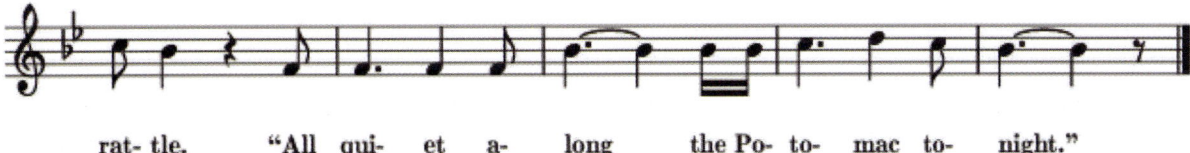

rat- tle. "All qui- et a- long the Po- to- mac to- night."

All quiet along the Potomac tonight,
Where the soldiers lie peacefully dreaming,
Their tents in the rays of the clear autumn moon,
O'er the light of the watch fires, are gleaming;
There's only the sound of the lone sentry's tread
As he tramps from the rock to the fountain,
And thinks of the two in the low trundle bed,
Far away in the cot on the mountain.

His musket falls slack, and his face, dark and grim,
Grows gentle with memories tender,
As he mutters a prayer for the children asleep,
For their mother, may Heaven defend her.
The moon seems to shine just as brightly as then
That night when the love yet unspoken
Leaped up to his lips when low-murmured vows
Were pledged to be ever unbroken.

Then drawing his sleeve roughly over his eyes,
He dashes off tears that are welling,
And gathers his gun closer up to its place
As if to keep down the heart-swelling.
He passes the fountain, the blasted pine tree,
The footstep is lagging and weary;
Yet onward he goes, through the broad belt of light,
Toward the shades of the forest so dreary-

Hark! Was it the night wind that rustled the leaves?
Was it moonlight so wondrously flashing?
It looks like a rifle—"Ah! Mary, good-bye!"
And the lifeblood is ebbing and splashing.
All quiet along the Potomac tonight,
No sound saves the rush of the river;
While soft falls the dew on the face of the dead-
The picket's off duty forever.

Sing the song correctly with lips slightly rounded, ensuring a clean emission, and loosen up your body for a perfect position. Sing the song while having students maintain the beat (patting their knees or doing other body movements that do not interfere with quality singing) to ensure that the sustained notes are held out at full value. Without speaking, clap the rhythm of a musical phrase from the song and ask the students to follow up with an echo. After they clap, make them identify the words of the song that match up with the rhythm.

The Treble Clef and Staff

At the beginning of each staff there is a clef. The treble clef or G clef looks like this:

The treble clef establishes the note G on the second line of the treble staff.

The five lines and four spaces are called the musical staff. We number these lines and spaces from the bottom to the top. Each line and space represent a different pitch.

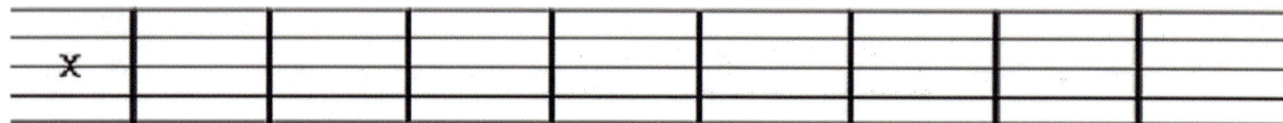

1. On the staff, mark an 'X' in the following locations.

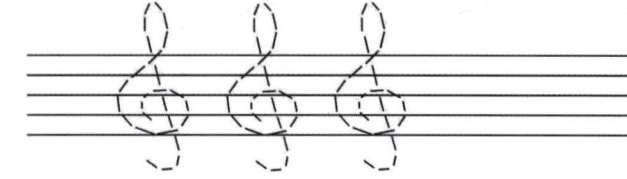

Line 3   Line 5   Space 2   Space 4   Line 1   Space 3   Line 4   Space 1   Line 2

2. By tracing over the dotted lines, try drawing the treble clef symbol. Then draw an additional five of your own.

In the beginning, you may wish to make up a saying that uses the letters of the spaces and lines to help you remember the lines and spaces. For example, remembering the lines of the treble clef: Every Good Boy Does Fine. Spaces of Treble Clef: FACE – FACE

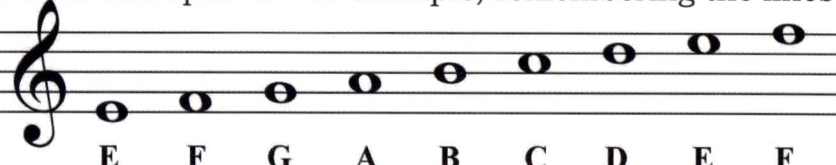

E   F   G   A   B   C   D   E   F

3. At the beginning of the staff, draw the treble clef and name the indicated notes.

4. At the beginning of the staff, draw the treble clef and draw the indicated notes. If the note can be drawn on more than one place on the staff, choose which one you want to write.

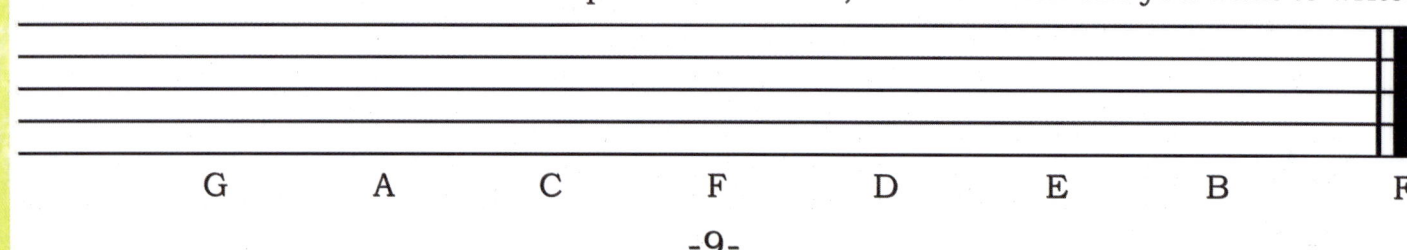

G   A   C   F   D   E   B   F

Brennan on the Moor

🔊 Audio G10

Traditional Song

It's of a fear-less high-way man, a sto-ry I will tell. His name was Wil-lie

Bren-nan in Ire-land he did dwell, And on the Li-me-rick Moun-tains he com-

menced his wild ca-reer, Where ma-ny a weal-thy gen-tle-man be-fore him shook with

fear And it's Bren-nan on the moor, Bren-nan on the moor, Oh,

bold and un-daun-ted stood Bren-nan on the moor.

Have the students sing the song once and evaluate their ability to sing in one breath each sentence. (If possible, record song singing.) Tell them that they can improve their singing of the song by focusing on breath control.

Ask students to stand with their shoulders down and their heads straight, hands-on their lower ribs. To feel the muscles that support breathing, have them bend over and pant. Explain that inhaling and exhaling are controlled by diaphragm muscles, and that breathing for singing needs to be much deeper than talking to support the singing tone. Have students stand up straight and, while lightly touching their lower ribs with their hands, inhale silently and without moving; to a count of five, ask them to relax their throats so that they feel space in the back of their mouth, almost as if they were yawning. Then, ask them to inhale as if they were sipping juice through a straw and filling the waist with an inner tube.

Let students sing this song again and take the time for the deep breath described above before each sentence, as it is four. Repeat the song and ask students to take in as much air before each sentence, but only count two.

Have the students sing the song again. Ask them to breathe in just one count this time. Have them reassess their ability to sing long phrases well, now that they are deeply and correctly breathing through each sentence. Repeat the above steps if necessary.

Let students sing the song once more, having them raise their hands every time they breathe so that you can see if they can sing each sentence in one breath.

Have the class set the criteria to judge the song's accurate performance (that is, with correct pitches and rhythms). Then, in small (2-4) groups, have students practice the song, working for pitch and rhythm accuracy and good breath control. Have students make suggestions for improving their singing within these groups.

Ask students once again to sing the song altogether and to assess their performance. (When possible, record their singing. Have students compare it to a recording of their singing at the beginning of the class.)

Circle all musical notes A in the song.

Measures & Bar Lines

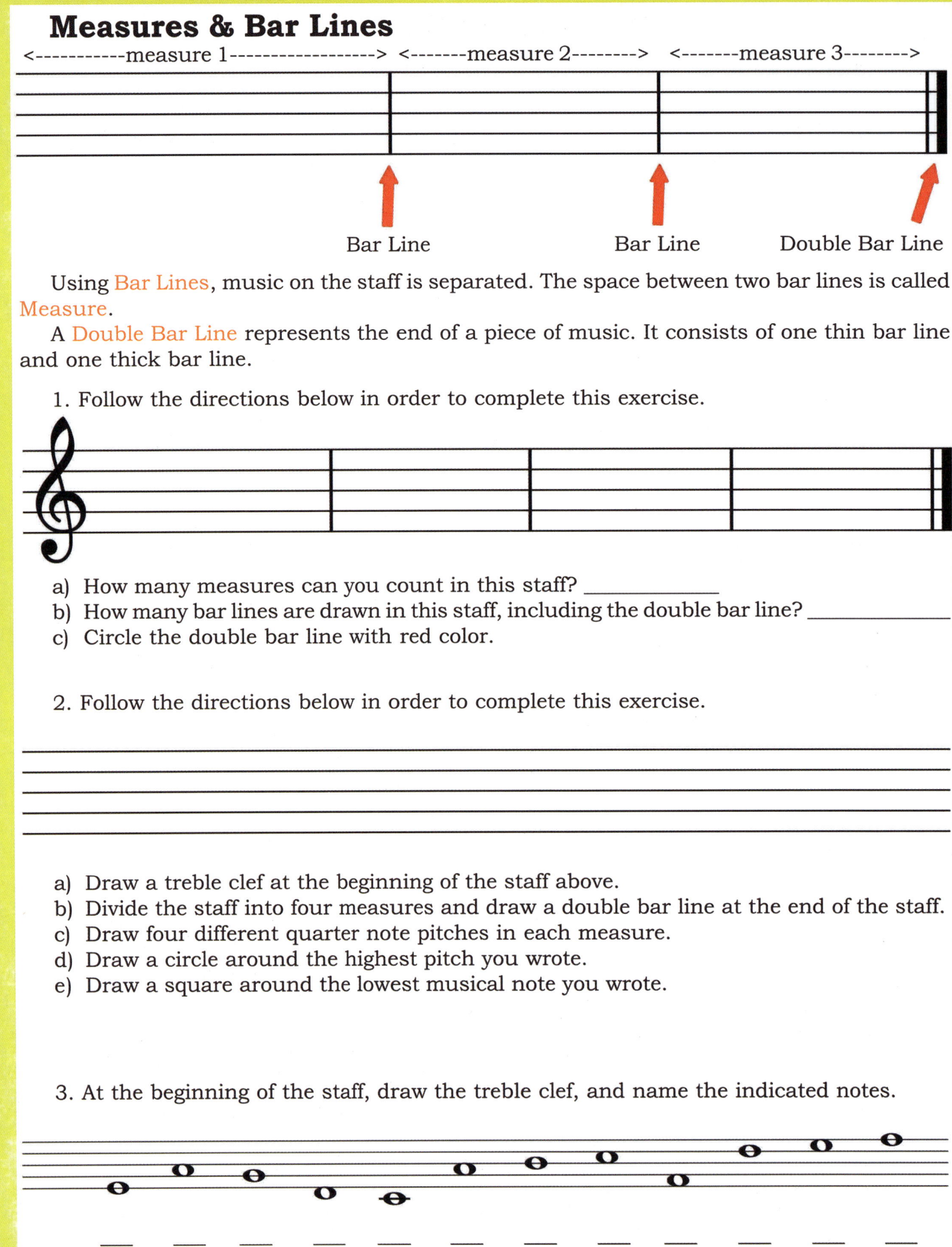

Using **Bar Lines**, music on the staff is separated. The space between two bar lines is called **Measure**.

A **Double Bar Line** represents the end of a piece of music. It consists of one thin bar line and one thick bar line.

1. Follow the directions below in order to complete this exercise.

   a) How many measures can you count in this staff? _____
   b) How many bar lines are drawn in this staff, including the double bar line? _____
   c) Circle the double bar line with red color.

2. Follow the directions below in order to complete this exercise.

   a) Draw a treble clef at the beginning of the staff above.
   b) Divide the staff into four measures and draw a double bar line at the end of the staff.
   c) Draw four different quarter note pitches in each measure.
   d) Draw a circle around the highest pitch you wrote.
   e) Draw a square around the lowest musical note you wrote.

3. At the beginning of the staff, draw the treble clef, and name the indicated notes.

Rhythm Activity

🔊 Audio G11

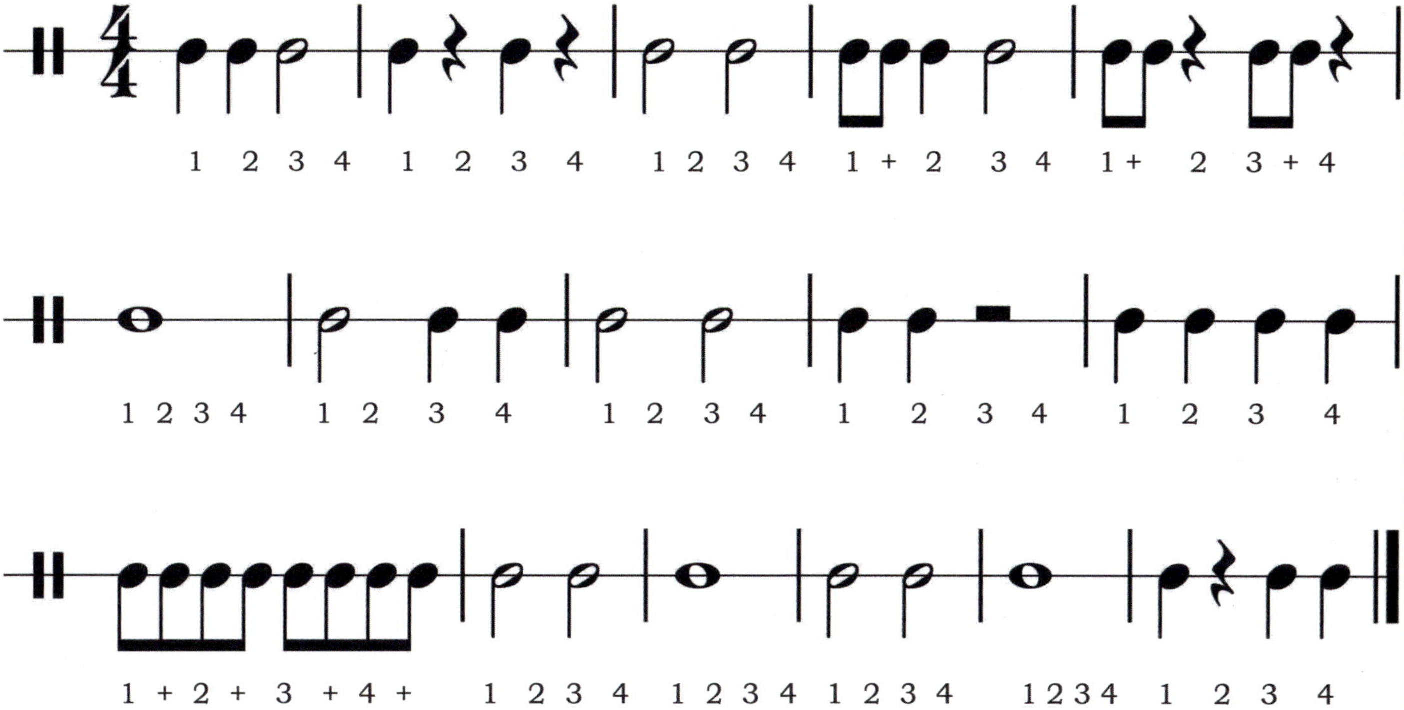

| Eighth Note | Quarter Note | Half Note | Whole Note |
| 1/2 Beat | 1 Beat | 2 Beats | 4 Beats |

One of the most critical abilities for developing a strong sense of rhythm is vocalization counting. Students will not understand how the rhythm is broken without it, and they will find it difficult to recreate musical rhythms that they see printed on the page. It is very important that vocal rhythm counting be used frequently.

• Clap (or play on a rhythm instrument like drums, shakers, or tambourine) this short rhythm.
• Rhythm has two components: the pulse and the rhythm that goes over the pulse. Establish the tempo first. Model the tempo and counting style you want your students to use during the rhythmic exercise. Explain that the students are to count the rhythm out loud.
• Practice the rhythm at a slow tempo, feeling four beats per measure.
• Determine which beats are weak and which are strong.
• Practice with a metronome.

Note Values

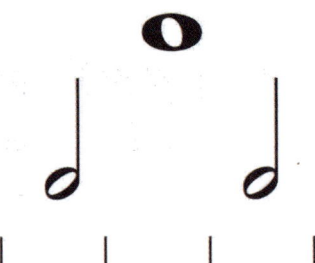 **Whole Note** (one whole note = 4 quarter notes)   **Whole note rest**

 **Half Note** (two half notes = 4 quarter notes)   **Half note rest**

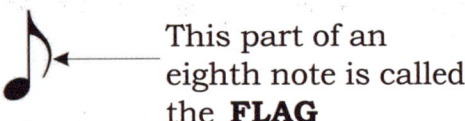 **Quarter Note** (four quarter notes = 1 whole note)   **Quarter note rest**

Eighth Note (eight eighth notes = 1 whole note)   **Eighth note rest**

This part of an eighth note is called the **FLAG**

Eighth notes and sixteenth notes can be grouped together by using **BEAMS**

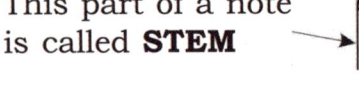 This part of a note is called **STEM**

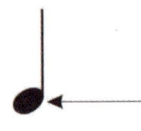 This part of a note is called **NOTEHEAD**

A dot placed after a note makes it longer by half of its own length.

 Fill in the missing notes.

-13-

Solfege - Jingle Bells

Sight-reading music is not meant to be perfect. And just like anything else you do, the more you practice, the better you get! So, do not focus on the mistakes you make during the performance, and do not feel like you have to stop and correct them. Just keep going, do the best you can, and remember that by testing your skills as a musician, you are going to make yourself better in the long run.

Solfege - Jingle Bells

Before You Start
• Orient yourself
• Check out the key signature. What kind of key are you in? Is this a major or minor key? How many beats are there in each measure? Is there an indication of a tempo?

Scan
• Scan the piece carefully in order to root out surprises. Is it in a mixed meter? Are there tempo changes? Any hidden high notes? All this is useful information.

Get Your Note
• Play Audio G12 for the solfege and sing along.

Tap the Beat
• Establish the beat by tapping your foot. This will help you stay in rhythm. It is better to practice singing with a metronome to get your rhythms as accurate as possible.

Practice sight singing Solfege-Jingle Bells. Circle all eighth notes. Examine all note values in this solfege and discuss it with your teacher or colleague. How many measures are in this solfege? What is the time signature?

How to Count and Sing in Cut Time Signature

When we have a 4/4 time signature, the quarter note gets the beat because 4 is the bottom number.

When we have a 2/2 time signature or Cut Time, the half note gets the beat, so the quarter note will only get 1/2 of a beat."When we divide a half note into two equals, we end up with two-quarter notes - so one-quarter note = only 1/2 of a beat now, instead of a whole beat in 4/4 time.

Remember that you have to make sure that you are giving the correct type of note the beat with each different time signature, and when that changes, so do your note values. Just cut everything in half when you play in **Cut Time**.

Once you master **Cut Time**, you will find it much easier to sing or play specific types of notes. Let us see what those are in the next step.

The bottom number in the time signature tells us what note value is equal to one beat. When the bottom number is 4, then the quarter note is equal to one beat. This lesson features a time signature in which the half note is equal to one beat. 2/2 is also called **Cut Time or Alla Breve**. It is represented with the symbol of a letter **C** with a line running through it, as shown above. The top number indicates that there are two beats in a measure and the bottom number indicates that the half note is equal to one beat.

The relative length of each note value remains the same, regardless of the time signature. For example, a whole note is always equal to the length of two half notes tied together. However, the number of beats a note is played in depends on the time signature. The chart below shows how many beats each note will be played in Cut Time. The patterns in this lesson demonstrate how they will be counted.

In Cut Time one half note equals 1 beat, therefore:

One whole note = two half notes = 2 beats

𝐨 = ♩ ♩ (tied)

One dotted half note = a half note tied to a quarter note = 1 and a 1/2 beat

𝅗𝅥. = 𝅗𝅥 ♩ (tied)

One dotted quarter note = a quarter note tied to an eighth note = 3/4 of a beat

♩. = ♩ ♪ (tied)

One quarter note = half of a half note = 1/2 a beat

♩ = half of a 𝅗𝅥

One eighth note = one fourth of a half note = 1/4 of a beat

♪ = one-fourth of a 𝅗𝅥

Practice the following rhythm exercise. Practice with a metronome and counting the beats out loud.

🔊 Audio G13

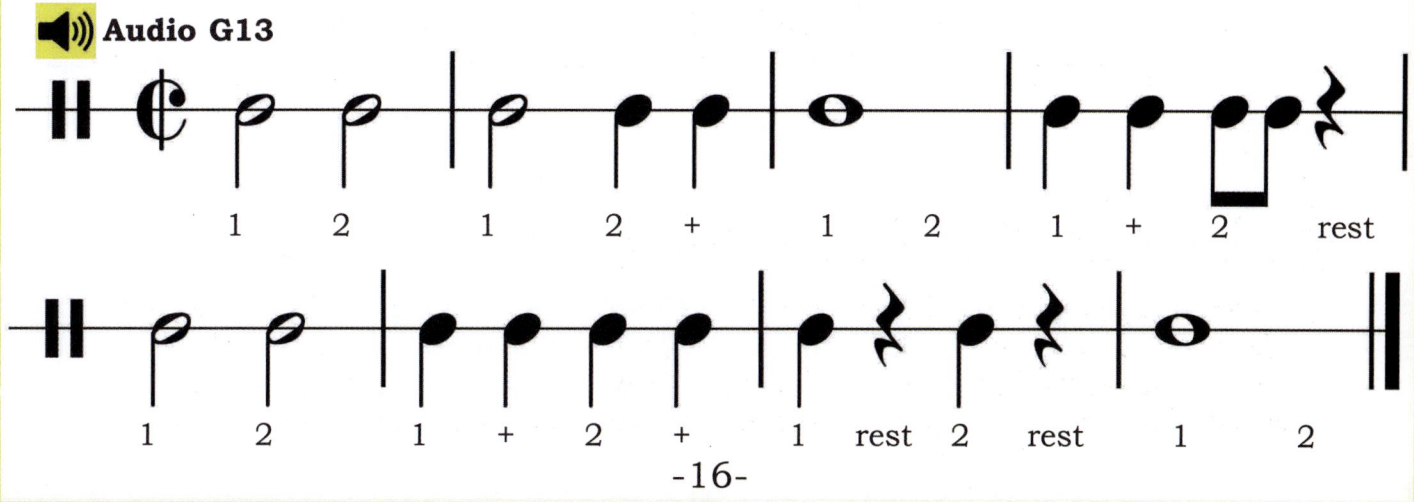

-16-

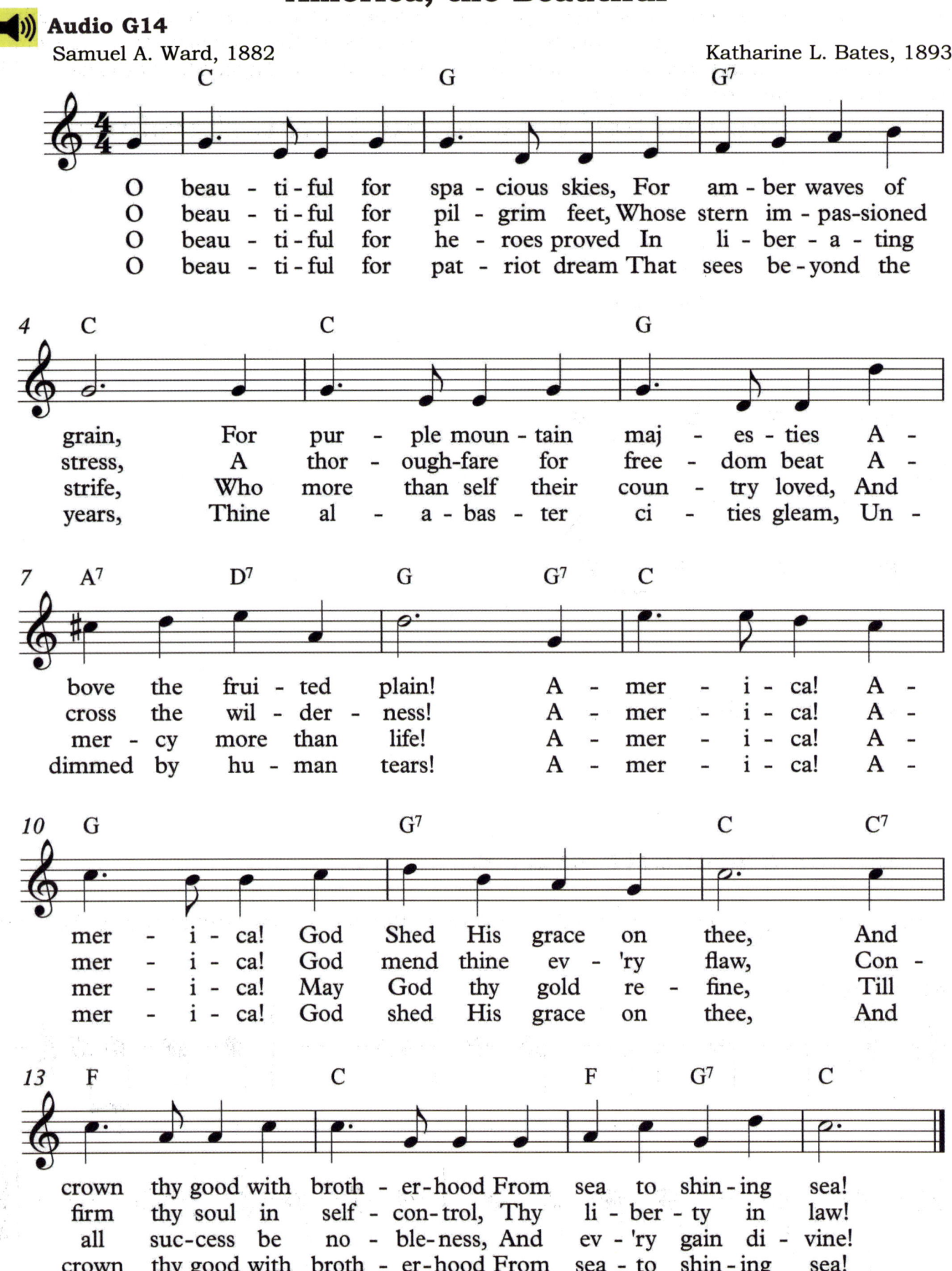

America, the Beautiful

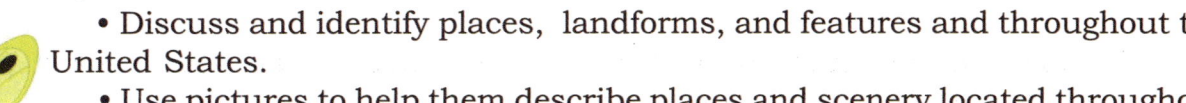

- Discuss and identify places, landforms, and features and throughout the United States.
- Use pictures to help them describe places and scenery located throughout the United States.
- Analyze the song for literal and symbolic content.
- Identify and analyze the time signature. What is the time signature?
- Before singing, form groups of 2 students. Practice pronunciation and learn lyrics. Analyze rhythm and count the beats out loud.
- Have your students put their pronunciation skills to the test by singing along to the song.
- Point to all the dotted half notes and dotted quarter notes.
- This song is written in C Major key. Let us sing the C major scale.
- Practice singing the song at a slow tempo. Listen to Audio G14 and sing along.
- Have students respond to music with movement.
- While listening or playing music, tap your foot to a steady beat.

C Major Scale
🔊 Audio G15

do re mi fa sol la ti do   do ti la sol fa mi re do

How to Count and Sing in Common Time Signature

When we have a 4/4 time signature, the quarter note gets the beat because 4 is the bottom number.

--------> 4 beats per measure
--------> Quarter note gets one beat

The time signature of a piece of music is one of the key clues that can help you understand the rhythm and structure of the piece. It tells us how many beats (pulses) are contained in each measure (bar) and which note value is equivalent to a beat.

In music notation, the time signature is placed at the beginning of the staff after the clef and the key signature. The time signature indicates how many beats there are in each measure and what the value of the beat is.

Common Time is another way of notating and referring to the 4/4 time signature, which indicates that there are four quarter-note beats per measure. It may be written in its fraction form of 4/4 or with a **C**-shaped semicircle.

The top number of the time signature determines how many beats there are per measure. The bottom number indicates the note value of the beats. In the case of our 4/4 example, the bottom "4" is referring to a quarter note.

Common Time and Cut Time (Alla Breve) Exercise

1. Complete the measures below. Use quarter notes or half notes and quarter or half rests. Clap the rhythm and count out loud.

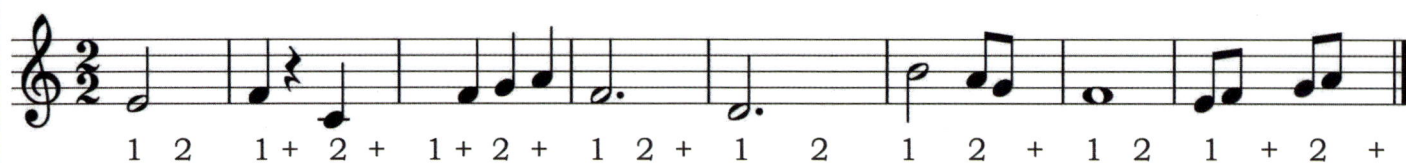

2. In the example below, circle the measures with the incorrect number of beats.

3. In the example below, draw bar lines. Count and clap the rhythm.

4. The Time Signature is a symbol that appears at the _____ of the staff just after the clef. It is made up of two numbers placed one above the other.

5. The upper number indicates how many _____ are allowed in each measure.

6. The lower number indicates what type of musical note receives one _____.

7. In this time signature:

a) How many beats are allowed in each measure? _____
b) What type of note receives one beat? _____

8. In this time signature:

a) How many beats does one quarter note get? _____
b) How many beats does one half note get? _____
c) How many beats does one whole note get? _____

Hildegard von Bingen

Born: 1098. Died: 1179. Lived in: Germany

Bingen's Hildegard was an outstanding woman, "first" in many fields.

Hildegard of Bingen, a German Benedictine abbess, writer, composer, philosopher, Christian mystic, visionary, and polymath, was also known as Sibyl of the Rhine and Saint Hildegard. She is one of modern history's leading and most widely documented writers of sacred monophony. She was considered to be the founder of scientific natural history in Germany by many in Europe.

She was elected Magistra by Hildegard's fellow nuns in 1136; she established the monasteries of Rupertsberg in 1150 and Eibingen in 1165. In Rupertsberg's first work manuscript, *Scivias*, she wrote theological, botanical, medicinal texts and letters, liturgical songs, and poems.

Hildegard has more surviving chants from the entire Middle Ages than any other composer, and she is among the few composers who have written both the music and the lyrics for a piece of music. The *Ordo Virtutum*, one of her works, is an early example of liturgical drama and arguably the oldest surviving play on morality.

Although her formal canonization history is complicated, for centuries, branches of the Roman Catholic Church have recognized her as a saint.

In recent decades, attention to the women of the medieval Church has led to a great deal of popular interest in the music of Hildegard. Sixty-nine musical compositions, each with its original poetic text, survive besides the *Ordo Virtutum*, and at least four other texts are known. Their musical notation, however, has been lost.

Hildegard composed many liturgical songs collected into a cycle called the *Symphonia armoniae celestium revelationum*, in addition to the *Ordo Virtutum*. Hildegard's text is set to the Symphonia songs and ranges from antiphons, hymns, and sequences, to responsories. Her music, which consists of exactly one melodic line, is described as monophonic. The style is characterized by soaring melodies that can push the boundaries of the traditional Gregorian chants' more staid ranges. Another characteristic of Hildegard's music that reflects the evolution of singing in the 12th century and drives them further is that it is highly melismatic, often with recurring melodic devices. Hildegard's music lacks any indication of tempo or rhythm, as with all medieval chant notation; the surviving manuscripts employ late German style notation, which uses very ornamental neumes. The reverence of the Virgin Mary reflected in music demonstrates how deeply the Virgin Mary and the saints influenced and inspired Hildegard of Bingen and her community.

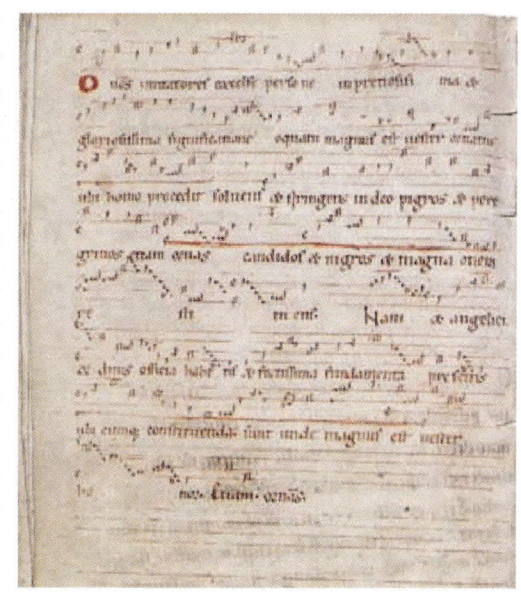

Hildegard von Bingen

🔊 **Audio G16, G17, G18**

While coloring, you may listen to "Ave Generosa", "O Eterne Deus" and "Instrumental on Kyrie" composed by Hildegard von Bingen.

Hildegard von Bingen Quiz

1. Where was Hildegard von Bingen born?
a) the United States
b) Germany
c) France
d) Romania

2. Hildegard von Bingen composed music during what period?
a) Romantic
b) Impressionist
c) Medieval

3. Hildegard von Bingen is known for writing the _____.
a) *Moonlight Sonata*
b) *Ordo Virtutum*
c) *Turkish March*

4. As with all medieval chant notation, Hildegard's music lacks any indication of tempo or rhythm; the surviving manuscripts employ late German style notation, which uses very ornamental neumes.
a) True
b) False

Botany Bay

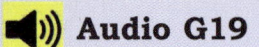
Traditional Song

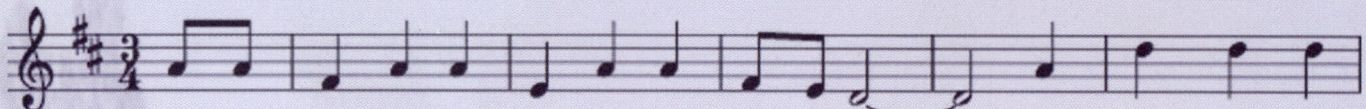
O there's Glas-gow and Ber-wick and Pen-ter-ville, There's Ports-mouth and

old Dart-moor, But they ain't of in-terest to none of us, For we're

bound for a far fo-reign shore. Sing-ing too-roo-loo oo-roo-loo

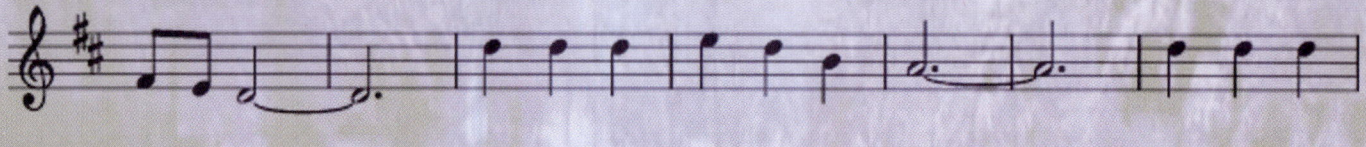
oo-roo-lay'(Also...) Too-roo-lie oo-roo-lie-ay'(Likewise) Too-roo-lie

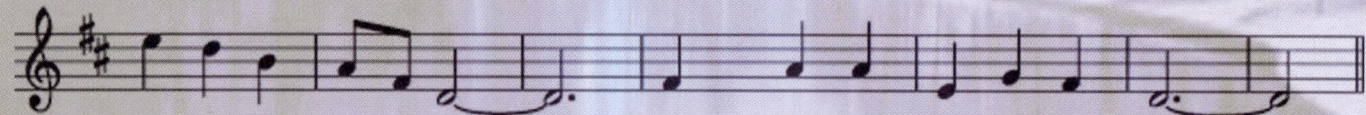
oo-roo-lie oo-roo-lay'(Not forgetting...) Too-roo-lie oo-roo-lie-

- Before singing this song, take a moment of silent study to identify challenging rhythms.
- Find the following musical items in the song "Shores of Botany:" sixteenth, dotted quarter note, musical note B flat.
- What is the time signature?
- What is the key signature?
- Is this song written in a major or minor key?
- How can you improve your performance? (Posture, pitch, rhythm, breathing?)
- As you sing, remember to take a full, relaxed breath and avoid throat tension.
- Practice singing this song until you feel confident about your performance.
- Analyze rhythm and count the beats out loud.
- Have your students put their pronunciation skills to the test by singing along to the song.
- Have students respond to music with movement.

Time Signature 2/4 and 3/4

Rhythm, Melody, and Harmony are the three major components of music as we know it today. We know that the first came to the rhythm in the history of music. By clapping their hands, our ancestors may have created rhythmic music. This could be traced back to the earliest musical instruments when someone discovered that smacking stones or sticks together causes less pain in the hands. Many of these instruments are unlikely to have survived because they were made of soft materials like wood or reeds. Instruments like bone pipes are what has survived. Between 39,000 and 43,000 years old, some of the earliest ever discovered bone pipes are made from swan and vulture wing bones. Other ancient instruments have been discovered in unexpected locations. For example, there is evidence that in caves dating from 12,000 years ago, people struck stalactites or "rock gongs" with the caves themselves acting as resonators for the sound.

Melody and harmony were not invented until much later in the history of music.

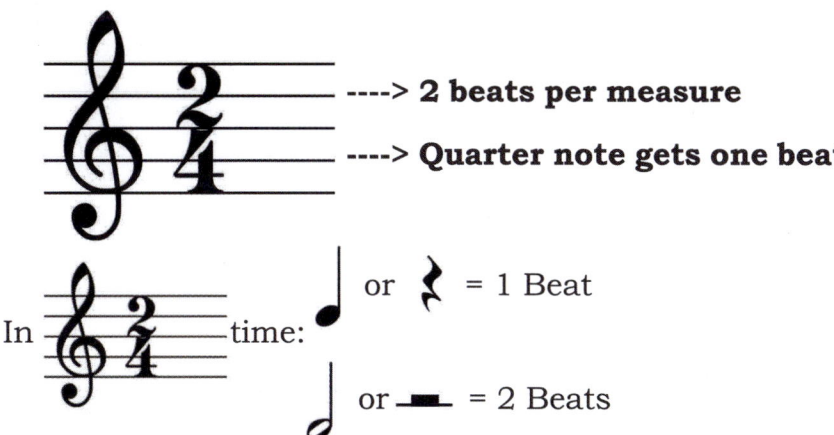

In every measure, the number of notes allowed is determined by the time signature. Each time signature has two numbers, as you saw in the time signature examples: the top number and the bottom number: 2/4 time, 3/4 time. The bottom number of the time signature denotes a specific note type, while the top note denotes the number of those notes in each measure!

• March around the classroom in March Time and count 1-2, 1-2, etc. Each such group is called a measure. Be sure to stress the first count in every measure.

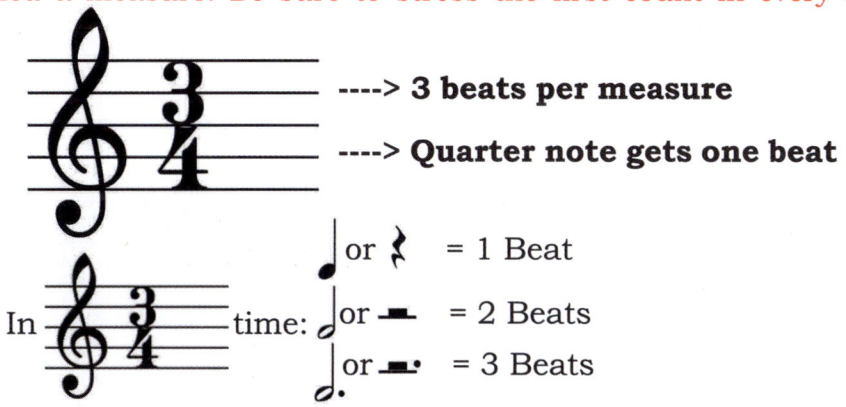

• Dance around the classroom in Waltz Time and count 1-2-3, 1-2-3, etc., while dancing. Be sure to stress the first count in every measure.

The basic definition of music itself is that music needs to move through time—it is not static. Music is, therefore, a sound that is organized through time. Time signatures manage this time-based organization of music in the Western music system! Time signatures allow us to record our music to play music from scores, hear their organizational patterns and converse with other musicians' common terminology. As stated by the time signature, the organizational patterns of beats are how we hear or feel the piece's meter. When discussing music, the terms time signature and meter are often used interchangeably. However, time signature specifically refers to the number and types of notes in each music measure. The meter refers to how those notes are grouped in a repeated pattern to create a cohesive sounding composition.

1. Count the beats out loud. Clap the rhythm of the notes and rests. After you feel comfortable with this rhythm exercise, choose a body movement pattern and dance while clapping this excerpt.

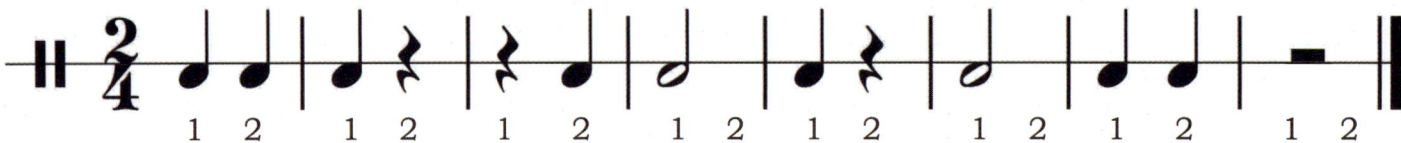

2. Write the beats under the notes or rests and then clap the rhythm.

3. Count the beats out loud. Clap the rhythm of the notes and rests. After you feel comfortable with this rhythm exercise, choose a body movement pattern and dance while clapping this excerpt.

4. Write the beats under the notes or rests and then clap the rhythm.

5. Complete the measures below. Use quarter notes or half notes and quarter or half rests. Clap the rhythm and count out loud.

Henry Martin

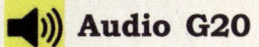

Traditional Song

There were three bro-thers in mer-ry Scot-land. In Scot-land there

lived bro-thers three. And they did cast lots which of them should go, should

go, should go. For to turn rob-ber all on the salt sea.

The lot it fell first upon Henry Martin
The youngest of all the three
That he should turn robber
all on the salt sea
For to maintain his two brothers and he
He had not been sailing but
a long winter's night
And part of a short winter's day
When he espied a rich lofty ship
Come a bibing down him straight away
Hello, hello, cried Henry Martin
What makes you sail so high
I'm a rich merchant ship
bound for fair London town
Won't you please for to let me pass by
O no, o no, cried Henry Martin
That thing it never can be
For I have turned robber
all on the salt sea
For to maintain my two brothers and me

So lower your topsail and bail up your mizzen
Bring yourself under my lee
Or I shall give you a fast flowing ball
And your dear bodies drown in the salt sea
Then broadside and broadside and at it they went
For fully two hours or three
Til Henry Martin gave to her the death shot
Heavily listing to starboard went she
The rich merchant vessel was wounded full sore
Straight to the bottom went she
And Henry Martin sailed away
... on the salt sea
Sad news, sad news to old England came
Sad news to fair London town
There was a rich vessel and she's cast away
And all of her merry men drowned

- Your teacher will play Audio G20 and sing the starting pitches of this song. Listen, tune, and blend your voice with other voices around you.
- First, practice the rhythms. Next, sing the pitches. Finally, add the words.
- Maintain a good singing posture. Activate the articulators (lips, teeth, tongue).
- Produce good tone by concentrating on vowel formation and vertical space inside the mouth.
- Sing with expression.
- Did you notice the 3/4 time signature?

Eighth Note & Eighth Rest
Sixteenth Note and Sixteenth Rest

The first subdivision that we will learn is the eighth note, which divides a quarter note beat into two equal parts. Single eighth notes look similar to quarter notes, but they have a flag extending from the stem of the note. When eighth notes occur on or above the middle staff line, the stem usually extends downward.

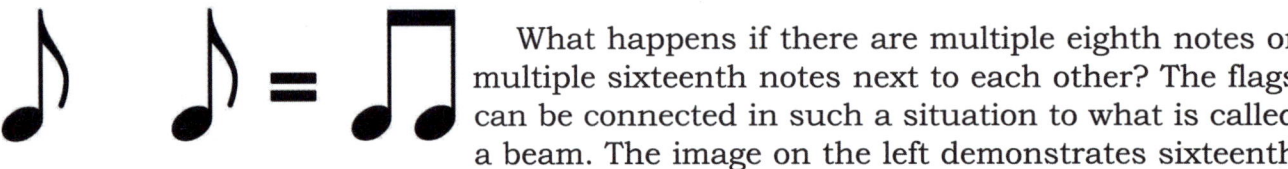

A sixteenth note is very short in terms of its time value. It is played for half of an eighth note's duration. A filled-in oval notehead is used to mark sixteenth notes. They have a straight stem and two flags. (They look almost like eighth notes, except that eighth notes have one flag). Two sixteenth notes equal one-eighth note. Four-sixteenth notes equal one-quarter note.

What happens if there are multiple eighth notes or multiple sixteenth notes next to each other? The flags can be connected in such a situation to what is called a beam. The image on the left demonstrates sixteenth notes that have been beamed together. This is also how eighth notes can be beamed together.

The sixteenth rest looks similar to an eighth rest, but it has two flags instead of one. It is the same duration as a sixteenth note, but it represents silence.

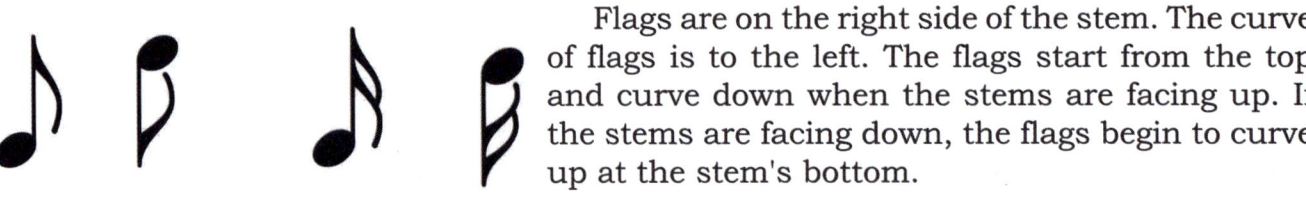

Stems can be drawn to the notehead's right when notes are below the middle line of the staff. The musical notes are drawn with stems on the notehead's left, facing down if they are on or above the middle line.

Flags are on the right side of the stem. The curve of flags is to the left. The flags start from the top and curve down when the stems are facing up. If the stems are facing down, the flags begin to curve up at the stem's bottom.

1. Let's learn to count this rhythm excerpt.

2. Let's learn to count this rhythm excerpt.

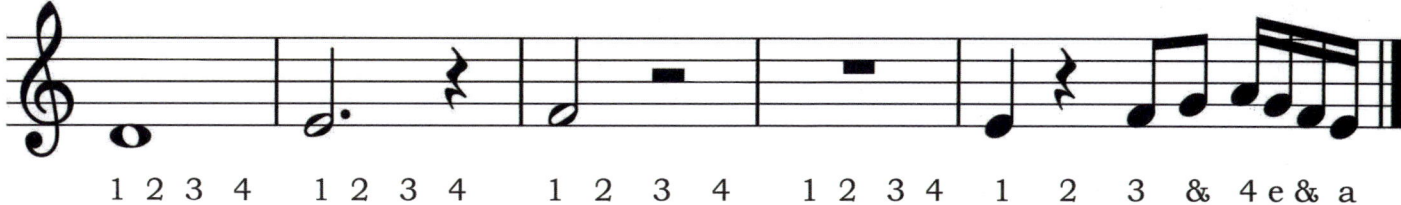

3. There are notes or rests missing from each measure below. Draw the note or rest on the appropriate beat to complete the measure. Clap the rhythm.

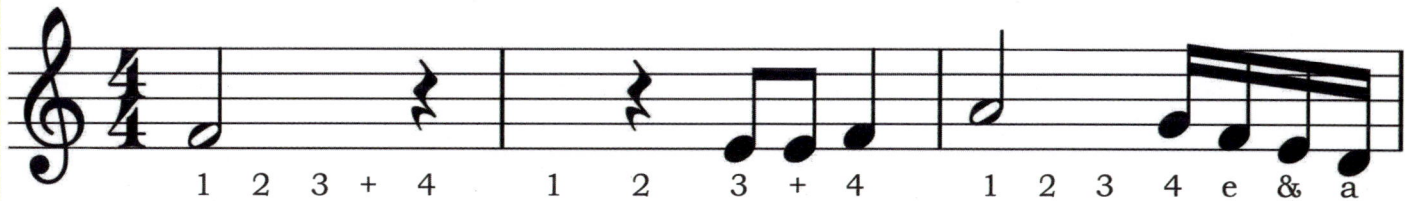

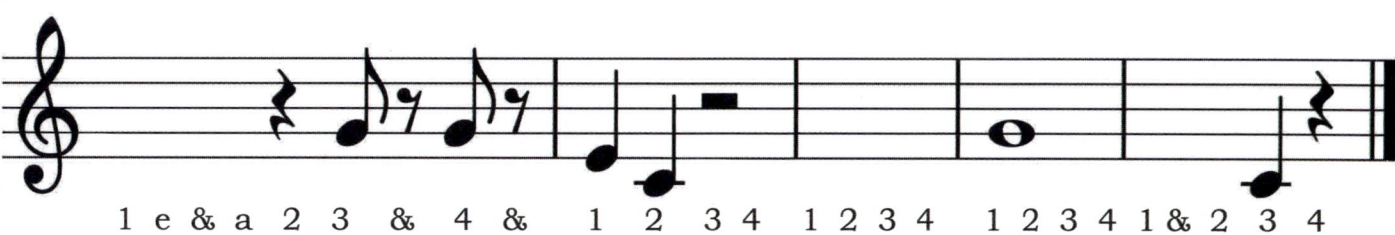

4. Draw bar lines in the following music. Write in the counting below the staff. Clap the rhythm.

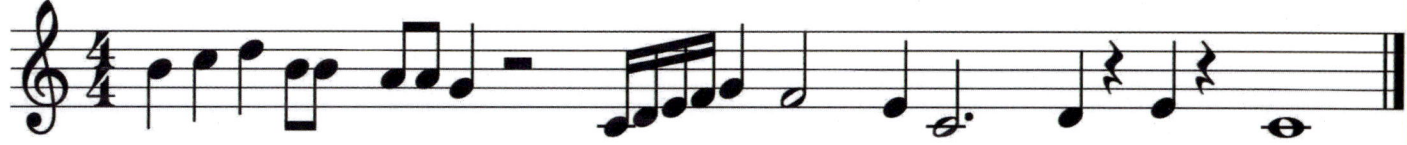

5. Complete the following exercises in drawing eighth or sixteenth notes.
  Trace the eighth note and draw five more.   Trace the sixteenth note and draw five more.

6. Complete the following exercises in drawing eighth or sixteenth rests.
  Trace the eighth rest and draw five more.   Trace the sixteenth rest and draw five more.

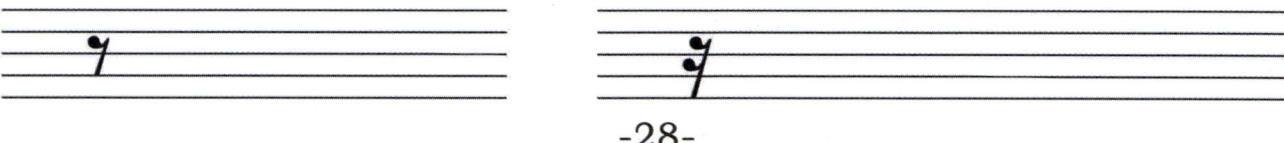

Rosebud in June

🔊 Audio G21

Traditional Song

It's a rose- bud in June, and vi- 'lets in full bloom, And the small birds sing- ing love

songs on each spray. We'll pipe and we'll sing, love, we'll dance in a ring, love, when each

lad takes his lass All on the green grass, And it's all to plough Where the

fat ox- en graze low And the lads and the lass- es to sheep shear- ing go.

• Before singing this song, take a moment of silent study to identify challenging rhythms.
• Review with students the content knowledge of time signature and the value of quarter notes, eighth notes, sixteenth notes, dotted quarter notes, dotted eighth notes in 3/4 time signature.
• Point out the fermata sign.
• Play Audio G21 and have the students work in pairs to guess what kind of song it is, for example --- fast, slow, happy, sad, etc.
• Analyze the song and discuss if it was written in a major or minor key?
• Review melody, melodic direction, tonal center/tonic, and key signature.
• What is the key signature?
• Students attempt to determine the meaning of the song through the expressive quality of the music. The teacher can drive conversation by using terms such as dynamics, major/minor key, tempo, legato, fermata.
• Ask students to come up with adjectives that describe the emotion behind the song. Compile a list of adjectives on a marker board, poster, or smartboard.
• Sing with expression, using any expressive elements (tempo, dynamics, articulation) students recommend would fit the intent of the song.
• Teach the melody and lyrics of the song.
• Demonstrate good singing technique by using a head voice, supportive posture, diction, and breath control.

Let's compose a little song

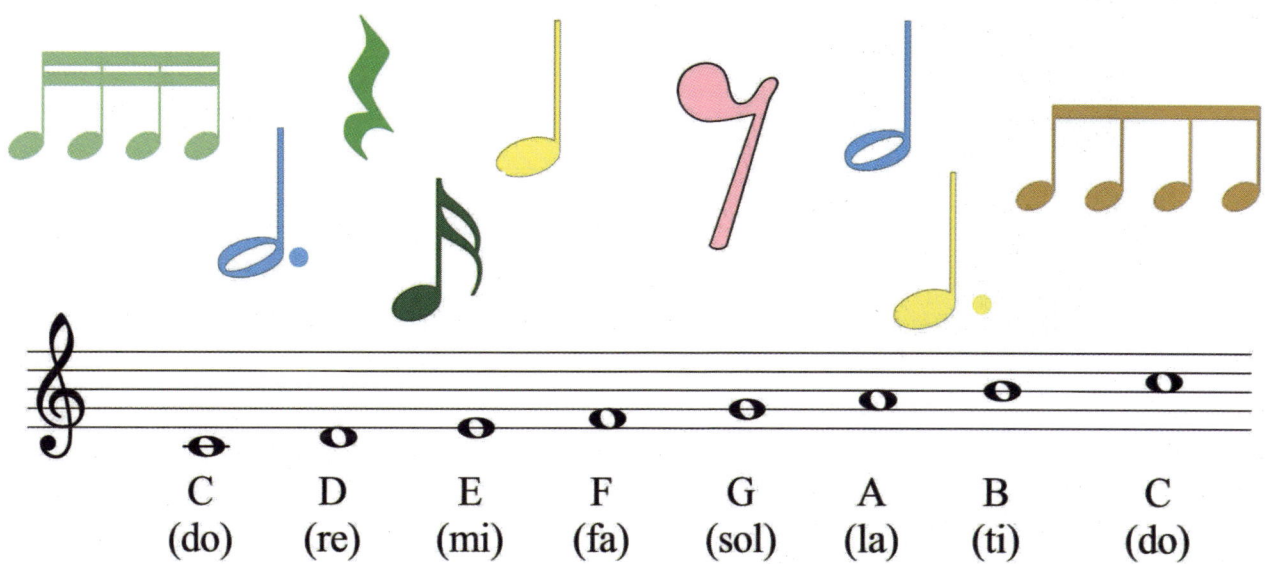

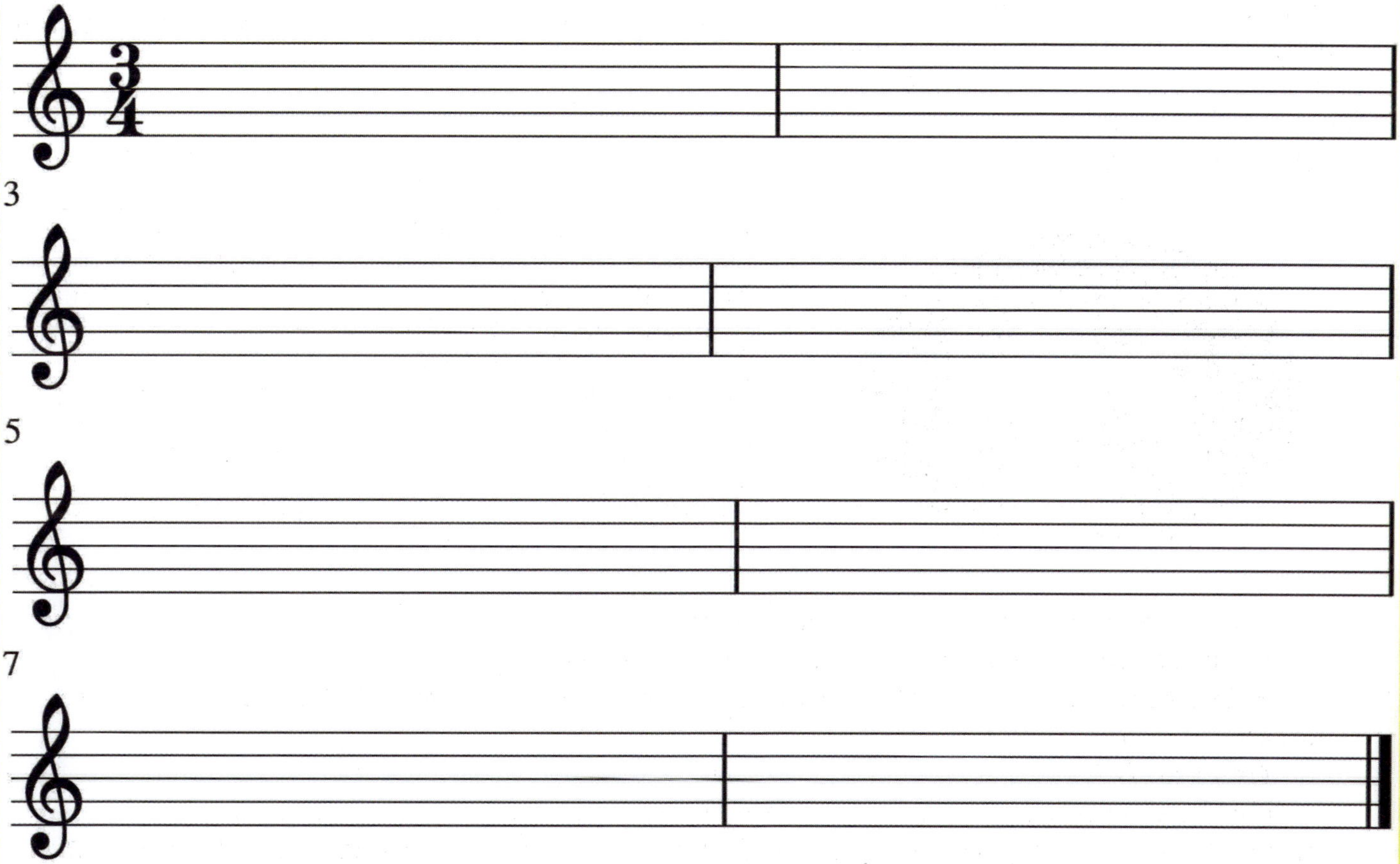

- Compose eight measures of melody, rhythm, and dynamics using musical notes do, re, mi, fa, sol, la, ti, do.
- The song will be written in a 3/4 time signature. Therefore every measure must have three beats.
- You may add text to your little song.
- Have fun composing this little song.
- Sing your song with expression, chant the rhythm.
- Your teacher can help you learn to play your composition on the xylophone.

Elements of Music
Rhythm

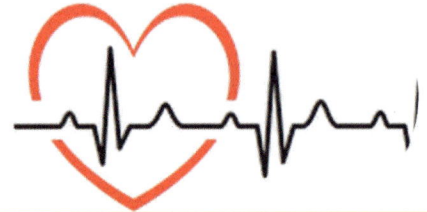

Rhythm is present in everyone's life. Some processes are carried out with a certain periodicity, such as rhythm in plant development, work rhythm, rhythm in nature, the rhythm of learning, and the poem's rhythm.

In music, rhythm refers to the musical organization of time. The combination of long and short duration in time is referred to as rhythm. Noteheads that are either empty or filled are used to note durations. Filled noteheads always have a stem, while empty noteheads may or may not have a stem. Adding flags to filled noteheads reduces the length of the note by half.

Form groups of 3 students and describe what activities do you see in the above pictures. What is the role or importance of rhythm in each case?

Rhythm is derived from the Greek word rhythmos, which means "measured motion." The length of notes used within each measure is an important component in determining the rhythm in music. Long and short notes can be used to create slow and fast rhythms. Whole notes (4 beats), half notes (2 beats), quarter notes (1 beat), and eighth notes (1/2 of a beat) are the basic building blocks of note lengths or note values. You are keeping the beat or following the music's structural rhythmic pulse by tapping your foot to the music.

There are many important aspects of rhythm:
• Duration: the length of a musical note (or silence).
• Tempo: the number of beats per second, can be used to describe the beat's speed.

Ties and Dots

The basic duration can be lengthened with dots and ties. A dot occurs after a musical note or a rest, increasing the pitch or rest duration. A dotted quarter note, for example, would be equivalent to three eighth notes in duration. In terms of duration, a quarter note is equal to two eighth notes.

A dotted note is the same as writing the basic note tied to a half-value note – a dotted half note, for example, is the same as a half note tied to a quarter note.

dotted eighth note = three sixteens

dotted quarter note = three eighth notes

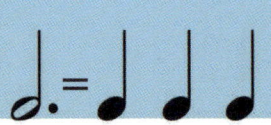

dotted half note = three quarter notes

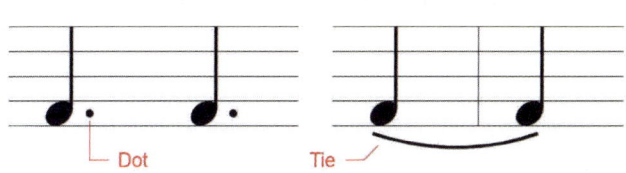

The time value of a note goes up by half when a dot is placed to the right of the notehead or a rest. There are two different ways to add time value to a note: dots and ties. A tie lengthens a duration by connecting two adjacent identical pitches. Ties are used to either sustain a pitch beyond the length of a single measure or to make a particular rhythmic grouping in a measure clearer.

The time value of a quarter note and an eighth note will be added together if they are linked. As a result, a quarter note (1 beat) tied to an eighth note (half beat) has a total time value of 1 and 1/2 beats.

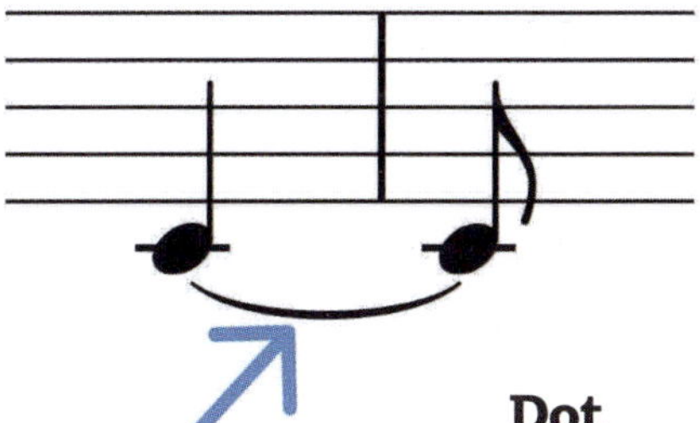

Ties are indicated at the top of notes with down-stems and below notes with up-stems.

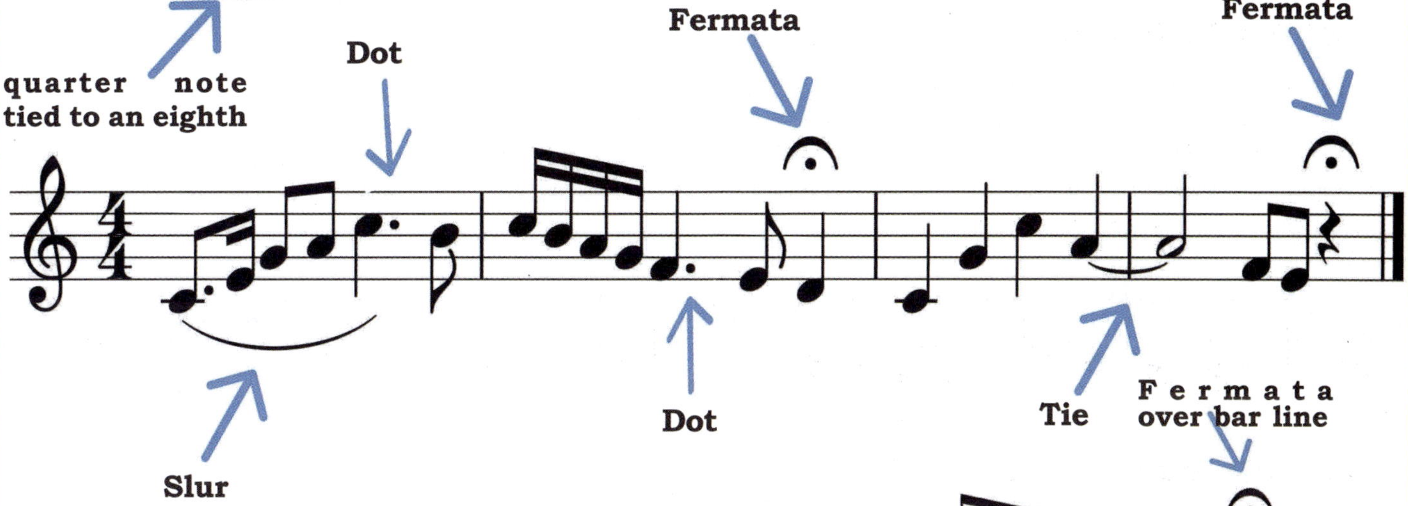

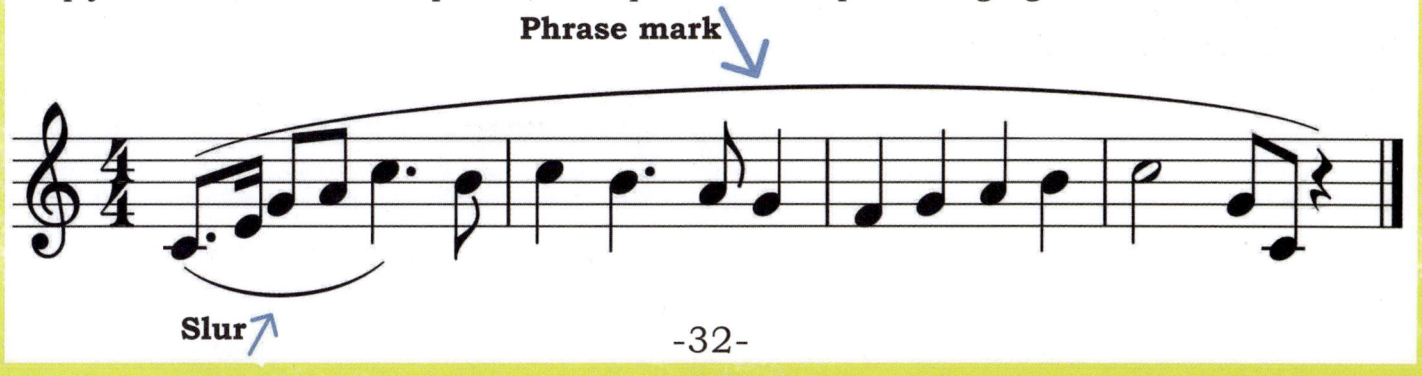

A tie extends the duration of a pitch by linking two adjacent identical pitches. Ties are used to extend a pitch beyond the length of a single measure or to make a rhythmic grouping in a measure more distinct.

The **fermata** is a semicircle containing a dot that may lie above or below a note or rest or over a bar (bar line). The fermata indicates that the note (or rest) should be prolonged beyond the normal duration. A fermata is an articulation mark that allows a note or chord to be held for as long as desired. If a fermata is written over a bar line, there will be a pause between the measures.

A **slur** is a symbol in musical notation that denotes that the notes it encompasses should be played together (that is, with legato articulation). A slur is denoted with a curved line generally placed above the notes if the stems point downward and below them if the stems point upwards. A slur may be difficult to distinguish from a phrase mark that looks like a slur but may cover a longer passage, and it simply indicates that this is a phrase, like a phrase in the spoken language.

1. Circle only the ties in the following excerpt. Write in the counting. Clap the rhythm.

2. Write the total number of beats each set of tied notes will receive. (The quarter note gets one beat.)

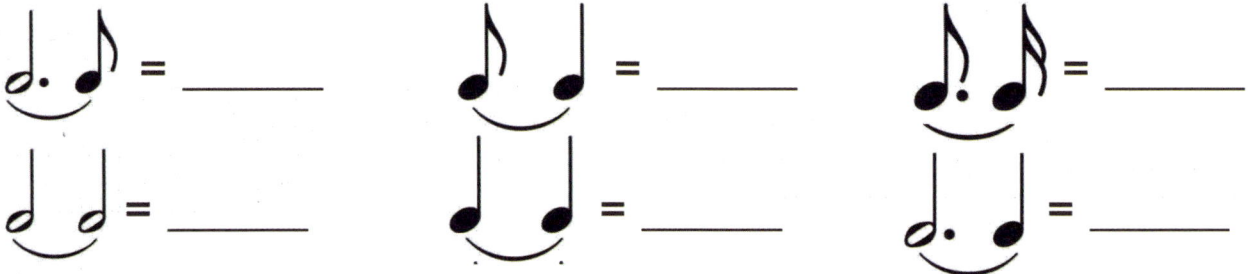

Syncopation

In pop, jazz, rock, as well as in classical music, the accents sometimes come on the weak divisions of the beat, adding new excitement to the music. This is called syncopation. Syncopation is the accenting of a note which would usually not be accented. Syncopation is when a normally unstressed beat is stressed. For example, music in common time (4/4) usually stresses the first and third beat.

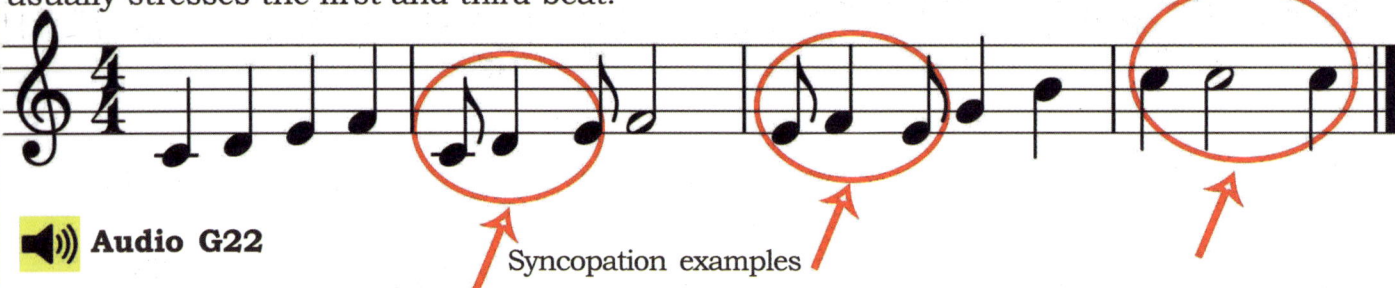

🔊 **Audio G22**   Syncopation examples

In contrast, a syncopated song may emphasize the second and fourth beats. When a note falls between two beats, syncopation can occur.

The red circles above show examples of syncopation.

Upbeat or Anacrusis

While an incomplete measure starts with unstressed notes, these notes are referred to as upbeat or anacrusis, which is also known as a pickup note (s). This marks the downbeat of the next measure, the first beat of the next measure.

The first complete measure (not the anacrusis) is counted as measure number one when numbering the measures. The final measure will also be incomplete. Together they equal one complete measure.

The well-known song "Happy Birthday to You" has upbeat. The word Happy appears before the first beat of the bar (making this the upbeat), and the word birthday lands on the bar line.

The Battle of New Orleans

Audio G23

Traditional Song

'Twas on the eighth of Jan-u-a-ry, just at the dawn of day; We spied those Bri-tish

of-fi-cers All dress'd in bat-tle ar- ray. Old Jack-son then gave or- ders, Each

man to keep his post, And form a line from right to left And let no time be lost.

With rockets and with bombshells, like comets we let fly;
Like lions they advanced us, the fate of war to try;
Large streams of fiery vengeance upon them we let pour,
While many a brave commander lay withering in his gore.

Thrice they marched up to the charge, and thrice they gave the ground
We fought them full three hours, then bugle horns did sound
Great heaps of human pyramids lay strewn before our eyes;
We blew the horns and rang the bells to drown their dying cries.

Come all you British noblemen and listen unto me;
Our Frontiersman has proved to you America is free.
But tell your royal master when you return back home,
That out of thirty thousand men, but few of you returned.

- Learn to sing the song and try to keep the rhythm using the drum.
- Sing the song correctly, be expressive, keep your lips slightly rounded, have a clean emission, and a loose body position.
- Play Audio G23 and have students echo phrase by phrase.
- Add movement. This can be simultaneous or while echoing.
- Put the song together. Sing it completely without echoing.
- Could you describe what do you see inside the red circles?
- Play Audio G23 and have the students work in pairs to guess what kind of song it is, for example --- fast, slow, happy, sad, etc
- Analyze the song and discuss if it was written in a major or minor key?
- Review each measure and discuss note values; legato as well count beats.
- What is the key signature?

Eighth Note Triplets

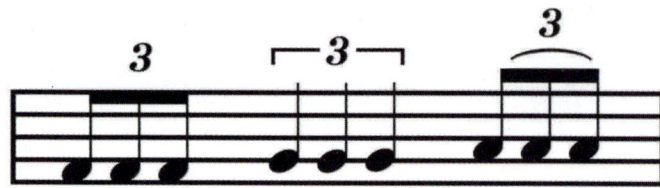

A triplet is formed when three notes are stacked together with a number "3" above or below the notes.

The three notes are played in the time of two notes of the same value. For example, an eighth note triplet spans two eighth note beats (one-quarter note); a quarter note triplet spans the length of a half note, a sixteenth note triplet spans the length of an eighth note, a half note triplet spans the length of a whole note, and so on.

These are the most commonly used triplets, along with their equivalent:

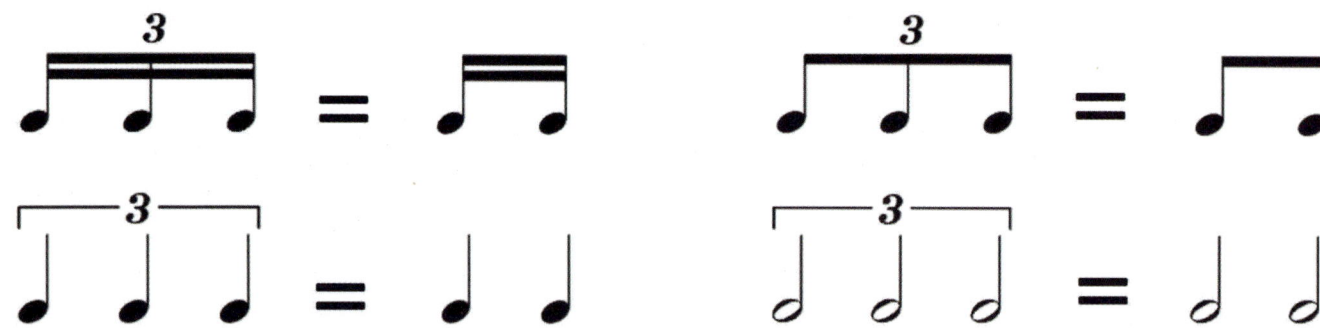

The triplet divides time into three equal parts. Note lengths, music rests, or rhythmic dots can be used to modify these parts as long as the total length of the note grouping remains intact.

Examples:

Counting eighth note triplets

There are many ways that musicians count triplets. It is not correct to assert that there is only one way to count triplets. For each triplet, you could simply say "1 – Ah – Lee – 2 – Ah – Lee – 3 – Ah – Lee – 4 – Ah – Lee."

Or, "One – Trip – Let, Two – Trip – Let, …"

🔊 Audio G24

1. Add bar lines, write the beats under the notes, and clap the rhythm.

Francesca Caccini

Born: September 18, 1587, Florence, Italy
Died: 1640, Florence, Italy
Nationality: Italian
Siblings: Settimia Caccini
Parents: Giulio Caccini, Lucia Gagnolanti

Francesca Caccini, called "La Cecchina," was an Italian composer and singer of the early Baroque era.

Francesca Caccini was born and raised in Florence, where she followed in her father's footsteps by becoming a musician for the Medici family. At the height of her career in the 1620s, she was the first woman to compose opera and the most well-paid musician on the court. Besides composing opera, she also composed songs, and music for the theatre, but the vast majority of her works were lost to time.

Francesca was born into a musical family in Florence on September 18, 1587. Her father was an upstanding composer, doing numerous notable works. Both her mother, Lucia Gagnolanti, and her younger sister, Settimia, were professional singers. Together they performed chamber music and entertainment for the court, including Jacopo Peri's *L'Euridice* and Giulio Caccini's *Il rapimento di Cefala*, and wedding music for Maria de' Medici and Henri IV of France. Beyond being a virtuoso singer, Francesca played guitar, lute, harp, and keyboard and taught the court's younger women to sing instrumental performance and composition. Caccini was also a poet, and it is known that she composed poetry in Italian and Latin, especially poems for the majority of her published songs.

Although there is evidence that Caccini had written at least 16 stage works, only one opera by Caccini is surviving, *La liberazione di Ruggiero dall'isola d'Alcina*, sometimes known simply as *Alcina*. This is the first opera by a woman that was also written in Italy. Opera was written by the first woman in history, Caccini.

During the reign of the Medici, Caccini was the highest-paid musician, earning a considerable sum.

Until May of 1637, Francesca continued to perform, compose, and teach for the Medici court. After that, conflicting reports of her location and death are in circulation. She is more than likely to have died in Florence, where it is said that she passed away in 1640. Francesca is buried with her father, Guilio, and her sister, Settimia, in San Michele Visdomini's family tomb. Francesca will forever be considered one of the greatest female composers.

Francesca Caccini

Audio G25

While coloring, you may listen to "La liberazione di Ruggiero dall'isola d'Alcina" by Francesca Caccini.

Francesca Caccini Quiz

1. Francesca Caccini was born in _____.
a) Germany
b) Italy
c) France
d) England

2. In the court of Medici, Caccini was the highest-paid musician at the time.
a) True
b) False

3. Francesca Caccini composed _____.
a) *Fur Elise*
b) *Sonatina in C major*
c) *La liberazione di Ruggiero dall'isola d'Alcina*

4. Francesca Caccini was a _____ composer.
a) Romantic
b) Baroque
c) Classical

3/8 and 6/8 Time Signature

6/8 is a meter that splits the beat into three eighth note groups rather than two.
What is the difference between 6/8 and 3/4?
Six eighth notes could be included in both. However, 3/4 time signature divides them into three groups of 2, while 6/8 time signature divides them into two groups of three.

6/8 = Six eighth notes per measure, eighth note gets the beat.
3/8 = Three eighth notes per measure, eighth note gets the beat.

3/8 includes one group of 3 eighth notes, and 6/8 includes two groups of 3 eighth notes. Two 3/8 measures put together would equal one 6/8 measure. 3/8 is counted the same way as 6/8.

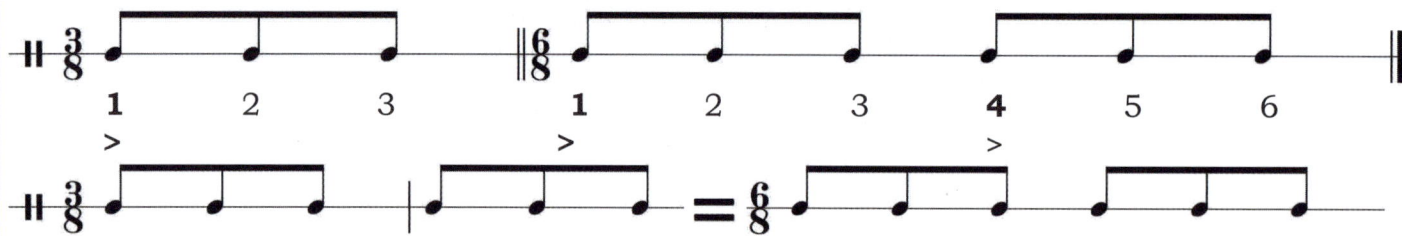

3/8 and 6/8 time signature can also be performed at fast tempos: count each 3/8 measure in 1 count and each 6/8 measure in 2 counts.

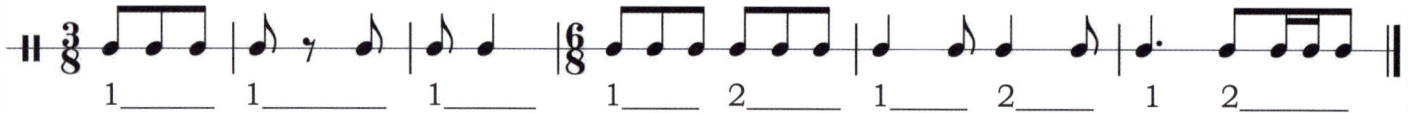

Count out loud each beat and tap your foot on beats **1** and **4**.   Audio G28

This is just another way of writing the triplet feel.
It could also be written: Audio G29

Solfege

🔊 Audio G30

Solfege is a system for sight-singing music that applies standard syllables to the notes. Singing with solfege syllables makes it easier to hear and remember the sound of intervals. Play Audio G30 and sing along each pitch as you hear it. When we are singing, our egos need to remember that we are developing our inner ear. The relative goodness or badness of our singing voice is not that important in this case. It is more important to simply learn how to match a pitch.

Form a group of 2 students and describe in writing the time signature, tempo, dynamics, marks of expression. Write the beats under each measure.

Warm-up your voice by sight-singing C major scale a few times.

The following syllables are common to most solfege systems in English-speaking countries: Do ("doh") Re ("ray") Mi ("mee") Fa ("fah") Sol ("soh"/ "soul") La ("lah") Ti ("tee") [or Si] Do ("doh")

C Major Scale

🔊 Audio G31

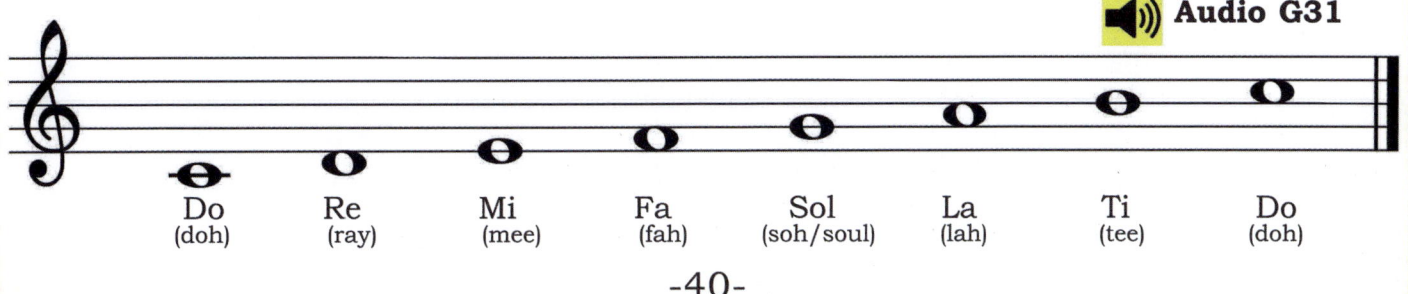

-40-

Ostinato

An **ostinato** is a melodic phrase that is repeated over and over throughout a musical composition. It usually occurs in the same voice and at the same pitch, but it can be transposed and moved to different voices. The word ostinato comes from the Italian word for obstinate, plural ostinatos, or ostinati and has been used by composers for centuries.

The **ground bass**, or **basso ostinato**, is an ostinato pattern in the lowest notes that keeps playing while the melodies in the higher notes change. This has often been used in baroque musical works. An example of ostinato is the famous "Canon in D" by Pachelbel. "Carol of the Bells" uses a repeated rhythm all the way through the piece.

Audio G32 "Canon in D" by Pachelbel
Audio G33 "Carol of the Bells"

Ostinato Solfege

Separate students into two groups. One group will sight-sing "voice 1" and the other group will sight-sing "voice 2." Your teacher will play Audio G34 and sight-sing the starting pitches of this solfege. Listen, tune, and blend your voice with other voices around you. First, practice the rhythms. Next, sight-sing the pitches. Maintain a good singing posture. Activate the articulators (lips, teeth, tongue). After both groups learn very well to sight-sing their part, you can have them sight-sing together. Sing with expression.
- Did you notice the mixed meters?
- What is the time signature? Form groups of 2 students and describe in writing the time signature, tempo, dynamics, marks of expression. Write the beats under each measure.
- Is this solfege written in a major or minor key?
- Point to all dotted sixteenth notes dotted half notes, and ostinato pattern.

-41-

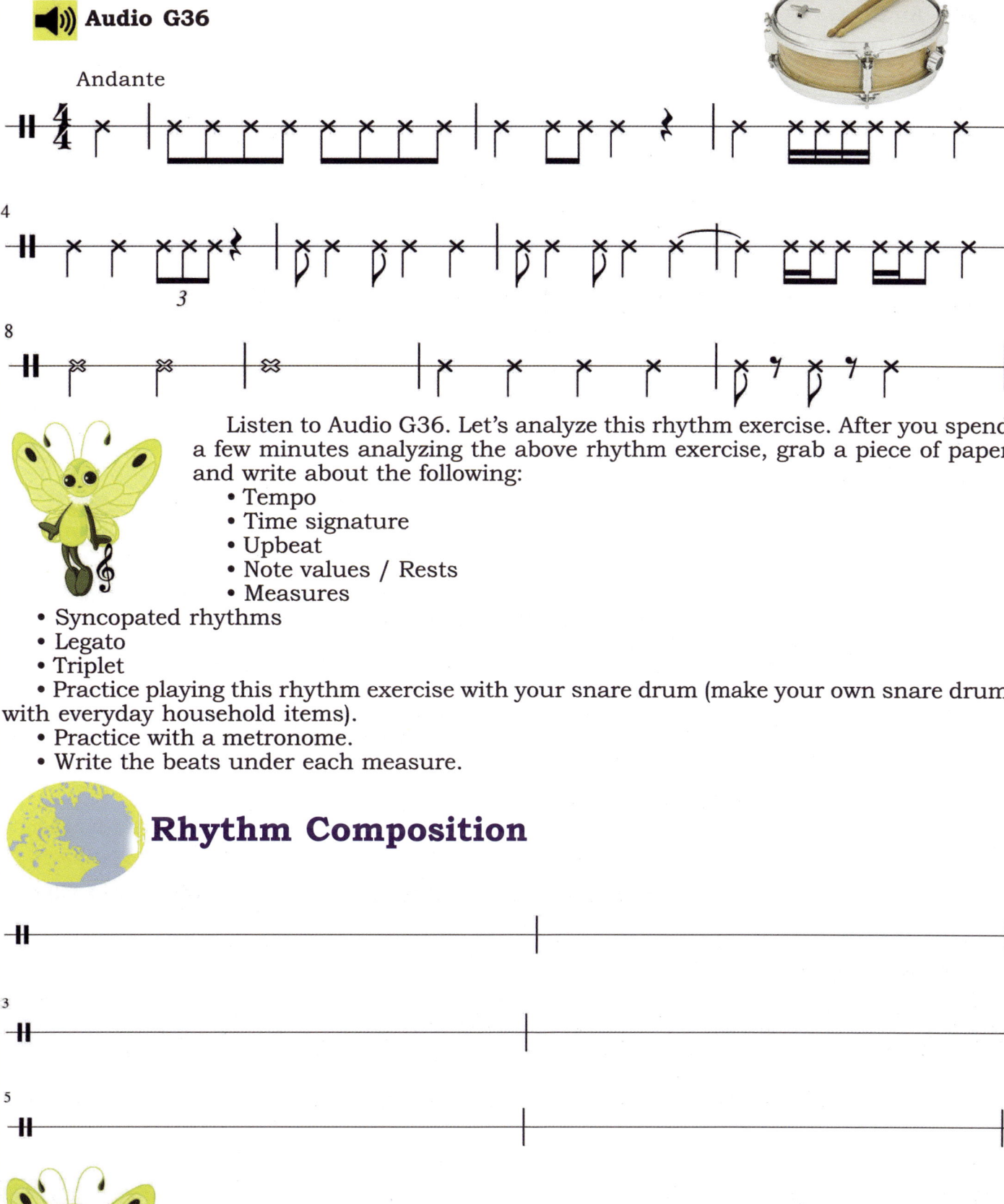

Fennario

 Audio G37

Traditional Song

As we marched down to Fen- na- ri- o, As we marched down to Fen-

na- ri- o, Our cap- tain fell in love with a la- dy like a

dove, They called her by name, pret- ty Peg- gy, O

Sing the song correctly, be expressive, keep your lips slightly rounded, have a clean emission and a loose body position. Sing this song and play the rhythm on a percussion instrument that you made.

Do a Think-Pair-Share activity in which students talk about:
• meaning of the song.
• what kind of feelings brings this song, happy/sad feelings
• major or minor key (there is a common assumption about music that major is happy, and minor is sad).
• describing what they like the most (rhythm, melody, lyrics, etc.) at this piece.
• identifying upbeat, legato, dotted notes, and mixed meters.
• improvising an accompaniment rhythm for this song and performing it while classmates sing "Fennario."

Warm-Up Exercise

 Audio G38

After this vocal warm-up exercise, you can continue to learn singing "Fennario."

F major & D minor scale

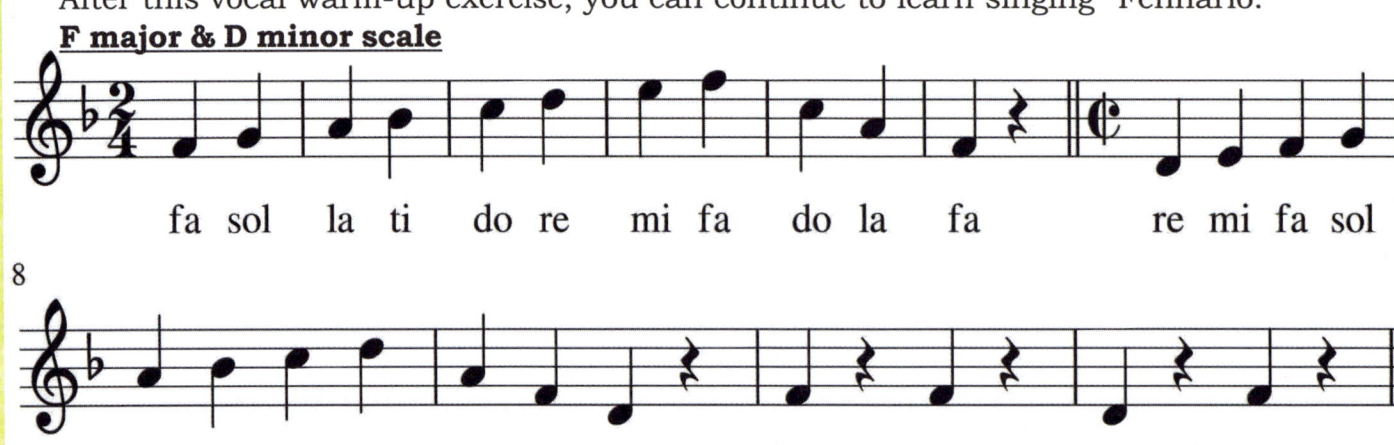

fa sol la ti do re mi fa do la fa re mi fa sol

la ti do re la fa re fa fa re fa

Bolero

Tempo di Bolero   Maurice Ravel

Ravel was born near the Spanish frontier in France. His father was an inventor of machines and engines, and his Spanish mother was an amateur musician. The family went to Paris when Maurice was only a few months old. However, his mother's Spanish heritage and the mechanical brain of his father greatly influenced Ravel in his Bolero composition of 1928. Joseph-Maurice Ravel had piano lessons from the age of 6 and moved on quickly to perform in public at the age of 14 and eventually study at the Paris Conservatoire.

Joseph-Maurice Ravel (March 7, 1875 - December 28, 1937) was a French composer and pianist, best known for his orchestral work, Boléro. He had described Boléro as "a piece for orchestra without music." Ravel's orchestrations are notable for his effective use of tonal color and various sounds and instrumentation.

Bolero is an orchestral piece composed in 1928 by Maurice Ravel and one of the most popular orchestral pieces. Bolero is the longest single idea crescendo in the history of music. It is the most repetitive piece ever written.

Listen to one of the most famous pieces, Bolero, composed by Maurice Ravel.

While listening, describe what you like the most about this piece. First, the student will think on his/her own, then share ideas with a partner, and then share ideas with the entire class.

Analyze measure by measure and describe rhythm, melody, dynamics, marks of expression, ostinato, tempo, time signature, tonality, etc.

Sol - Mi Duet

🔊 Audio G40

♩ = 70

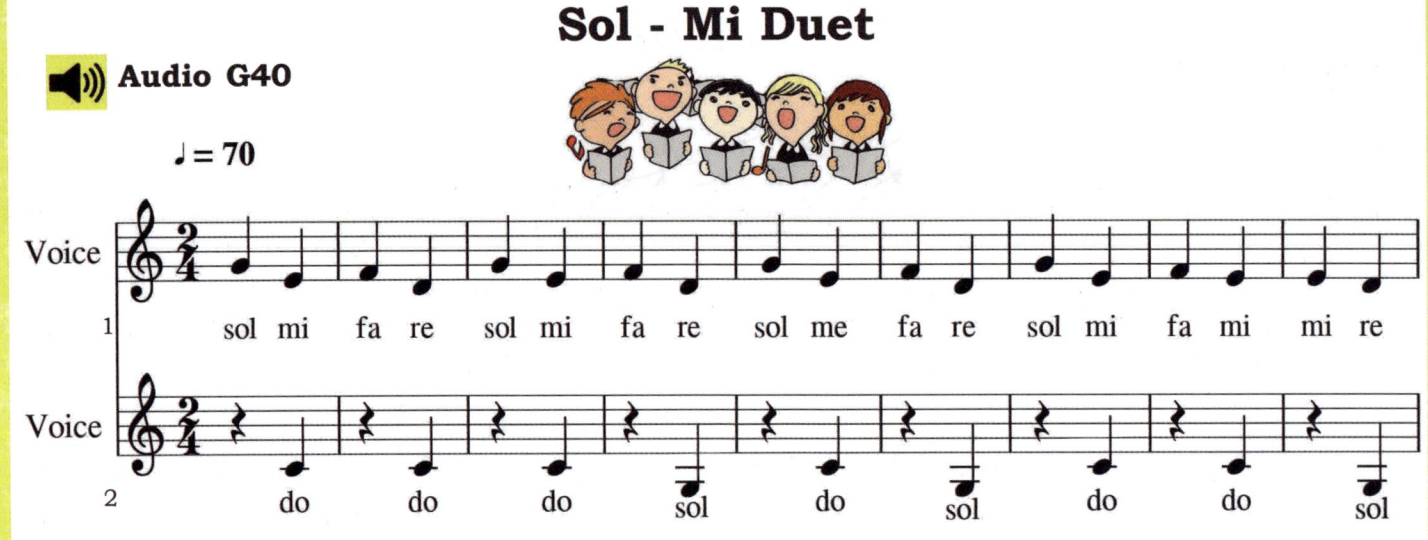

Separate students into two groups. One group will sight-sing "voice 1" and the other group will sight-sing "voice 2." Your teacher will play Audio G40 and sight-sing the starting pitches of this solfege. Listen, tune, and blend your voice with other voices around you. First, practice the rhythms. Next, sight-sing the pitches. Maintain a good singing posture. Activate the articulators (lips, teeth, tongue). After both groups learn very well to sight-sing their part, you can have them sight-sing together. Sing with expression. Practice with a metronome.

Let's play a ball game. The student throws the ball at another student. The student that catches the ball must answer a question from his/her classmates and then throws the ball further down to another classmate and asks a question. The student that does not know the answer to the question has to throw the ball back to the student that asked the question. That student will have to throw the ball at another student that might know the answer to his/her question.

Examples of questions:
• How many beats does a one-quarter note get?
• What is syncopation in music?
• What is an upbeat?

Let's Practice More Fun Rhythm

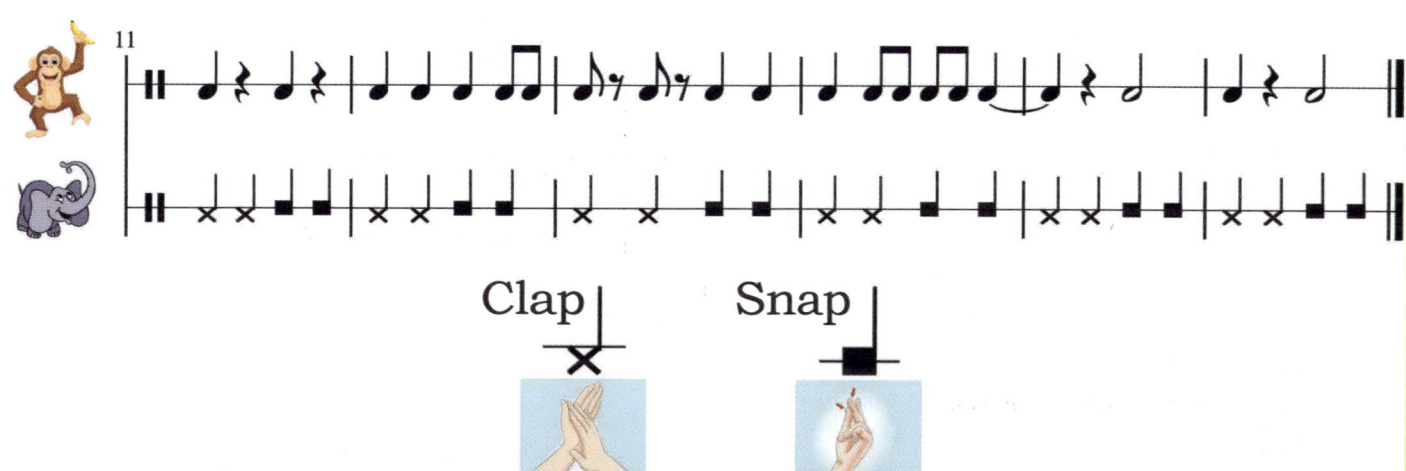

Listen to Audio G41. Let us analyze this rhythm exercise. After you spend a few minutes analyzing the above rhythm exercise, grab a piece of paper and write about the following:
- Tempo
- Upbeat
- Measures
- Time signature
- Note values / Rests
- Syncopated rhythms
- Legato

Practice with a metronome.
Write the beats under each measure.

Let us get into two groups—the monkey group and the elephant group. The monkey group will play Group 1 rhythm, and the elephant group will play Group 2 rhythm. In the beginning, you may practice the rhythm with each group. When both groups play the correct rhythm, have them play the rhythm together.
- Monkey group works together to compose lyrics for their part and chant lyrics on rhythm.
- Elephant group follows the clap and snap rhythm markings.

Music Theory Crossword

 Fill in the crossword puzzle.

Across:
1. Note that it gets two beats.
6. Silence in music.
7. This note gets four beats.
9. Distance between two bar lines.
10. How fast or slow the steady beat is moving is called the _____.

Down:
2. How many lines are in a music staff?
3. Increases the value of a note by half of its original value.
4. A group of 3 notes performed in the space of 2 is called a _____.
5. A quarter note tied to a half note gets how many beats?
8. An _____ is a melodic phrase that is repeated over and over throughout a musical composition.

Note Values

Sixteenth Note and Sixteenth Rest (continue writing same sixteenth notes/rest)

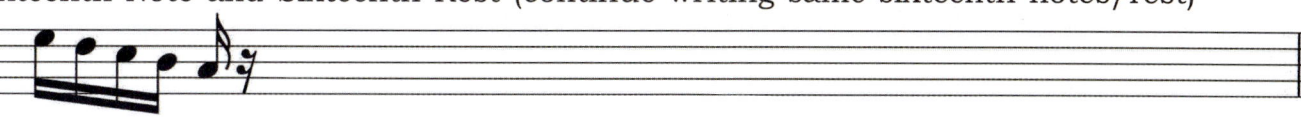

Eighth Note and Eighth Rest (continue writing same eighth notes/rest)

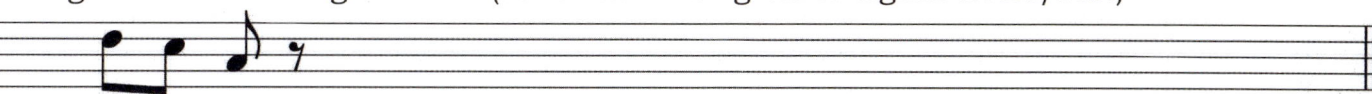

Quarter Note and Quarter Rest (continue writing same quarter note/rest)

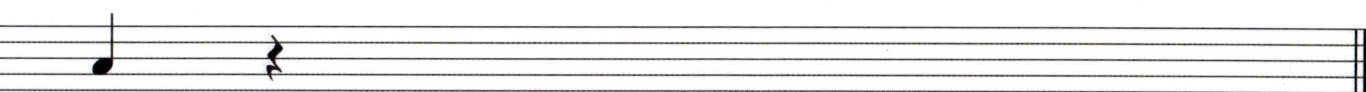

Half Note and Half Rest (continue writing same half note/rest)

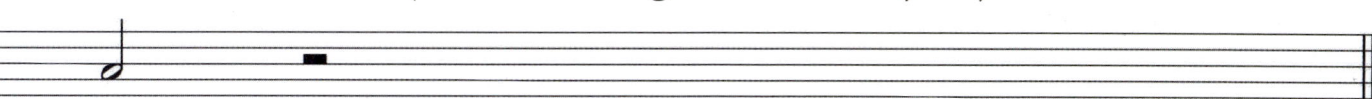

Whole Note and Whole Rest (continue writing same whole note/rest)

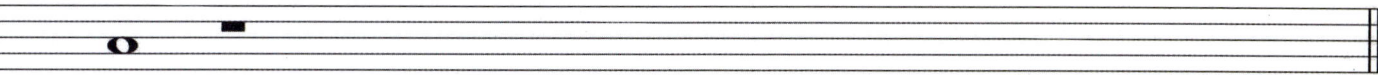

Eighth Note Triplet (continue writing same eighth note triplet)

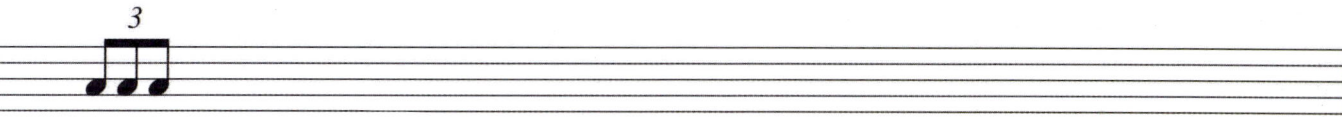

Quarter Note Triplet (continue writing same quarter note triplet)

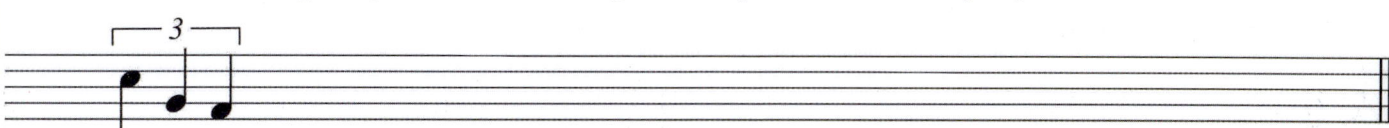

The meter of a song is indicated by its time signature. The time signature (also known as meter signature or measure signature) is made up of two numbers stacked on top of each other. The top number represents the number of beats in a measure. The lower number represents a certain note or sound that gets a beat. You can use notes and rests on marking rhythms. The notations for each note are listed below, together with the equivalent rest (rest is silence when no sound is played.)

Name	Note	Rest	Beats	1 $\frac{4}{4}$ measure
Whole	𝅝	𝄻	4	𝅝
Half	𝅗𝅥	𝄼	2	𝅗𝅥 𝅗𝅥
Quarter	𝅘𝅥	𝄽	1	𝅘𝅥 𝅘𝅥 𝅘𝅥 𝅘𝅥
Eighth	𝅘𝅥𝅮	𝄾	½	𝅘𝅥𝅮 𝅘𝅥𝅮 𝅘𝅥𝅮 𝅘𝅥𝅮
Sixteenth	𝅘𝅥𝅯	𝄿	¼	𝅘𝅥𝅯 𝅘𝅥𝅯 𝅘𝅥𝅯 𝅘𝅥𝅯

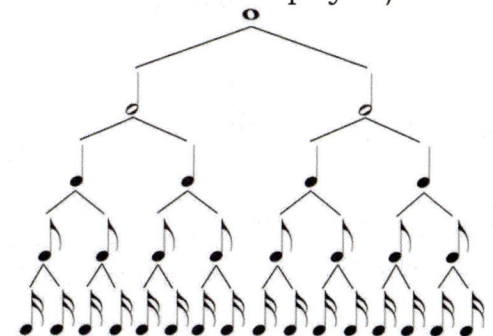

Time Signature

Continue writing 2/4 time signature in each measure

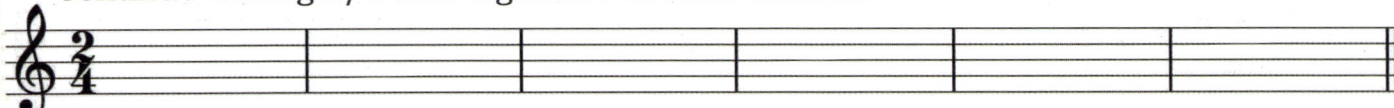

Continue writing 3/4 time signature in each measure

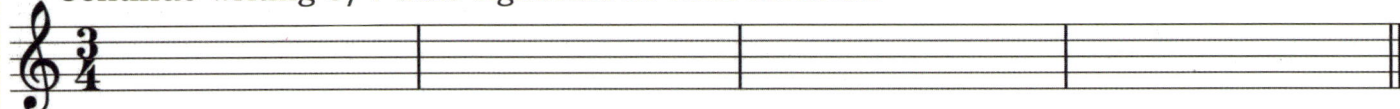

Continue writing 4/4 time signature in each measure

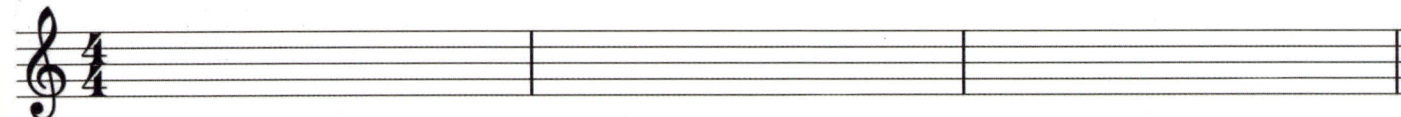

Continue writing Cut Time (Alla Breve) time signature in each measure

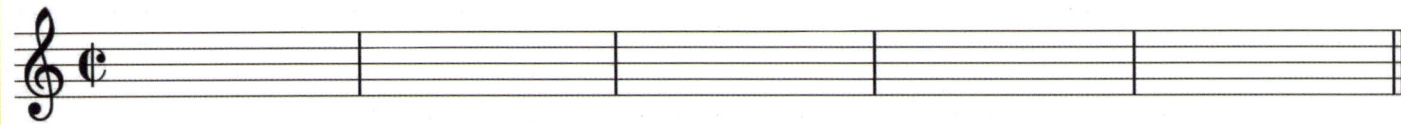

Continue writing Common time signature in each measure

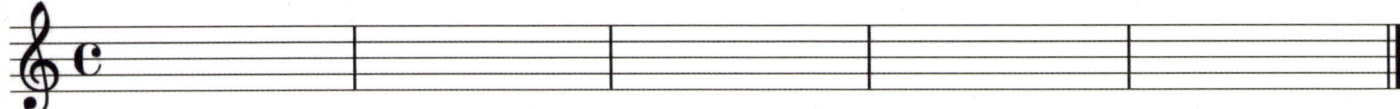

Continue writing 3/8 time signature in each measure

Continue writing 6/8 time signature in each measure

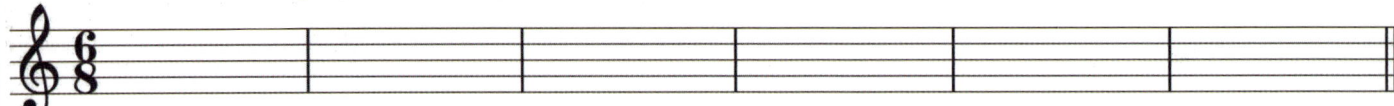

Add the bar lines and write the beats under each measure.

Assessment

1. In 3/8 time, an _____ note receives one beat.
2. In 3/8 time, there are _____ beats in each measure.
3. In 6/8 time, there are six beats in each _____.
4. In 6/8 time, an eighth note receives _____ count.
5. When 3/8 is played fast, it is counted in _____.
6. When 6/8 is played fast, it is counted in _____.
7. _____ is the symbol for common time.
8. _____ is the symbol for cut time.
9. Cut time is also called ____ Breve.
10. A triplet is a group of _____ notes.
11. When accents are placed on week beats, it is called _____.
12. Four sixteenth notes equal _____ eighth notes.
13. One whole note equal _____ sixteenth notes.
14. A tie is a curved line that connects two notes of the same _____.

15. Circle the example that starts with an upbeat.

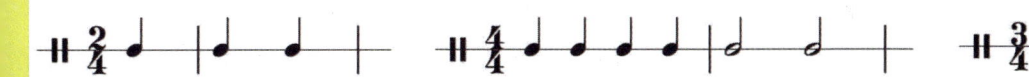 

16. Copy this example exercise below and rewrite the syncopation another way.

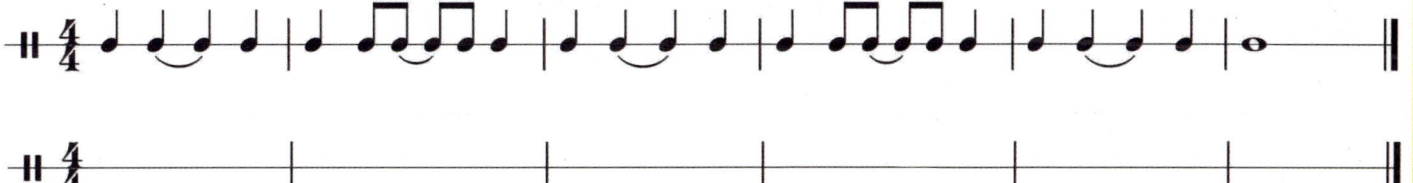

17. First, add the bar lines, and then write the counting under each measure. Count the beats and clap the rhythm.

18. Listen to the following piece and circle the appropriate time signature.
a) 2/4 time signature
b) 3/4 time signature
c) 6/8 time signature

-50-

Poor Old Crow

 Audio G43

Traditional Song

Peter Peter Pumpkin Eater

 Audio G44

- "Poor Old Crow" is a useful song for preparing, making conscious, or practicing the rhythmic element dotted quarter note followed by an eighth note.
- Sing to children alone, rocking your body or clapping or stomping to the beat.
  - Have children echo, phrase by phrase.
  - Add movement. This can be simultaneous or while echoing.
  - Put the song together. Sing it completely without echoing.
  - Practice chanting "Peter Peter Pumpkin Eater" with a metronome.
  - Separate students into groups of 5 and create Halloween music and theme composition.
  - Turn your Halloween into a frightful and mysteriously musical fun time. Improvise a dance movement on this song. Make sure to step up the game by wearing your Halloween costumes and enjoy them with your students, family, and friends. Happy Halloween! Awooo!

Let's Learn Piano

Middle C is positioned in the middle of an 88-key keyboard. The piano's keyboard is made up of sets of white and black keys that between two notes on the and black keys) and another made up of two half-steps. follow the note-by-note they reset to A on the next called accidentals. C# (sharps are placed a half-step below) are a half-step above a key, depending on the context of seven letters of the alphabet of seven white keys from C to called an octave, and this pattern is repeated on the piano. repeat. A half-step is a distance piano, one-note (including the white note directly above it. Whole-steps are Starting from middle C, the white keys alphabet until they reach G, where note. The black keys to the piano are are a half-step above a key, and flats can refer to C sharp or D flat (sharps and flats are placed a half-step below) whatever you are playing. The first are used in all white notes. The group B, with five black keys in between, is

The C position entails placing your right-hand thumb on middle C and the rest of your right-hand fingers on the four white keys that follow. Using your right hand in the C position, play the melody of "Frere Jacques," one note at a time.

Be sure to pay attention to the numbers above the notes. This set of numbers is called fingerings, and they show you which finger to use for each note.

Move your right hand up the keyboard to get to G so that RH 1 rests on G. (This is the same G in position C occupied by RH 5.) Check out this new position, as well as the staff notes that you play in it. Note that RH 5 is now resting all the way up to D. You have learned how to find the notes on your piano keyboard.

In the center of an 88-key keyboard, middle C is found.

The piano's keyboard is made up of sets of white and black keys that repeat. In music, a half-step is a distance between a white or black key and the key directly above it. Two half-steps are also referred to as whole-steps. From Middle C, the white keys follow the note-by-note alphabet until they reach G, where on the next note, they reset to an A.

Happy, Scary, Halloween!

Video L30

Florentina Alexandru

Watch Video L30 and follow instructions on how to play "Happy, Scary, Halloween."

Start by practicing right hand only and then continue with the left hand. Once you learn to play separate hands, try to put hands together. Approach a slow tempo at the beginning and speed it up once you get more comfortable playing this song. It is very important before you start practicing right-hand and left-hand to analyze the rhythm and prepare your hand position, fingers position too.

Have fun learning to play "Happy, Scary, Halloween" on the piano. Try to practice singing it as well once you learn the piano part. Can you improvise a dance movement on this piece?

Henry Purcell

Henry Purcell, who was born in 1659, was the finest and most original composer of his time. Despite his short life, Henry Purcell was able to fully appreciate and utilize the renewed flowering of music that followed the Monarchy's Restoration. As the son of a musician at the Court, a chorister at the Royal Chapel, and the holder of royal appointments until his death, Purcell worked for three different Kings in Westminster for over twenty-five years. When Henry Purcell was five, his father died, forcing his mother to resettle the family of six children into a more modest home and lifestyle. Purcell sang as a young child at King Charles II's chapel and subsequently became an organist of the Abbey of Westminster. Henry Purcell wrote many works for the stage, but his masterpiece is *Dido and Aeneas* (1689). Over the final ten years of his life, he produced over 400 works, including his most well-known works. *The Ode to St. Cecilia's Day*, *The Queen of Fairy*, and his *Funeral Music to Queen Mary* all date back to these years. People love to play his *G minor Chaconne* for Strings, which he wrote in the early 1800s. Purcell is regarded as the finest baroque composer in England.

Purcell married in 1680 or 1681. We know of six children, three of whom survived into adulthood. One of the three, Edward, became a musician, as did his son, Edward Henry.

Henry Purcell died at the age of 36 of tuberculosis on November 21, 1695, in London. To honor his stature as the most important English composer of his day, he was buried under Westminster Abbey's organ. His wife continued to publish his music posthumously, including the famous collection of songs known as *Orpheus Britannicus*.

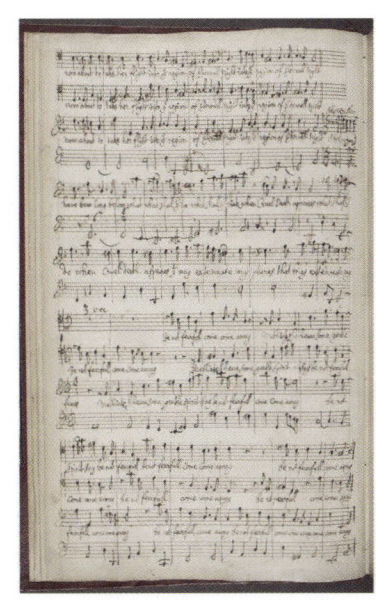

Purcell's manuscript copy of When on my sick bed I languish (c.1680)

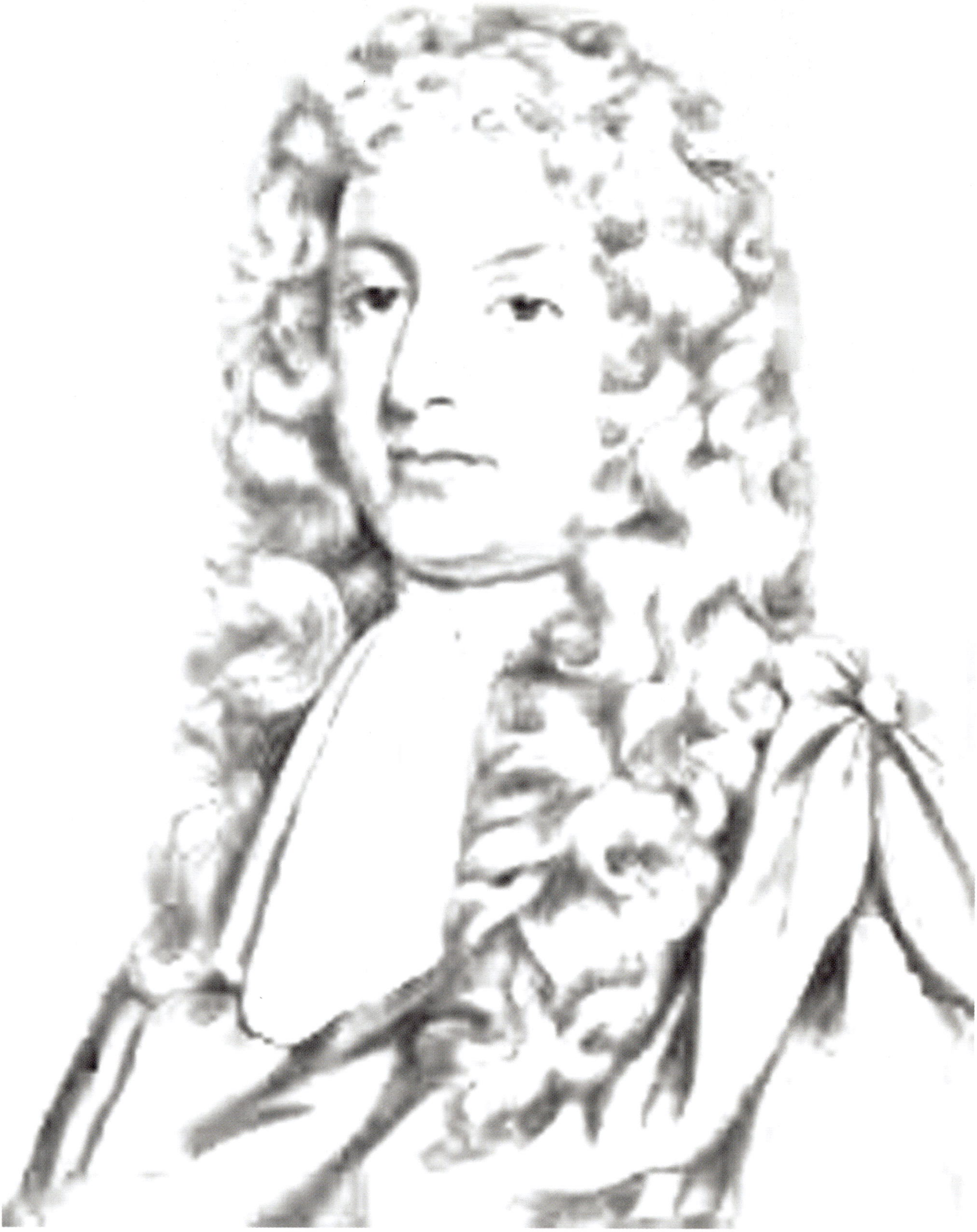

Henry Purcell

While coloring, you may listen to the opera "Dido and Aeneas" by Henry Purcell.

Henry Purcell Quiz

1. Purcell is considered England's finest composer of the _____ era.
   a) Romantic
   b) Baroque
   c) Classic

2. At what age did Purcell die?
   a) 52
   b) 36
   c) 27

3. Henry Purcell wrote many works for the stage, but only one opera _____ (1689), which is his masterpiece.
   a) *Dido and Aeneas*
   b) *Orpheus Britannicus*
   c) *Dioclesian*

4. At which famous London cathedral did Purcell work as an organist and composer?
   a) St. Paul's
   b) St. Mark's
   c) Westminster Abbey

The Origins of Blues Music

W. C. Handy (1873-1958)

The Blues began at the end of the 1800's in the levee camps or plantations in places like Mississippi, Louisiana, and Texas, where many African Americans lived. Country blues was the name given to the blues at the time. It was a mixture of African music, work songs, religious music, and ragtime.

The musical genre known as the blues is difficult to define, but you know it when you hear it: a simple progression of the chord, a deep bass line, and lyrics that evoke wisdom, sadness, and resignation. In the twelve-bar blues, the lyrics are repeated twice in the first eight bars and then further developed in the last four bars.

The first blues sheet music Antonio Maggio published in 1908 was called "I Got the Blues." It was the first time that the word "blues" had been used in a published song. In 1912, W.C. Handy, who was referred to as the "Father of the Blues," helped increase the public profile of the blues when he published and distributed sheet music for a blues song called "Memphis Blues." Mamie Smith's 1920 rendition of Perry Bradford's "Crazy Blues" was the first blues recording of an African American singer.

The blues had taken the form widely recognized today:
· 12 bars
· AAB lyrical structure
· a distinctive scale with the third and seventh notes flatted

What are the characteristics of the blues?

Although most bands use instrumental backing, the blues is primarily a vocal form. In contrast to many popular songs, blues songs are lyrical, not narrative. Blues singers, on the other hand, express feelings rather than communicate stories. The emotion expressed is generally one of sadness or melancholy, often due to problems of love.

The texture of blues is usually homophonic in that a single melodic line is accompanied by a guitar or, later, a band. The most important instrument besides the voice is the guitar (originally acoustic, then electric). Sometimes a blues player will use a "slide" on the left hand.

The most commonly used blues pattern is a 12-bar chord progression. This indicates that a repeated twelve-bar chord progression is being used. This is known as the "12-Bar Blues." You should keep this in mind: a bar is equal to a measure. In blues, the most commonly used time signature is 4/4, in which each bar consists of four beats. A 12-bar blues riff is reprised endlessly as the song progresses. A blues song may play the sequence of notes (the blues progression) no fewer than 20 times. It depends on the particular song. The blues can be played in any key, regardless of the key signature. It is the same sequence of I, IV, and V chords in 12-bar blues, regardless of key. This pattern is generally viewed as being made up of three 4-bar sections, the first four, the middle four, and the last four bars. To play the blues in A, we use the I, IV, and V chords from the key of A. That means that A is I, D is IV, and E is V. Then, in the blues form, we plug these three chords into the corresponding places. We are going to end up with this set of chord changes:

Here it is an example of **I** (A)   **IV** (D)   **V** (E)

🔊 **Audio G46, G47, G48**

• "Beale Street Blues" by W. C Handy
• "Crazy Blues" - Mamie Smith And Her Jazz Hounds
• "Arkansas Blues" - Mamie Smith And Her Jazz Hounds

🔊 **Audio G49**   12 Bar Blues

-57-

Backwater Blues

🔊 Audio G50

American Folk Song

Lyrics

When it rains five days and the sky turns dark as night, (repeat)
There's trouble takin' place in the lowlands at night.

I woke up this mornin', can't even get out my door. (repeat)
There's enough trouble to make a poor girl wonder where she wants to go.

Backwater blues done caused me to pack my things an' go, (repeat)
'Cause my house fell down and I can't live there no mo'.

They rowed a little boat about five miles 'cross the pond, (repeat)
I packed all my things throwed 'em in, and they rowed me along.

When it thunders and lightnin's and the wind begins to blow, (repeat)
There's thousands of people ain't got no place to go.

Backwater Blues is a standard song for blues and jazz. Bessie Smith penned the piece. "Backwater Blues" analyzes the flood of the Mississippi River in 1927 through the lenses of race and charity, blues music, mobility, and labor. Many of the song lyrics use the AAB blues formatting. Words vary from performer to performer; this opening verse is representative: "When it rains for five days, and the skies turn dark as night (repeat) There is trouble going on in the lowland that night."

Sing the song correctly, be expressive, keep your lips slightly rounded, have a clean emission and a loose body position.

Do a Think-Pair-Share activity in which students talk about:
• meaning of the song.
• describing what they like the most (rhythm, melody, lyrics, etc.) about this piece.
• major or minor key (there is a common assumption about music that major is happy, and minor is sad).
• describing what they like the most (rhythm, melody, lyrics, etc.) about this piece.
• identifying upbeat, tie, dotted half notes, dotted half rests, and quarter rests.

Brown's Ferry Blues

 Audio G51

American Folk Song

Hard luck pa-pa a- coun-tin' his toes, You can smell his feet where- e-ver he goes,

Lord Lord, and he's Got them Brown's Fer-ry blues; Hard luck pa-pa done

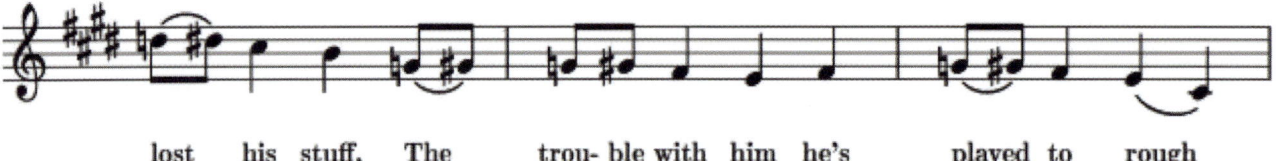

lost his stuff, The trou-ble with him he's played to rough

Lord, Lord, and he's got them Brown's Fer-ry blues.

Two old maids a-sitting in the sand,
Each one wishing that the other was a man,
Lord, Lord, got those Brown's Ferry Blues
Two old maids done lost their style,
If you want to be lucky you got to smile.
Lord, Lord, got those Brown's Ferry Blues

Early to bed and early, to rise,
And your girl goes out with other guys.
Lord, Lord, got those Brown's Ferry Blues
If you don't believe me try it yourself,
Well I tried it and I got left.
Lord, Lord, got those Brown's Ferry Blues

Hardluck poppa standing in the rain,
If the world was corn he couldn't buy grain.
Lord, Lord, got those Brown's Ferry Blues
Hardluck poppa standing in the snow,
His knees knock together but he's raring to go.
Lord, Lord, got those Brown's Ferry Blues.

- Sing the song correctly, be expressive, keep your lips slightly rounded, have a clean emission, and a loose body position.
- Sing the song and clap to the beat and rhythm.
- Identify the beat or pulse in this song and join in at a faster or slower tempo.
- Identify the rhythm of the words.
- What is the time signature? Write the beats under each measure.
- Describe what you like the most (rhythm, melody, lyrics, etc.) about this piece.
- Can you name a few blues songs that you know?
- Can you name the instruments present in the blues song you like?
- Can you find a dance movement while listening to the blues song you like?

Title: Composer:
                                                     Lyrics:

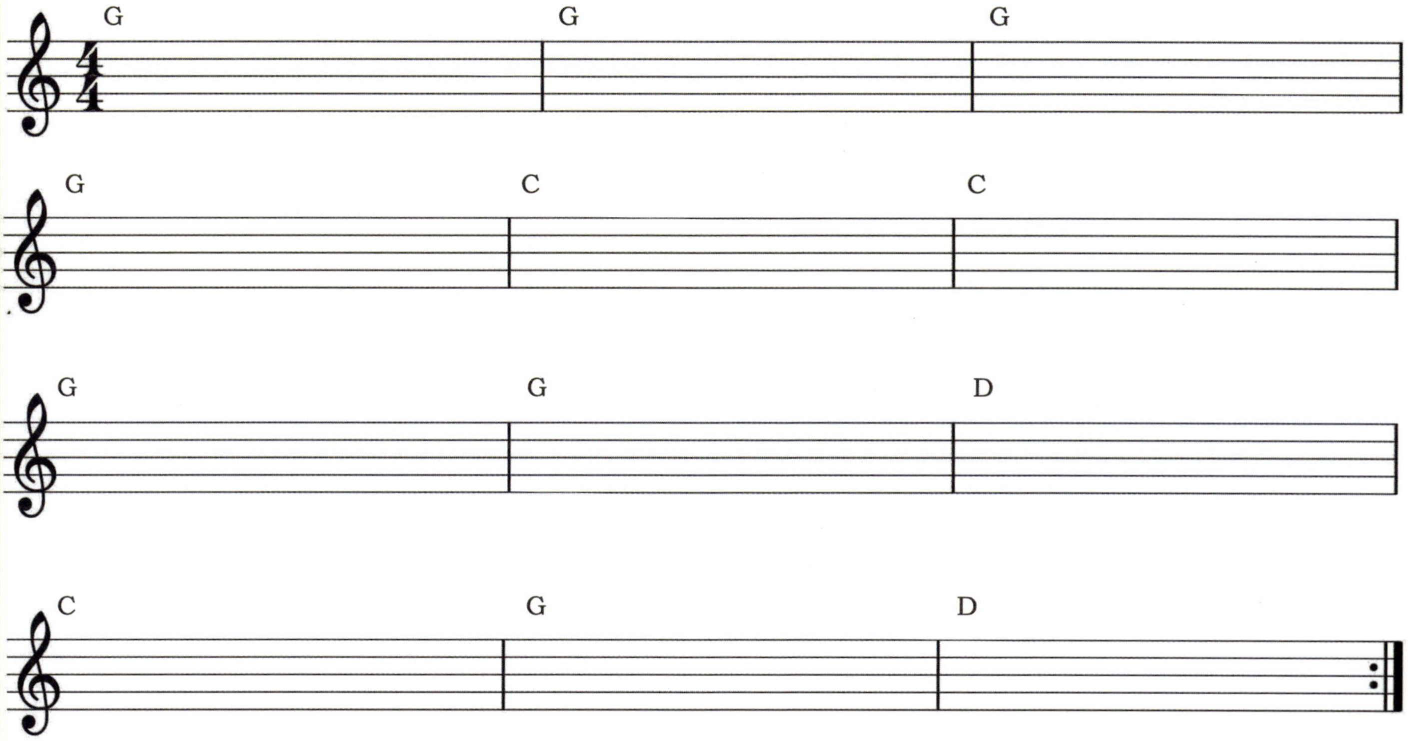

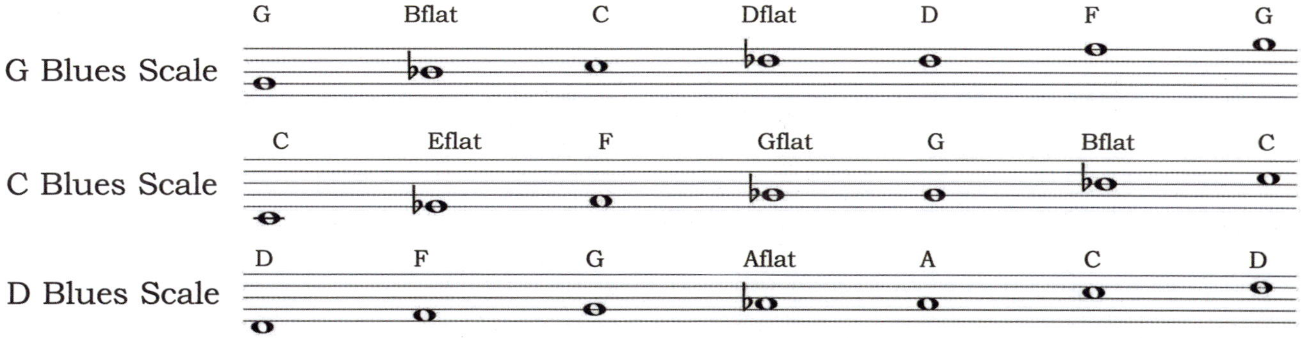

(12-bar blues chord chart in 4/4:)
G	G	G
G	C	C
G	G	D
C	G	D :

G Blues Scale: G, Bflat, C, Dflat, D, F, G
C Blues Scale: C, Eflat, F, Gflat, G, Bflat, C
D Blues Scale: D, F, G, Aflat, A, C, D

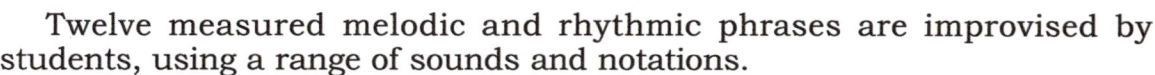

Twelve measured melodic and rhythmic phrases are improvised by students, using a range of sounds and notations.

Composition rules:
• Give your piece a proper title. Put your name where it says the composer.
• If you are using a poem for lyrics, put the poet's name where it says lyrics.
• You may use musical notes of the G, C, or D blues scale.
• Your tune must be a 12-bar standard blues piece (I is G, IV is C, V is D).
• Be creative with your melody, rhythm, dynamics, lyrics.
• Your tune should be easy to play or sing. Upon finishing your composition, you may play it or sing it.

Students may apply accepted criteria for critiquing musical performances of self and others.

Melody

Melodies are the most recognizable and significant aspect of a song. They are, however, the most difficult to write. The sequence of notes that we hear as a single entity is called "melody." A song's melody is the main focus of the musical piece, and it is a combination of pitch and rhythm. Also, sequences of notes that comprise the melody are often very enjoyable and will stay with the listener longer.

Melodies are produced through human voices or other instruments, as well: flutes, synthesizers, clarinets, guitars, trumpets, etc.

What Are Some Melodies You Know?

Melodies are everywhere, and there are tons of simple melodies that we all recognize in addition to those we hear in our favorite music. For example, when we sing a song called "Happy Birthday," we sing a melody.

🔊 **Audio G52**

What Is the Difference Between Melody and Harmony?

Now we know the definition of melody, but how does harmony compare? Harmony is when multiple notes are stacked on top of each other, creating a unique sound. Two or more sounds are played simultaneously in harmony, and the result should be sonically pleasing, with the sounds complementing one another. The main difference between harmonies and melodies is that harmony builds on a melody that already exists and needs a melody to exist.

The music line consists of notes starting at the left and traveling to the right. Western music has 12 notes (and seven intervals).

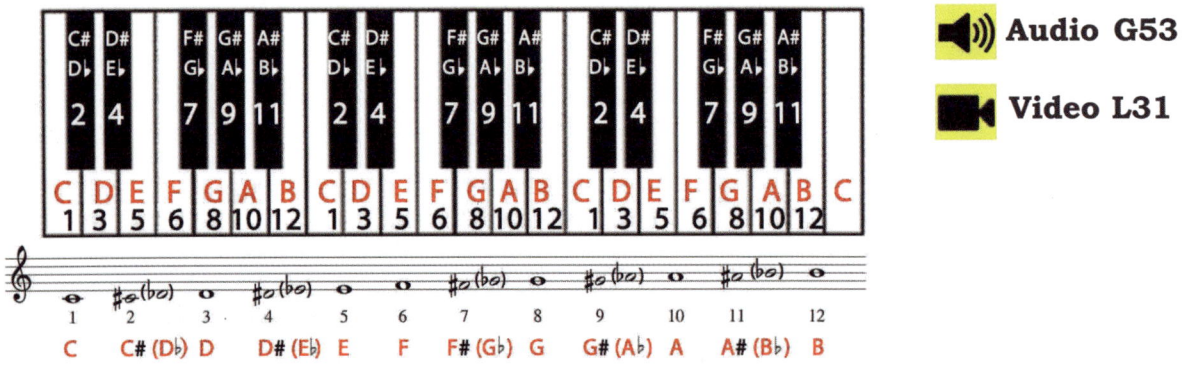

🔊 **Audio G53**

🎥 **Video L31**

These 12 tones are sometimes referred to as the chromatic scale. In combination with other symbols, we use the first seven letters in the alphabet to represent the tones commonly referred to as notes. The pattern of notes repeats every twelfth note, as you can see from the above picture. It is called the octave, the distance between the first C (Note 1) and the second C.

Accidentals

If you study the picture above sufficiently well, you will notice that seven of the 12-note names consist of only alphabetic symbols, the first seven alphabet letters. These notes are referred to as natural notes. The symbols known as sharps (#) and flats (♭) represent the remaining notes. These symbols are referred to as accidentals. Please read more on page 62.

Sometimes we need to cancel or negate a sharp or flat - that is, turn a "sharped" or "flatted" note back into a natural note. To do this, we use the natural sign (♮). This symbol cancels out any previous occurrences of a sharp or flat for that note in a measure of music. Do not worry if the previous sentence doesn't make complete sense right now. I will elaborate on this subject in a later lesson. For now, simply realize that seven of the twelve notes are natural notes while the others are not because they contain accidentals.

Please Note: A natural sign also falls under the category of accidentals.

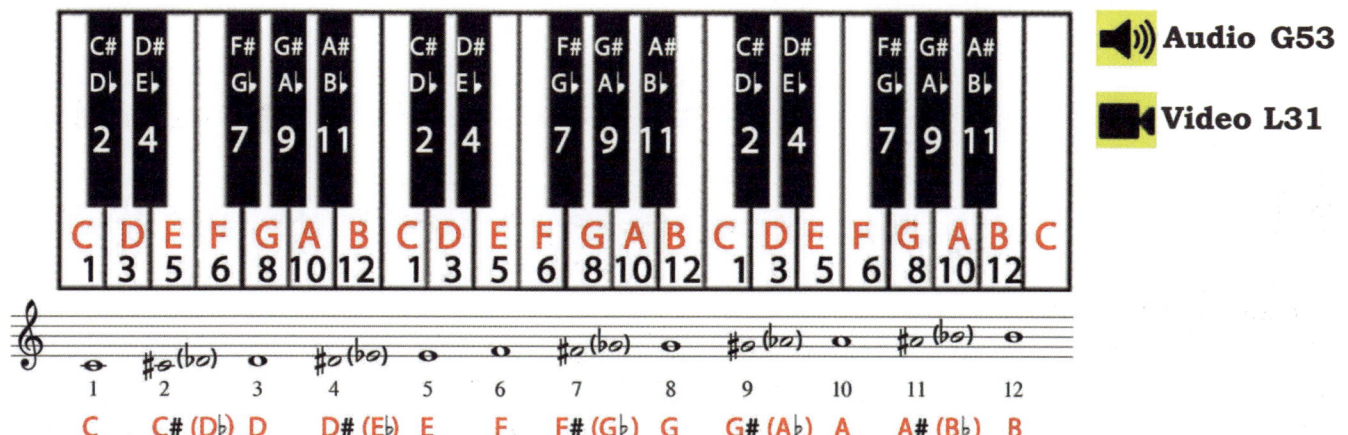

Intervals

The distance between any two notes is called an interval. There are many kinds of intervals, but for now, we will just study two:
• half-steps
• whole-steps

If we take a closer look at the chromatic scale, we see (in the above picture) that the distance between each adjacent note in the scale is the same. We call this distance a semitone or a half-step.

For example, the distance between A and A# is a half-step. The distance between A# and B is also a half-step. So is the distance between B and C, C and C#, C# and D, and so on. Study the above picture again to be sure you understand this idea. The distance between each adjacent note in the chromatic scale is the same, a half-step.

Remember fractions from school? 1/2 + 1/2 = 2/2 = 1. Right? It works the same way with half-steps. Two half-steps equal one whole-step.

For instance, we know that the distance between C and C# is a half-step. We also know that the distance between C# and D is a half-step. So, it only makes sense then that the distance between C and D is a whole-step.

Playing or singing the chromatic way means to "make use of semitones or half-steps."

You may watch Video L31 understand better and learn to play a chromatic scale on the piano.

How accidentals relate to intervals

A sharp raises a note's pitch by a half-step while a flat lowers it by a half-step. For instance, let's examine the interval between C and D♭. It is a half-step. But if we raise the D♭ (the top note of the interval) to a D♮, the interval increases and becomes a whole-step. If we take the whole-step interval and raise the bottom note, the C, to a C#, the notes' distance gets smaller again and becomes a half-step. Consult the picture below.

▶ Video L32

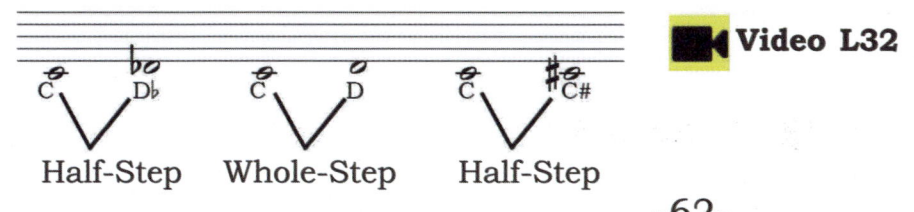

Enharmonic Notes

Enharmonic equivalencies or enharmonic spellings are notes that sound the same but are written differently. Another way of saying this is different names for the same note.

As we will see later, this concept also applies to intervals.

C# is enharmonically equivalent to D♭
D# is enharmonically equivalent to E♭
E# is enharmonically equivalent to F
F# is enharmonically equivalent to G♭
G# is enharmonically equivalent to A♭
A# is enharmonically equivalent to B♭
B# is enharmonically equivalent to C

 **Video L31**

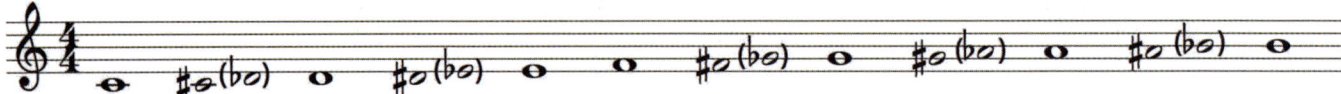

Musical Intervals

In music, an interval is the pitch difference between two notes. The interval is counted from the lowest to the highest note, with the lowest note being counted as one. With two exceptions, intervals are named after the upper note's number (2nd, 3rd, etc.). The interval between identical notes is called the unison (also called the prime interval); the 8th interval is called the octave.

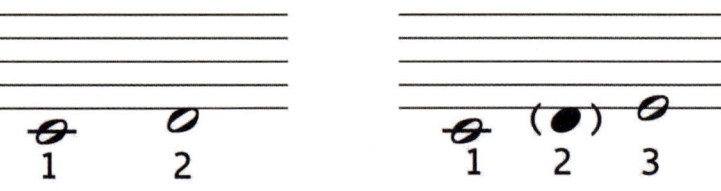

Unison or perfect unison (also called prime or a perfect prime) refers to the interval formed by a tone and its duplication, e.g., C–C.

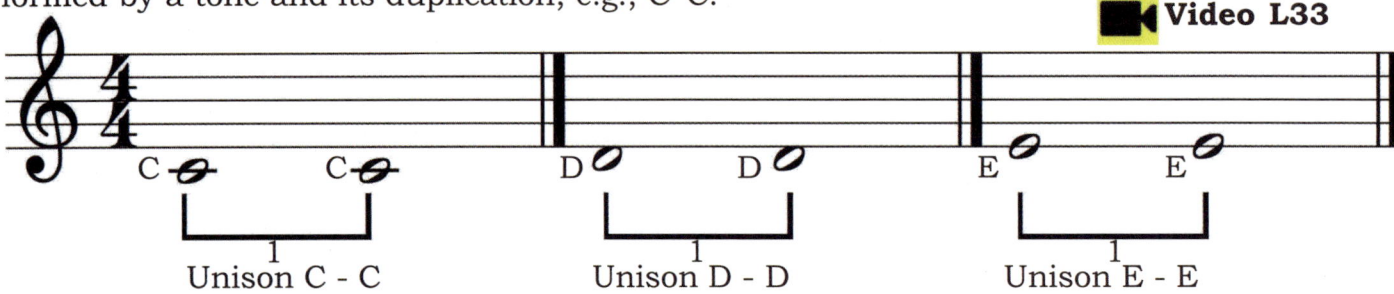

Video L33

Major and Minor Seconds

Two semitones make up a major second interval (or a whole step), whereas a minor second interval consists of a semitone. An example of a major second is C - D. Example of a minor second interval is B-C.

Melodic Intervals

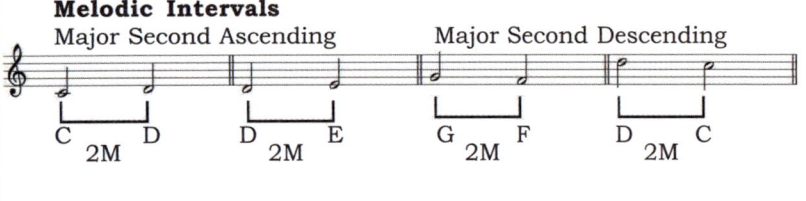

Intervals are known as melodic intervals when they are sounded separately and harmonic intervals when they are sounded together.

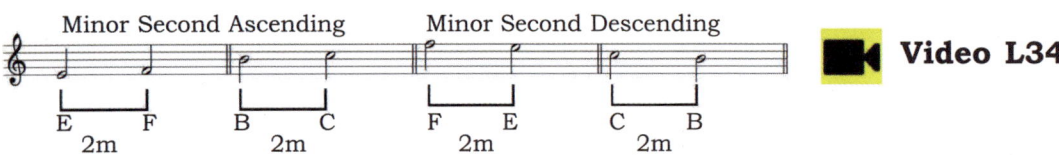

Video L34

Harmonic Intervals

Video L35

1. Indicate whether the following are melodic (M) or harmonic (H) intervals.

2. Write the melodic or harmonic interval indicated above the following notes.

harmonic   melodic   melodic   melodic   harmonic   melodic

3. Sing the following exercise using solfege syllables. Find and circle unison, major and minor second intervals, as well name them.

🔊 Audio G54

sol la sol   fa mi re mi fa   sol la ti   ti do re   do ti la la sol fa   mi re do ti   do   re   do

4. For each example, you will hear a whole step that moves up or down. Draw the second note on the staff using a half note.

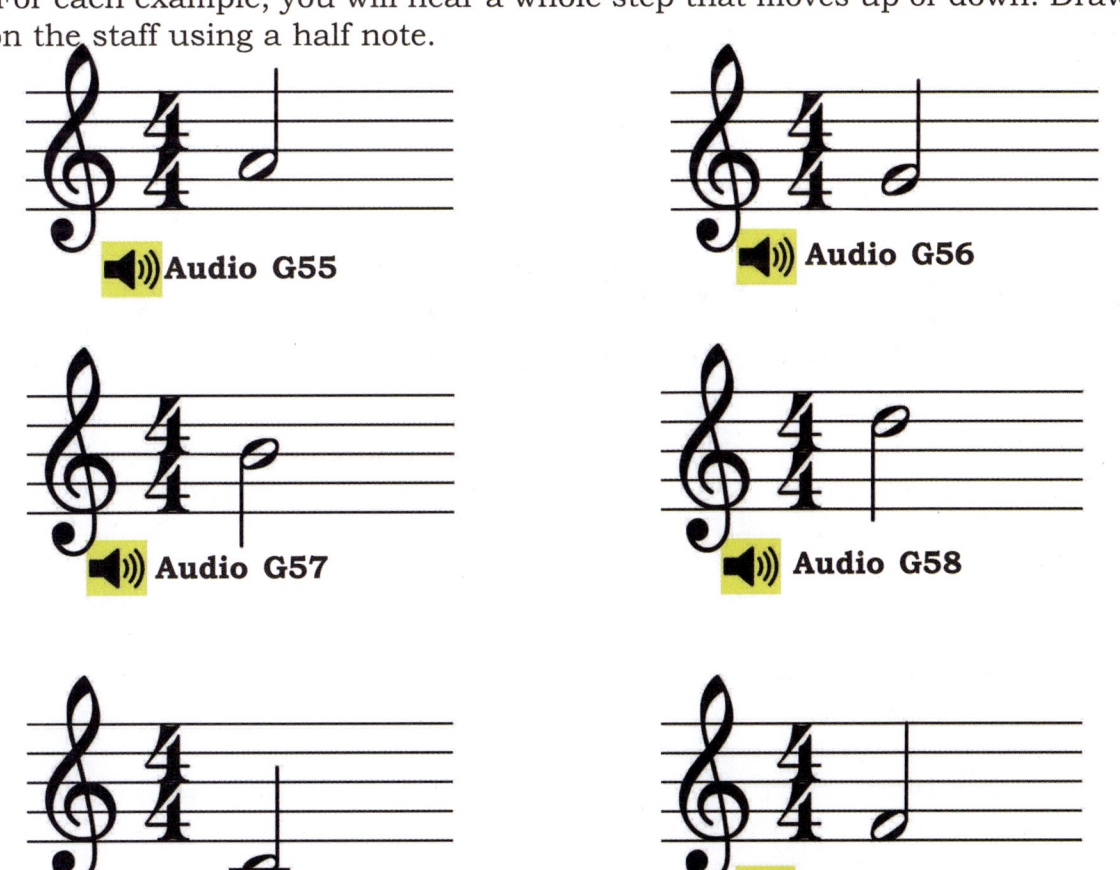

🔊 Audio G55

🔊 Audio G56

🔊 Audio G57

🔊 Audio G58

🔊 Audio G59

🔊 Audio G60

Wait for the Wagon

Audio G61 Traditional Song

Will you come with me, my Phyl- lis dear, to yon blue moun- tain free? Where the

blos- soms smell the swee- test, Come rove a- long with me. It's ev- 'ry Sun- day

mor- ning, When I am at your side, We'll jump in- to the wa- gon And we'll all take a ride.

Wait for the wa- gon, Wait for the wa- gon, Wait for the wa- gon and we'll all take a ride.

C Major Scale Warm-up Exercise   Audio G62

do re mi fa sol la ti do do ti la sol fa mi re do do mi sol do do sol mi do do

You are using the C major scale notes as a guide, sight-sing the following exercise while paying attention to the repeat sign. Before singing "Wait for the Wagon," it is necessary to study each note of the song separately to acquire a good emission of the voice, perfect intonation, purity, and unbroken continuity of vocal tone. Develop an awareness of the direction of the melody (melodic contour). Use movement to reinforce your inner feeling for the rhythmic pulse.

This song starts with an upbeat. A note or series of notes preceding the first complete measure of composition is known as an anacrusis. The number of beats expressed by the time signature is not held in this introductory (and optional) measure.

The anacrusis, also known as the upbeat, prepares your ears for the next measure's downbeat. In traditional notation, the number of beats in the anacrusis is taken out of the song's very last measure to even out the difference.

Can you circle major/minor seconds and unison intervals?

C Major & A Minor Chord

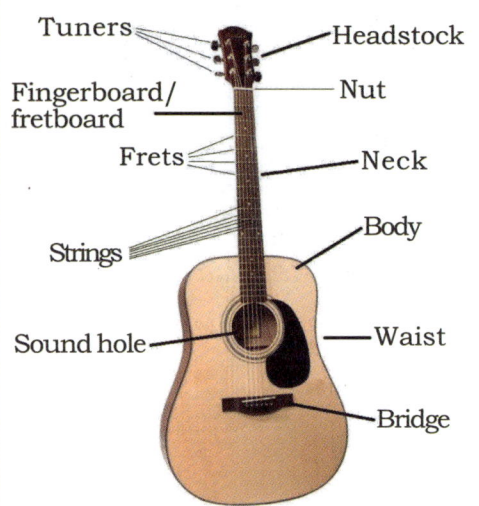

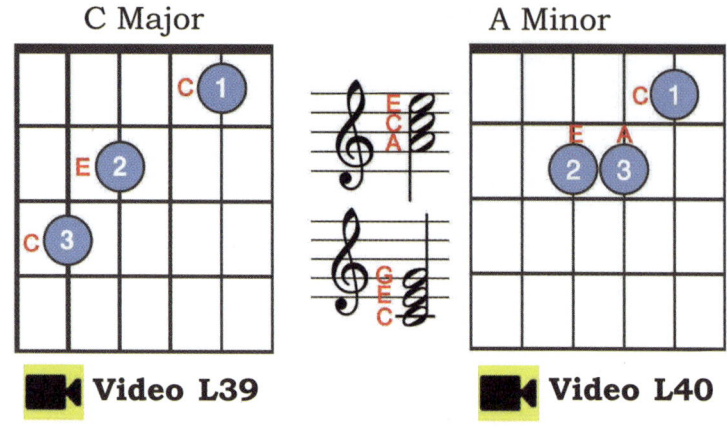

One of the most basic ways you can play chords is with a strum. Strumming the guitar is the simple act of brushing the strings with a pick, thumb, or the back of your fingernails. A strum can be slow, fast, hard, or gentle, or any of the infinite shadings in between.

Downstrokes: You are "executing a downstroke" when you go to naturally strike the strings on a guitar. A downstroke (indicated with an open-bottomed box, shown in the following figures) is played with a downward motion of the pick toward the floor — the way you naturally strike a guitar. You can strum multiple strings or pick an individual string with a downstroke.

Upstrokes: The upstroke (indicated with a V-shaped symbol) is played up towards the ceiling. Begin at the bottom of the first string and drag your pick up the strings, from the first to the sixth. You do not have to worry about hitting all the strings on an upstroke. Usually, the top three or four strings are enough.

How to play C major chord on the guitar

- Begin by making a C major shape with your fingers on the strings, then counting to four and strumming on each beat.
- Then, for four beats, take your fingers off the strings.
- Put your hands back on the keys and repeat the cycle.
- Taking your fingers off and on again in this way will help your brain to memorize the shape, while the four beats will give you time to place your fingers.
- When you are ready, go ahead and attempt the same approach, experiment by using a C major and A minor chord

How to play an A Minor chord on the guitar

- On your guitar, on the first fret of the second string, place your 1st finger.
- On the second fret of the fourth string, put your second finger.
- On the 2nd fret of the 3rd string, put your 3rd finger.
- Strumm all six strings at the same time.

Quarter-note striking: For quarter-note striking, play four strums for each bar of music. The quarter notes tell you that the strums occur once per beat. Note that quarter notes have just a stem attached to them.

All the strum patterns we will be looking at in the below Solfege-Guitar exercise are in a 4/4 time signature. In short, that means that every measure consists of four beats. For this first pattern, simply play a downstroke on every beat.

Solfege- Guitar (8 measures exercise)

🔊 Audio G63

🎥 Video L41

Form two groups. One group will sight-sing with solfege syllables, and the other group will accompany by playing the guitar.

Strum pattern: Downstroke C major chord on every beat on the first four measures and downstroke A minor chord on the last four measures. You may practice with each group separately, and once everybody feels comfortable, you may have them practice together. Practice with a metronome.

Homework: Compose similar eight measures exercise voice and guitar. Be creative with your melody and accompany rhythm.

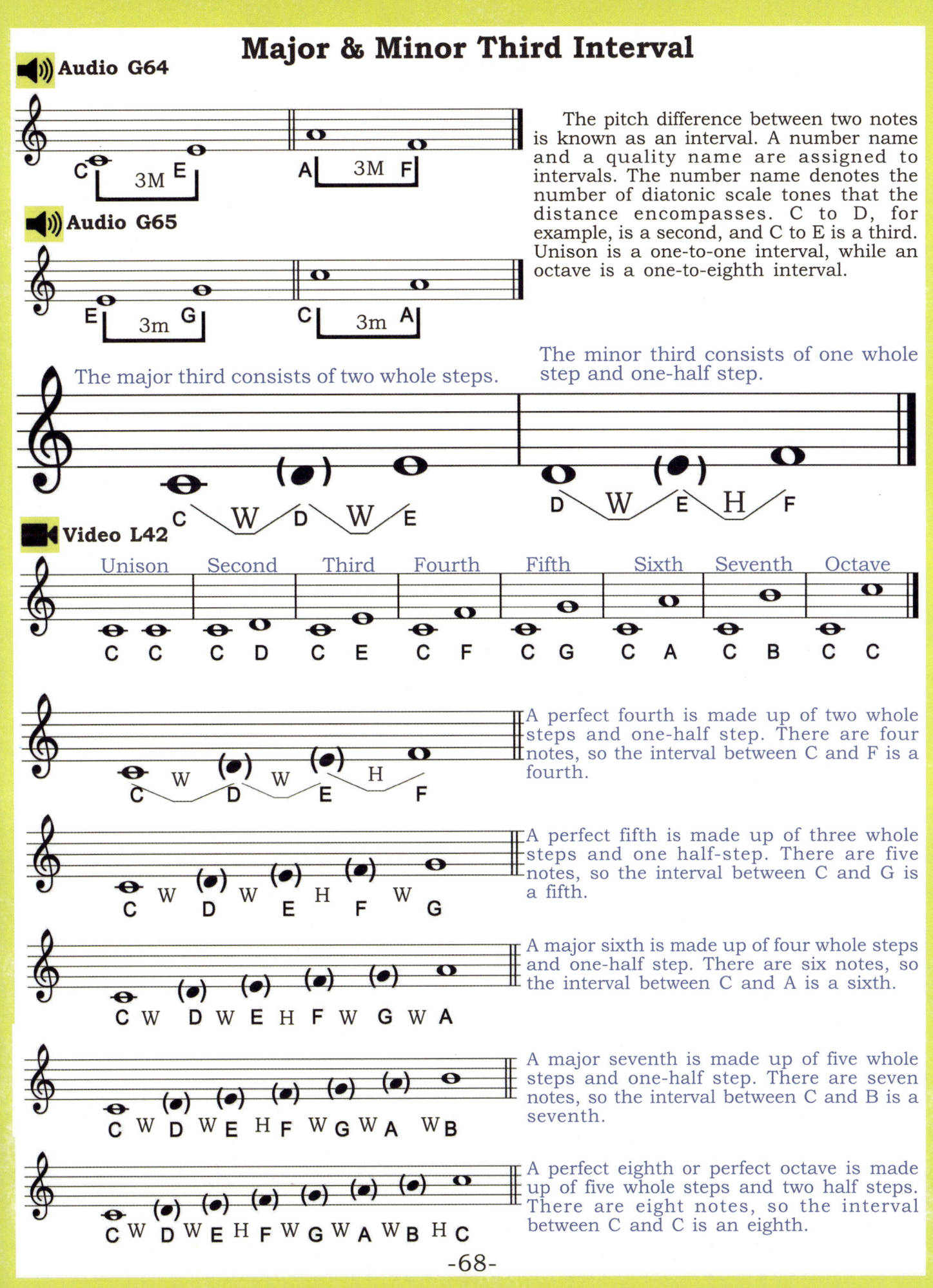

Thanksgiving Day

Homer H. Harbour

🔊 Audio G66

(Musical notation with lyrics:)

1. Oh, Thanks-gi-ving mor-ning is a time of glee, With our kit-chen bu-sy as a place can be. When the mince pies are a-ba-king, And the pud-dings are a-ma-king, That's the time for me.

Annotations on score: "Unison" (circled), "Phrase 1", "4th interval" (circled), "Phrase 2". Chords: F, C, F, C7, F, C, F, C7, F, D7, Gm, C7, F, Dm, Gm, C7, F.

In the afternoon it's time at last to eat
Of a dinner splendid as a king might greet;
There's a turkey full of spices,
There are puddings, there are ices,
Cake and candies sweet.

On Thanksgiving night when dark the shadows fall,
A great fire is lighted in the fireplace tall,
When the apples are a-roasting,
And the chestnuts are a-toasting,
That is best of all.

- Slowly learn melody and words and pick-up speed!
- Students learn and sing all verses while listening to Audio G66
- Play Audio G66 and have students echo phrase by phrase.
- Add movement. This can be simultaneous or while echoing.
- Students can sing-song with reasonable pitch accuracy and continue to build good posture.
- Review each measure and discuss note values as well as count beats. For example:
  - time signature is 2/4; the key signature is F major
  - this song starts with an upbeat, and there is also a perfect unison interval C-C at the beginning
  - second measure consists of musical notes F-G, quarter notes, major second interval...continue doing the same by analyzing each measure.
- There are two highlighted musical phrases. Can you find more musical phrases in this song?
- Circle other musical intervals that you might recognize and name them.

-69-

Swing Low, Sweet Chariot

🔊 Audio G67   **Traditional Song**

A phrase is a musical line that conveys a complete idea. In music, phrases are formed by the interaction of melody, harmony, and rhythm.

Although phrasing is a rather ambiguous term with many variations, it is critical to music making because it tells us how notes relate to one another rather than isolated dots on a page.

The concept itself is well known to us as we speak in phrases daily. We recognize that to speak a phrase/sentence/idea convincingly and clearly; we must first have a conceptual understanding of it; otherwise, it may come across as disorganized. The place where you take a breath is often the end of a phrase if there is a melody (something you might hum to yourself after hearing it).

    Choose a blue color crayon and mark the phrase on the page. Sing the song correctly with lips slightly rounded, ensuring a clean emission, and loosen up your body for a perfect position. When the students are comfortable with the song, move on to the next step, have them sing it while paying attention to all musical phrases.

    Knowing how to phrase your words as you sing is a huge part of delivering a song with a feeling, and it is one of the techniques that really sets great singers apart. Changing the phrasing of a song can change its meaning. Have you ever heard a cover song that did not sound anything like the original? (Students can comment on and give examples of their favorite singers). Some of the cover songs show deeper meaning through emphasis. You draw attention to a word or sound when you emphasize it. This implies significance, and the ensuing questions create tension for the listener.

    Paying attention to phrasing will make your singing better!

Slurs, Ties and Phrases

A slur is marked by a curvy line that runs from the first note of the slur group to the last note. The tie is a similar curved line, which joins two notes of the same pitch. The second note carries on from the first.

A slur can be difficult to distinguish from a phrase mark, which resembles a slur but may cover a longer passage and only indicates that this is one phrase, similar to a phrase in spoken language.

Musical phrasing is like telling a story. When speaking, you might emphasize certain words or speed up and slow down to make the story sound more interesting; when singing, you can do the same thing with musical phrasing.

Musical phrasing includes deciding when to breathe, how fast or slow to sing, and which words to emphasize. All these things can help you communicate the meaning of the song and create a certain feeling or emotion.

Musical terms are frequently written on music by composers to aid in phrasing and to help you understand how they want it to sound. Normally, these words are written in Italian.

You can completely change the mood of a song by changing your phrasing.

Often, a choir will use dynamics in their sound by adding more or less volume or intensity to a phrase. For example, singing "piano" is when you sing quietly and use your breath to support the sound. The Forte is the exact opposite of the piano. It is when you sing loudly while being careful not to overwork your voice. Another term you may come across is "legato." It is the Italian word for tied together and means the phrase rolls on smoothly. "Staccato" is the opposite. It's the Italian word for detached. This is when the musical notes are short and have a lot of space between them. Phrasing can also refer to the volume at which you are singing. When you sing a phrase that gradually gets louder, it is called a "crescendo," and when you sing a phrase that gradually gets quieter, it is called a "diminuendo."

Listen to your favorite singers in your preferred genre and pay attention to how they use phrasing. It will differ on the basis of the genre, and some styles intentionally use unusual phrases. With some observation, you will notice the phrases of your favorite singers that make their style distinctive.

Choose a song that has many different cover versions for a listening exercise. On the same song, compare how different singers use phrasing.

Listen to the following examples Audio G69 and G70, and discuss slur, phrases, ties, dynamics.

Treble Clef (G Clef)

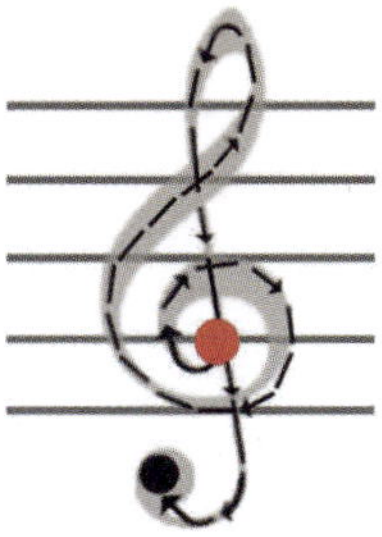

A staff is used to notate music. The staff is made up of five horizontal lines and spaces where musical notes can be written.

The pitch of the notes written on staff is indicated by a musical clef, placed at the left-hand end of the staff. A musician's ability to read the music in front of them is crucial because it tells them which lines or spaces represent each note. Clefs are commonly used in modern music, but four are commonly used: Treble, Bass, Alto, and Tenor.

The "G clef." is another name for the treble clef. The easiest way to remember this is to look at the clef and notice how it circles the note G. (second line from the bottom).

The violin, flute, oboe, bagpipes, all clarinets, all saxophones, horn, trumpet, cornet, vibraphone, xylophone, mandolin, and recorder are among the instruments that use the treble clef. Besides, it is also utilized on the guitar, which plays an octave lower than written.

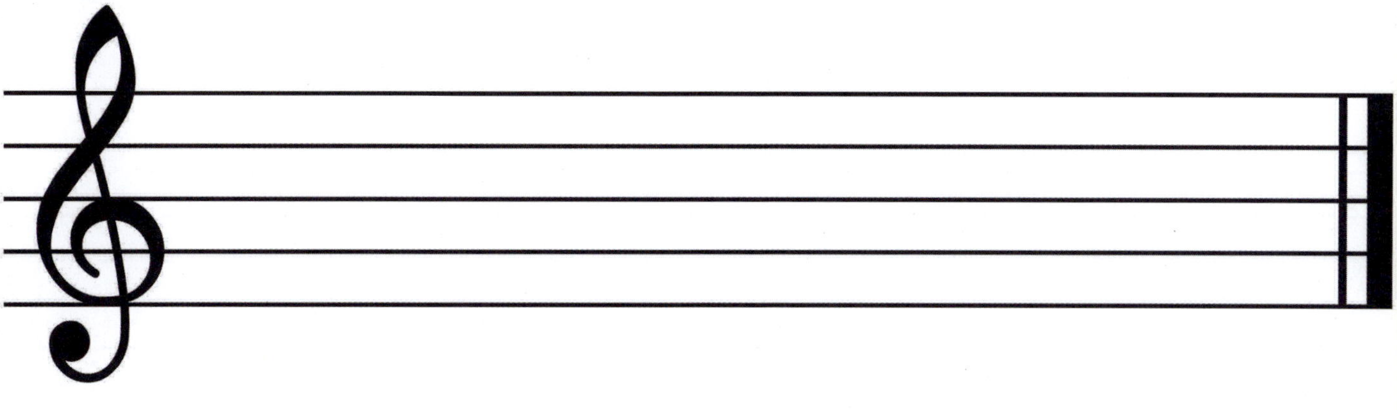

How to draw a treble clef Start on the **G** line (2nd line up) where the red dot is and follow the arrow around, up, and back down.

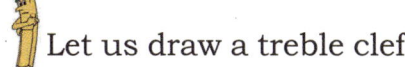 Let us draw a treble clef.

Bass Clef (F Clef)

This clef is also known as the "F clef." The line between the two dots is F, so that is one way to remember it (the fourth line from the bottom). It is usually the second clef that musicians learn after treble because it is on the bottom staff in the grand staff for piano.

The instruments that use the bass clef include cello, euphonium, double bass, bass guitar, bassoon, bassoon, trombone, baritone horn, tuba, and timpani. It is also the bottom staff in the grand staff for harp and keyboard instruments, and it is used for the lowest notes of the horn.

Although the tenor voice can be notated on the bass clef when bass and tenor are notated on the same staff, both bass and baritone voice parts are notated on the bass clef.

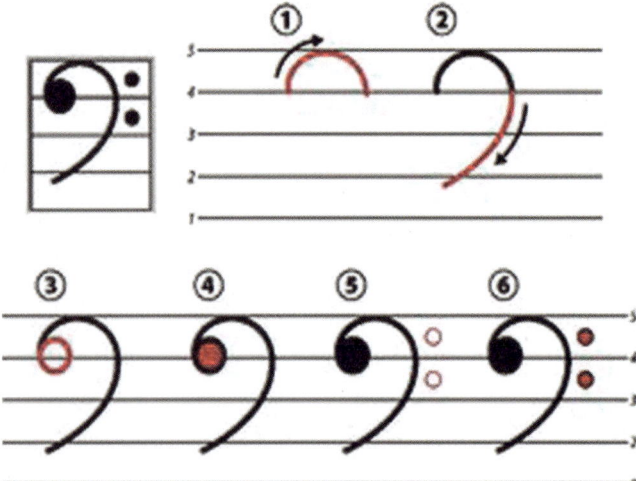

Begin on the fourth line with a dot.
Curve up to the top line and touch it.
Curve downward until you reach the second line or just below it.
In the spaces above and below the fourth line of the staff, draw two dots.

 Let us draw a bass clef.

Treble Clef and Bass Clef Notes

Treble clef line notes

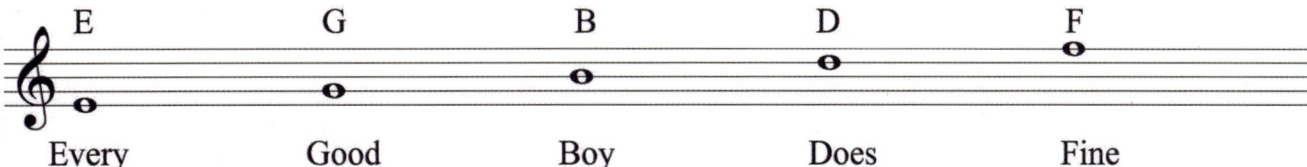

Treble clef space notes

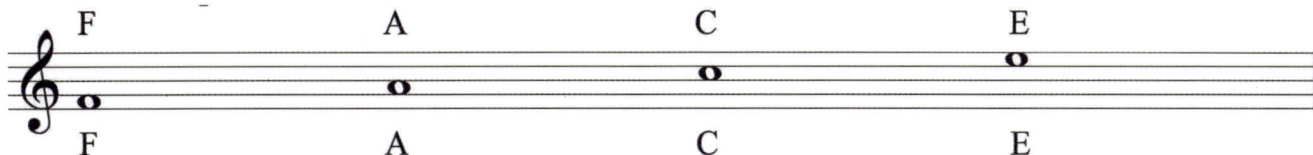

Bass clef line notes

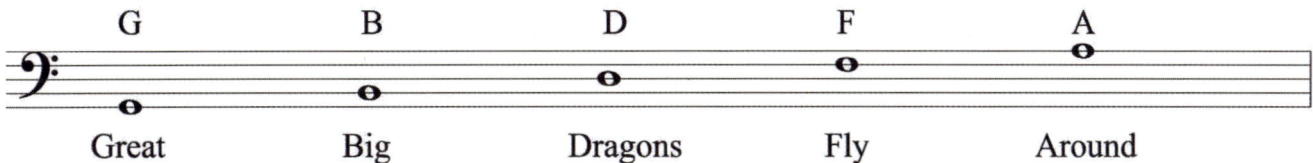

Bass clef space notes

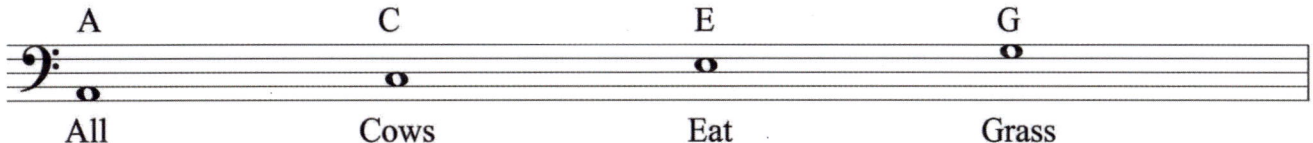

Treble clef notes

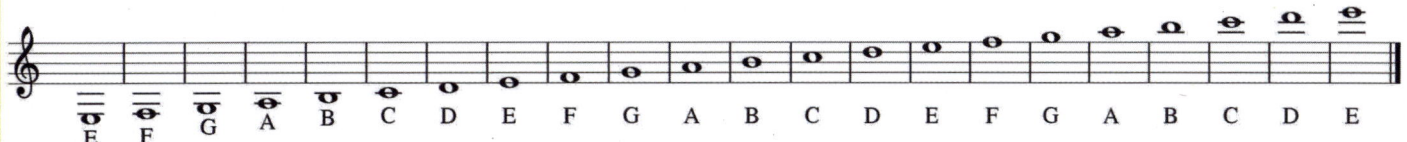

Bass clef notes

Grand Staff

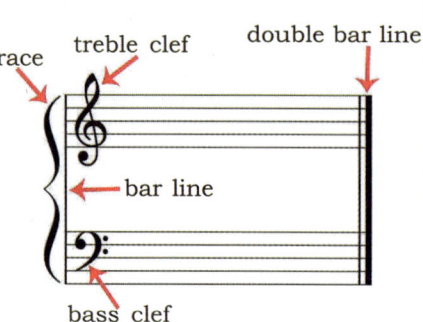

The grand staff is made up of the treble clef and bass clef staves combined. The treble and bass staves are joined by a curved line and bar line known as the brace.

These musical examples demonstrate all the notes on the grand staff. When the note is either above or below the staff, a ledger line is added. The Middle C note is on the ledger line between the treble and the bass staff.

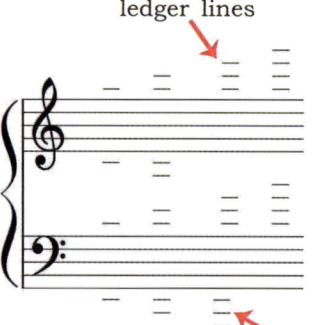

Ledger lines extend the staff up and down to allow notes to be written beyond the staff's five lines. The examples below show how ledger lines can be used to write notes above and below the staff.

1. Trace the braces, bar lines, and clefs to create the grand staff.

 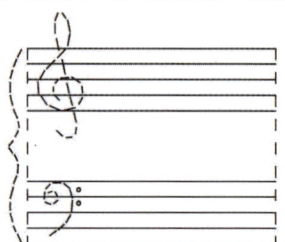 

2. Add braces, bar lines, and clefs to the following staff to make it a grand staff.

 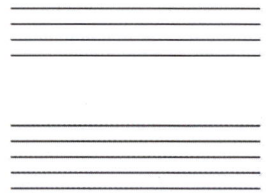 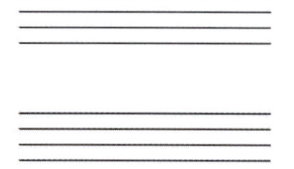

3. For each note, write the letter name.

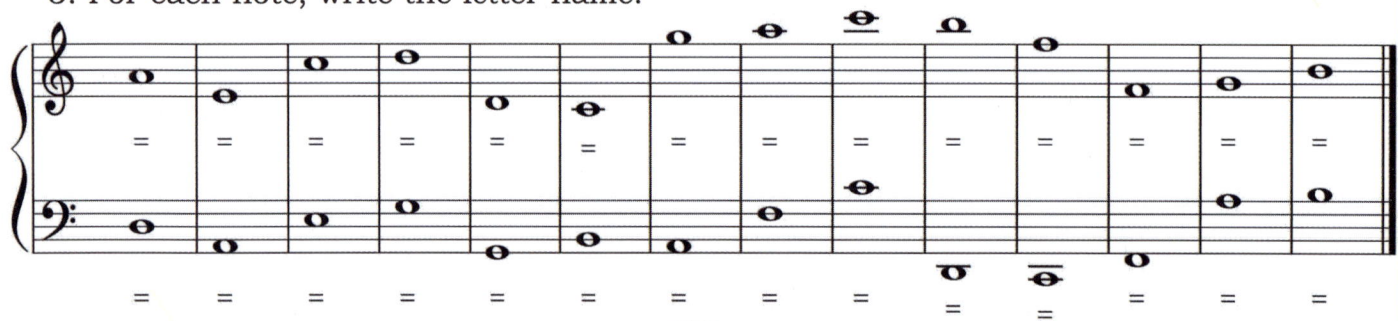

-75-

1. Draw the correct notes. When you find 2 or 3 same letters, choose a higher or lower position for that note than the previous one on the staff.

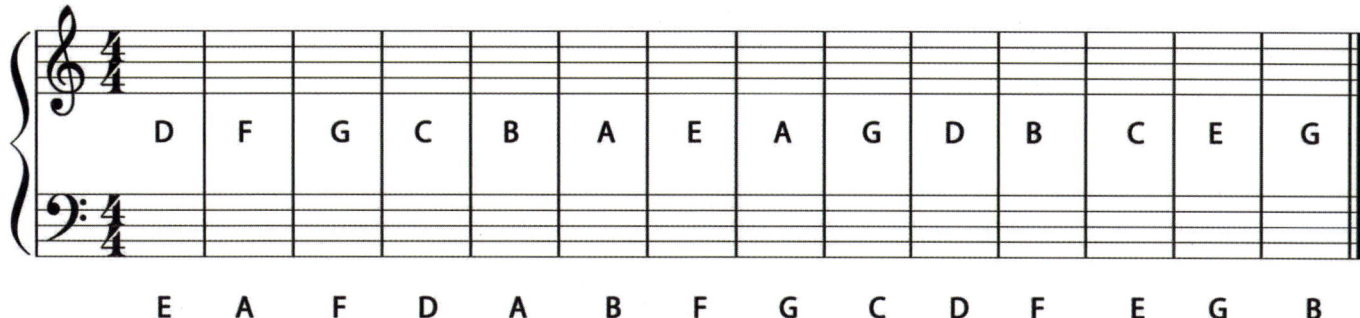

Have a good time writing a song. If at all possible, play it on the piano.

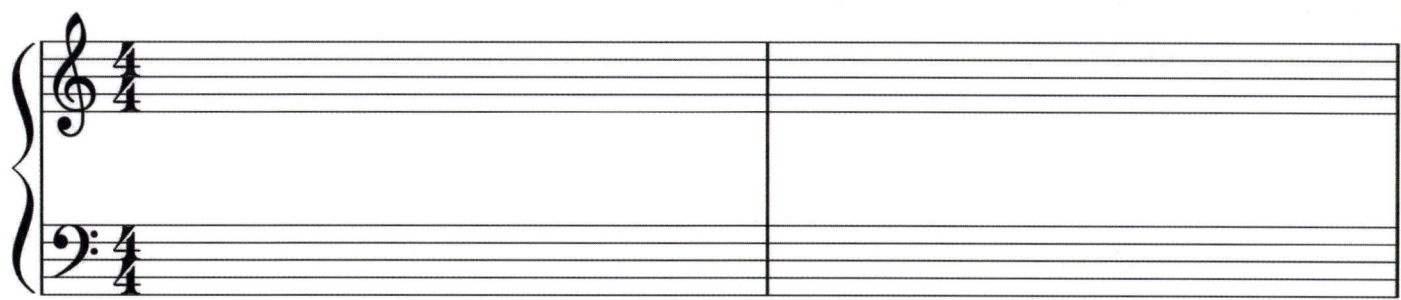

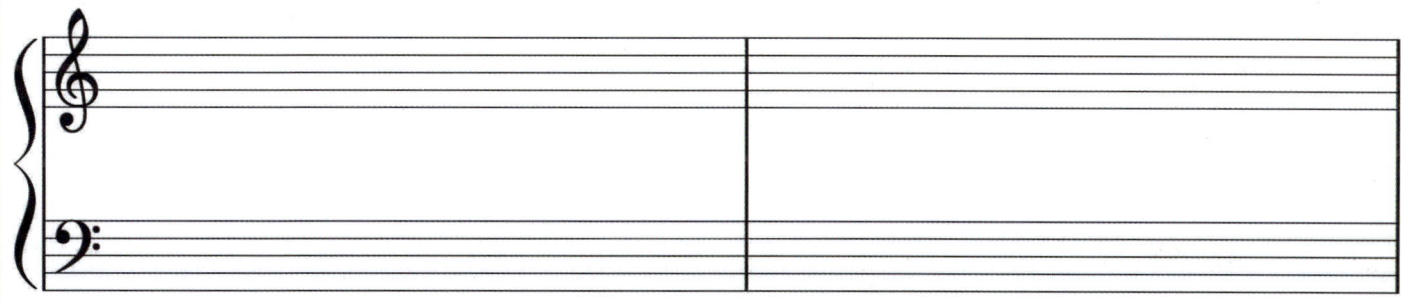

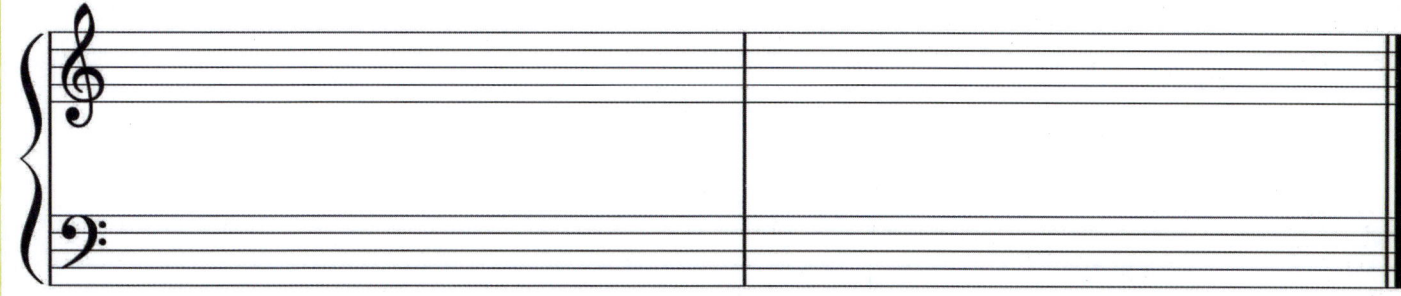

Key Signatures

In musical notation, a key series of sharps or flats are used to indicate the notes which are consistently one step higher or lower than the corresponding notes unless otherwise indicated (for example, the white keys on the piano). The key signature is usually written after the clef at the start of a musical notation line. However, they can appear in other parts of a score, notably after a double bar.

A key signature is a symbol used in music notation telling you what key a song or piece of music is in. A key is a major or minor scale around which a piece of music revolves. Every key has a unique set of seven notes. For example:

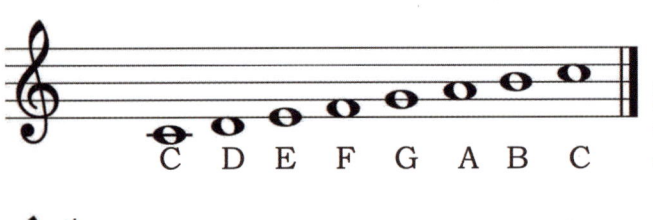

🔊 Audio G71
The notes C, D, E, F, G, A, B, and C are used in C major's key. There are no sharps or flats in the key of C major. You may play this scale on the xylophone.

🔊 Audio G72
Key of G Major uses the notes G, A, B, C, D, E, F sharp, and G. The key of G Major uses one sharp. You may play this scale on the xylophone.

🔊 Audio G73
Key of D Major uses the notes D, E, F sharp, G A B C sharp, and D. The key of D Major uses two sharps. You may play this scale on the xylophone.

🔊 Audio G74
Key of A Major uses the notes A, B, C sharp, D, E, F sharp, G sharp, and A. The key of A Major uses three sharps. You may play this scale on the xylophone.

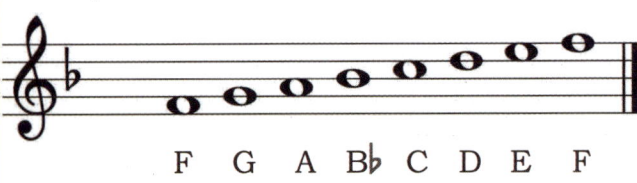

🔊 Audio G75
Key of F Major uses the notes F, G, A, B flat, C, D E, and F. The key of F Major uses one flat. You may play this scale on the xylophone.

🔊 Audio G76
Key of B flat Major uses the notes B flat, C, D, E flat, F, G, A, and B flat. The key of B flat Major uses two flats. You may play this scale on the xylophone.

🔊 Audio G77
Key of E flat Major uses the notes E flat, F, G, A flat, B flat, C, D, and E flat. The key of E flat Major uses three flats. You may play this scale on the xylophone.

Accidentals - Sharps, Flat and Natural

In music theory, an accidental is a musical notation used to change the pitch of a note. When an accidental appears in a measure, every note that is the same as the note being changed is changed the same way. In a key signature, accidentals retain their effects for the entire piece (unless a natural has been used to cancel it).

A **sharp** raises the note by a half-step. It is written as ♯.
A **flat** lowers the note by a half-step. It can be written as ♭.
A **natural** sign cancels a flat or a sharp. It can be written as ♮.

The accidental is always written on the staff before the note. But the accidental is after the note name when the note is written down. You say the accidental after the letter name when you say the note's name aloud (F sharp, B flat, A natural).

Trace the sharps, flats, and naturals listed below.

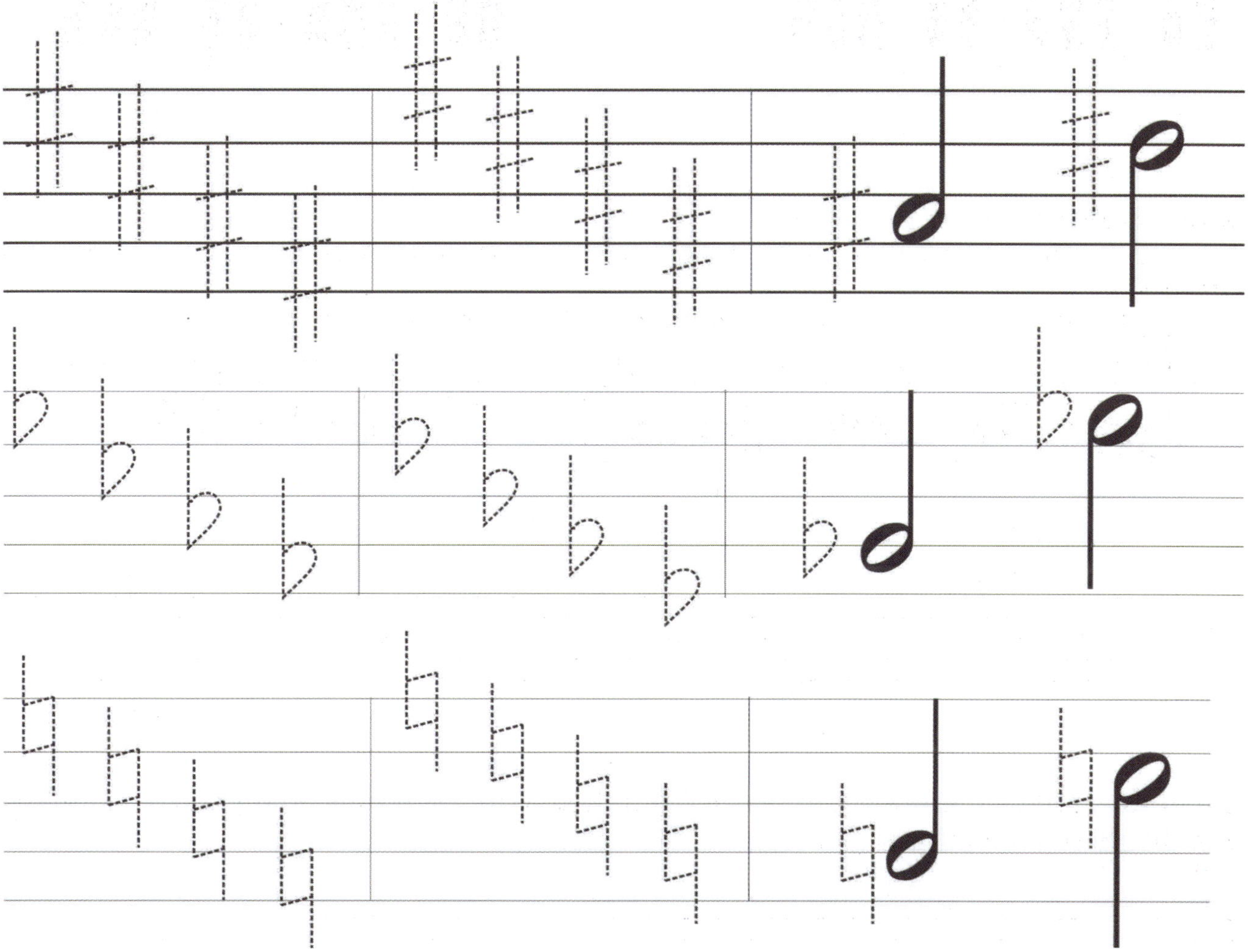

We discussed reducing the number of sharp and flat signs when writing music in a specific key in the previous lesson. In the key of A major, C, F and G are sharpened. Every sharpened note must be marked with a sharp sign if the notes are written without a key signature. If we write the A key signature (three sharps) at the beginning of the staff, it is no longer necessary to place sharp signs in front of those notes. The key signature shall apply to all relevant notes in every octave.

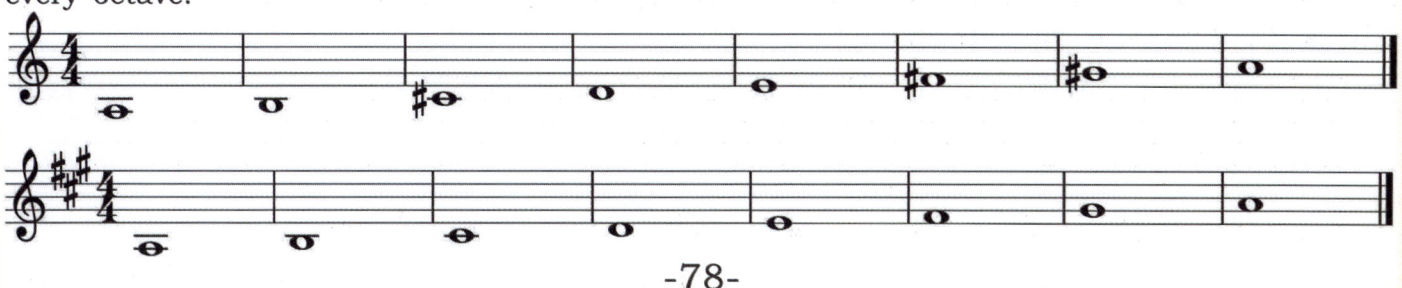

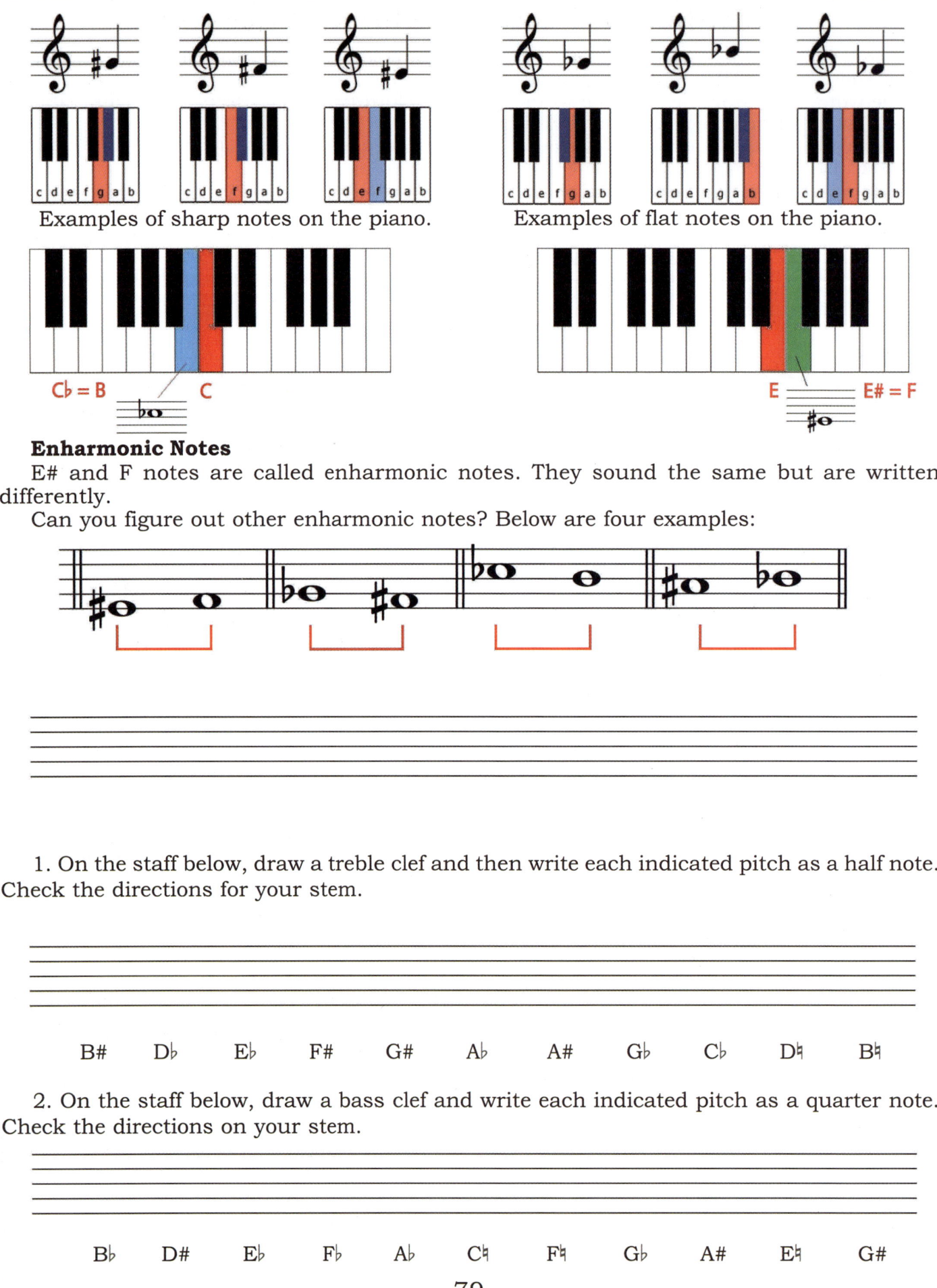

Major and Minor Pentatonic Scale

A pentatonic scale has only five notes, as the name suggests. It can be constructed using either the major or natural minor scales.

The word "pentatonic" is derived from the Greek word pente, five, and tonic, which means tone. A five-tone scale or a five-note scale are terms used to describe this scale. It is believed to have been used back in ancient times. The major pentatonic scale is the fundamental scale of Chinese and Mongolian music.

The 1st, 2nd, 3rd, 5th, and 6th notes of a major scale make up the major pentatonic scale. Take a look at the C major scale, for example. C – D – E – F – G – A – B - C are the C major scale notes. Therefore, the C major pentatonic would be the 1st note, C, the 2nd note, D, the 3rd note, E, the 5th note, G, and the 6th note, A, or C – D – E – G – A.

The natural minor scale's 1st, 3rd, 4th, 5th, and 7th notes make up the minor pentatonic scale. That is a natural minor scale without the second and sixth degrees. A Scale Degree is a name given to each pitch on a scale. From lowest to highest, the scale degrees are numbered.

1. Create major and minor pentatonic scales.

Twelve Days Of Christmas

🔊 **Audio G82**

Traditional Song

A Major Scale   🔊 **Audio G83**

- Practice singing the song "Twelve Days Of Christmas."
- Since this song is written in A major, start by warming up your voices with A major scale.
- Play Audio G82 and have students echo phrase by phrase.
- Add movement. It can be simultaneous or while echoing.
- Circle the change of time signature. Write the counting of beats under the notes.
- After you spend a few minutes analyzing the above song, grab a piece of paper and write about tempo, key signature, time signature, note values, measure.
- What do you feel while singing this song?

Orchestral Instruments

The majority of music is performed with musical instruments or voices. Most musical instruments are grouped according to the type of music they make. We will learn in this lesson about the greatest instrumental group: the orchestra symphony. The orchestra is divided into four groups of instruments: strings, woodwinds, brass, and percussion. An orchestra is a group of musicians who play together. There are about 100 musicians in a symphony orchestra. A symphony orchestra usually plays pieces of classical music.

Cello (G86), Bass (G87), Violin (G84), Viola (G85)

Strings
Four stringed instruments are commonly used in the modern orchestra: the violin, viola, cello, and bass. All are usually played by drawing a bow across the strings but are sometimes played by plucking the strings. These instruments are made from wood, with four strings of sheep gut, nylon, or wire. They are tuned by tuning pegs at the top and stroked by bows made of horsehair.

🔊 Audio G84, G85, G86, G87

Flute (G88), Bassoon (G91), Oboe (G89), Clarinet (G90)

🔊 Audio G88, G89, G90, G91

Woodwinds
Flute, oboe, clarinet, and bassoon are the woodwind members of the orchestra. There may be two, three, or four of these woodwinds in the orchestra, depending on the orchestra's size and the composition being played. All modern orchestral woodwinds are played by blowing into them and fingering various notes with keys covering various holes. Most of them, but not all of them, are made of wood and have at least one piece of reed in the mouthpiece.

🔊 Audio G92, G93, G94, G95

Trumpet (G92), Trombone (G93), Tuba (G94), French Horn (G95)

Brass
The orchestral brass is made of metal, although the metal can be a silver alloy instead of brass. The sound is produced by "buzzing" the lips against the mouthpiece; the rest of the instrument only amplifies and refines the sound from the lips so that it is a beautiful, musical sound when it comes out of the bell at the other end of the instrument. A slide or three or four valves aid in producing different notes, but players rely heavily on their instruments' harmonic series to achieve the full range of notes. The trumpet, French horn, trombone, and tuba are orchestral brass instruments. The number of these instruments, like the woodwinds, varies depending on the size of the orchestra and the piece being performed. Typically, there are two to five trumpets, horns, and trombones, as well as one or two tubas.

🔊 Audio G96, G97, G98, G99, G100, G101

Xylophone (G97), Snare Drum (G96), Tambourine (G98), Timpani (G99), Cymbals (G101), Triangle (G100)

Percussion
The largest group in the orchestra is the percussion family. Percussion instruments shall include any instrument that makes a sound when it is hit, shaken, or scraped. The orchestra's most common percussion instruments include the timpani, xylophone, cymbals, triangle, snare drum, bass drum, tambourine, maracas, gongs, chimes, and celesta.

1. Draw a line between each instrument and its orchestral family.
- string family

- brass family

- woodwind family

- percussion family

2. Listen. Circle some of the instruments you hear.

🔊 **Audio G102**

3. Listen to the following piece of music performed by string instruments.
With your partner, talk about which instruments you think you can hear and which ones you cannot hear in the music.

Expressions to use:
I think I heard .....
I do not think there is a............
When the melody is like this (sing) I think I heard.......
The melody is performed by the ....

🔊 **Audio G103**

4. Now, see what the other students think, and ask your teacher for the right answer.

5. Work in pairs. One of you must think of an orchestral instrument. The other must ask questions to guess which instrument their partner is thinking of. Be careful! The questions can only be answered by "yes" or "no."

Example questions:
Is it a string instrument?
Is it big?
Is it the highest/lowest of its family?
Is it played with a bow?

Keyboard Instruments

Musical instruments, such as pianos and organs that use a keyboard for producing sound, are called keyboard instruments. A keyboard is a system of levers or keys from which the player selects the notes to be played. The player strikes a key to make the instrument sound. To stop the sound, the player releases the key. The pitch for each note on a keyboard instrument is fixed and cannot be changed by the player. Some keyboard instruments may have more than one keyboard, like the organs and harpsichords.

Nearly all keyboard instruments, particularly those associated with Western music, have keys that correspond to notes in the chromatic scale and run from bass to treble on the keyboard.

Keyboards have grown in importance and popularity as one of the most versatile musical instrument families. The keyboard allows the performer to play several notes at once and in close succession to each other, a feat that few other instruments can do. Because a keyboard can play nearly any composition, whether it is chordal harmonies, a single melody, or a combination of the two, nearly every major composer since the 16th century has used it.

🔊 **Audio G104**

Piano
Did you know that the word piano comes from the word pianoforte? Because of its versatility, this musical device has a lot of classical and jazz music performances. The typical modern piano has 88 keys and a range of seven full octaves plus a few extra keys. The piano was invented by Bartolomeo Cristofori (1655-1731) from Italy.

Organ A pipe organ has one or more keyboards (known as manuals) that are played with the hands, and a pedal clavier played with the feet; each keyboard controls its division or group of stops. In the organ console are the keyboard(s), the pedalboard, and stops.

🔊 **Audio G105**

The organ was first labeled the "king of instruments." by none other than Mozart. He was most likely swayed, as so many others have been, by the immensity and nobleness of the organ's sound and the enormous variety of sounds that the instrument could produce.

Pipe organs are installed in synagogues, churches, concert halls, schools, other public buildings, and private properties. They are used to perform classical music, sacred music, secular music, and popular music.

🔊 **Audio G106**

Harpsichord is a keyboard instrument in which strings are plucked rather than hammered (the piano mechanism, a more recent development). The distinctive tone of the clapping is almost immediately related to the baroque age. The earliest references to such instruments date back to about 1400. The oldest surviving harpsichords date back to the 1500s when the complex mechanism of the instrument was perfected. The harpsichord's demand remained steady until the 18th century when it was gradually replaced by the fortepiano and then by the modern piano.

Clavichord is a stringed keyboard instrument that dates from the late Middle Ages to the Renaissance, Baroque, and Classical periods in Europe. It was used historically as a practice tool and as a composition aid. The clavichord produces sound by striking brass or iron strings with tangents. Vibrations are passed to the soundboard via the bridge(s).

🔊 **Audio G107**

Making Music

For thousands of years, people have been using sound to make music. There are several musical instruments they have invented. However, despite their diversity, musical instruments have certain similarities.

• By causing matter to vibrate, all musical instruments produce sound. Most instruments use resonance to increase the amplitude of the sound waves and make the sound louder. Resonance occurs when the object vibrates at a certain frequency in response to sound waves. In a musical instrument such as a drum, the entire instrument and the air inside it may vibrate when the drum head is struck.

• The frequency of the sound waves produced by most musical instruments can be changed. This modifies the sound pitch or how high or low a listener feels.

We use a wide range of instruments to produce sounds and make music. Some of them are simple pieces of solid wood or hollowed-out seashells. Others are highly technical or electrical. Instruments vary around the world, and each of them has its character.

How are musical instruments classified?

Acoustic instruments generate physical sound, and electronic instruments generate electrical sound. Percussion (hit or shaken), string (bowed or plucked), wind (woodwind and brass; blown), and keyboard (played with fingers) are the four acoustic groups.

How are the instruments generating sound?

When a part of an instrument vibrates rapidly, it produces sound. The column of air inside the wind instrument, the string of a string instrument, or the drum's stretched skin all vibrate when played. This vibration produces sound waves in the air that we hear as musical notes.

How is the sound produced on a piano?

When the key to a piano is pressed, it moves a hammer which strikes a string or a set of strings. The strings then create a vibration, and the sound's strength depends on the amount of force used to press the key. The piano also has three pedals called the una corda, sostenuto pedal, and damper pedal. The una corda pedal softens the note, the sostenuto pedal sustains the notes that are played when the pedal is pressed, and the damper pedal vibrates the notes, which makes the sound ring even after the key has been released.

Orchestral instruments seating chart

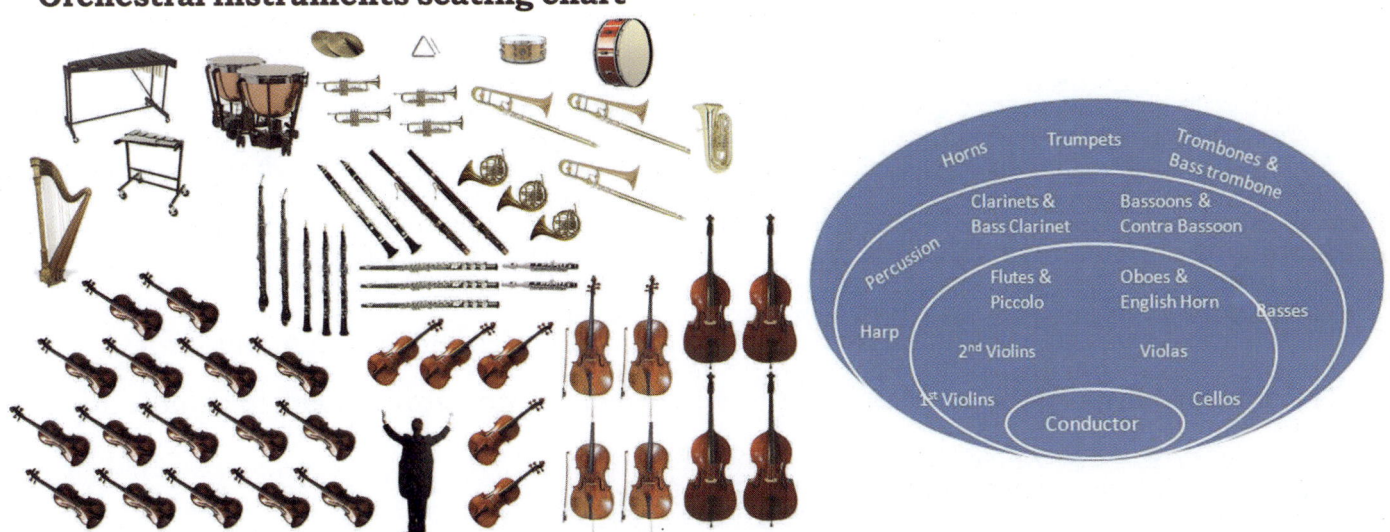

Vocal Types and Ranges

A voice type is a voice identified as having certain qualities or characteristics of vocal range, vocal weight, tessitura, vocal timbre, and vocal transition points, such as breaks and lifts within the voice. Singers, composers, venues, and listeners use voice classification to categorize vocal properties and assign roles to voices.

Soprano, mezzo-soprano, and contralto are the three vocal ranges for women. Countertenor, tenor, baritone, and bass are the four vocal groups for men.

A typical choral arrangement divides women into higher and lower voices and men into higher and lower voices. Most voices can be placed in one of these four ranges, giving the composer four vocal lines to work with, usually sufficient.
- Soprano – a high female voice
- Alto – a female voice with a low pitch.
- Tenor – A male voice with a high range.
- Bass – A male voice with a low pitch.

SATB is the abbreviation for arrangements for these four voices (for Soprano Alto Tenor Bass).

The perceived "lightness" or "heaviness" of a singing voice is referred to as vocal weight. Within classical music, the voice's quality is one of the most important determining factors in voice classification. Lighter voices are often linked to the term "lyric" and are generally more luminous and more flexible; heavier voices are often linked to a "dramatic" word and are often stronger, richer, and darker.

Spinto (from Italian, "pushed") is a vocal term used to characterize a soprano or tenor voice of a weight between lyric and dramatic, capable of handling large musical climaxes in opera at moderate intervals.

🔊 **Audio G108, G109, G110, G111, G112, G113, G114, G115**

The vocal weight of other voice types, such as the spinto, is more medium. Overall vocal agility is influenced by vocal weight; heavier voices have a harder time maneuvering through florid coloratura passages than lighter voices, as their weight and power compromise agility. Dramatic roles, likewise, are frequently written with larger orchestras in mind, as dramatic voices can easily carry over larger ensembles.

As a singer, it is important to know your voice type to understand what notes you can achieve and what you can expect from your voice. You might think you can figure out what kind of sound you have, but many people are surprised to learn that the precise results are far more complicated. The following vocal variables are the result of your specific type:

The notes you can produce, from low to high, are referred to as range.
Your voice's weight refers to how light or heavy it is.
Tessitura – part of the range where you are most comfortable with singing
Timbre – Your voice's unique quality and texture
Transition points: These are the points where you switch from chest to middle to head registration.
Vocal records – How large or small is your register extended?
Your speech voice determines your speaking range.
Physical Characteristics – Your Voice and Body Anatomy

Listening Examples:
Lyric Soprano (G116)   Lyric mezzo-soprano (G118)
Dramatic Soprano (G117)   Dramatic mezzo-soprano (G119)

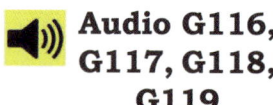

1. In this listening piece, you will hear a singer. As you listen, determine the vocal range for the singer.
   a) soprano
   b) mezzo-soprano
   c) tenor
   d) bass

🔊 Audio G120

2. This vocal range is classified as:
a) soprano
b) mezzo-soprano
c) tenor
d) bass

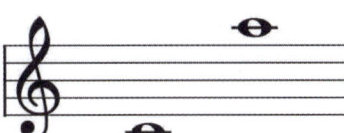

3. This vocal range is classified as:
a) soprano
b) mezzo-soprano
c) tenor
d) bass

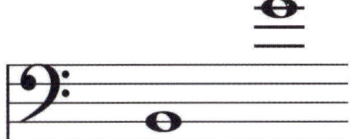

4. What are the different types of male voice?

_____

5. What does the term soprano mean?
a) The highest-pitched human voice type.
b) A singer who possesses the highest-pitched human voice type.
c) The smallest and highest-pitched variety of an instrument (like the saxophone).

5. In this listening piece, you will hear a singer. As you listen, determine the vocal range for the singer.
   a) lyric soprano
   b) dramatic mezzo-soprano

🔊 Audio G121

6. Which female voice type has the lowest vocal range?
a) Contralto
b) Mezzo-soprano
c) Soprano
d) All-female voice types have an equal range.

7. What are the different types of female voices?

_____

Reading Treble Clef and Bass Clef Notes

 Name the notes below.

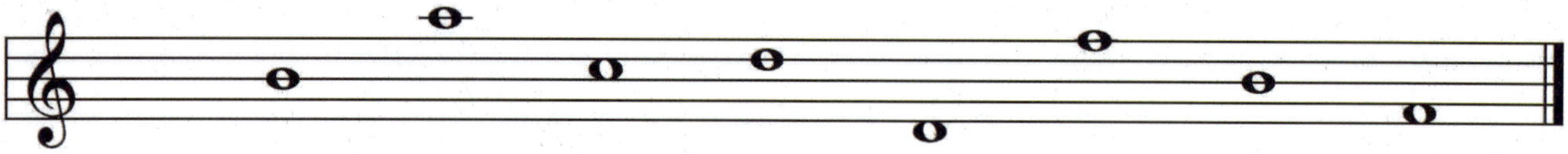

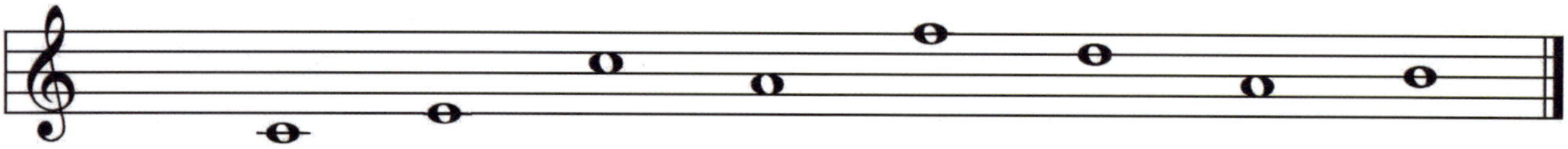

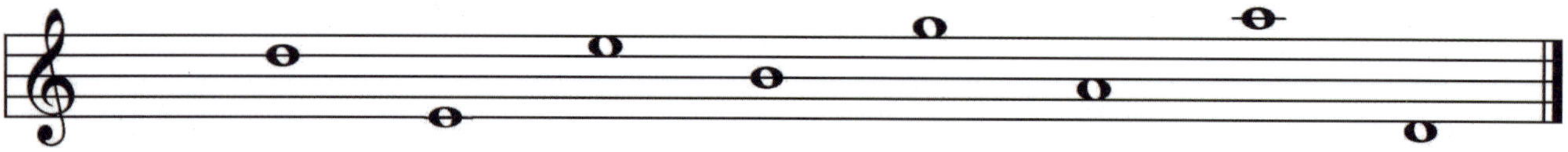

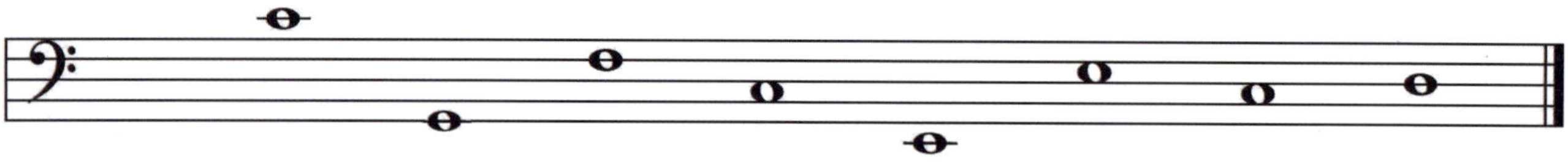

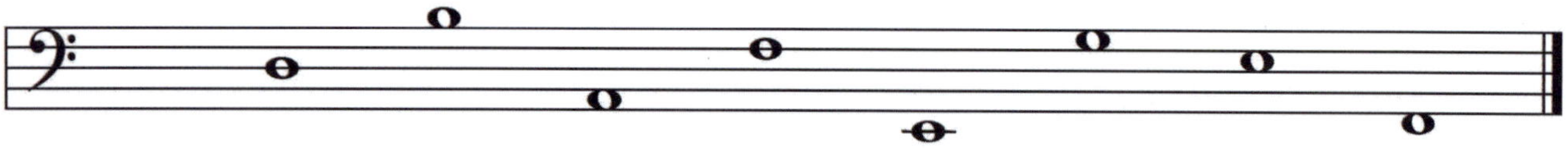

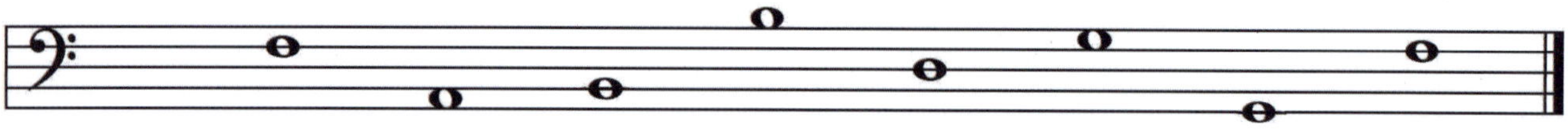

 Copy key signature, time signature, musical notes, and rhythm from the first grand staff to the second grand staff.

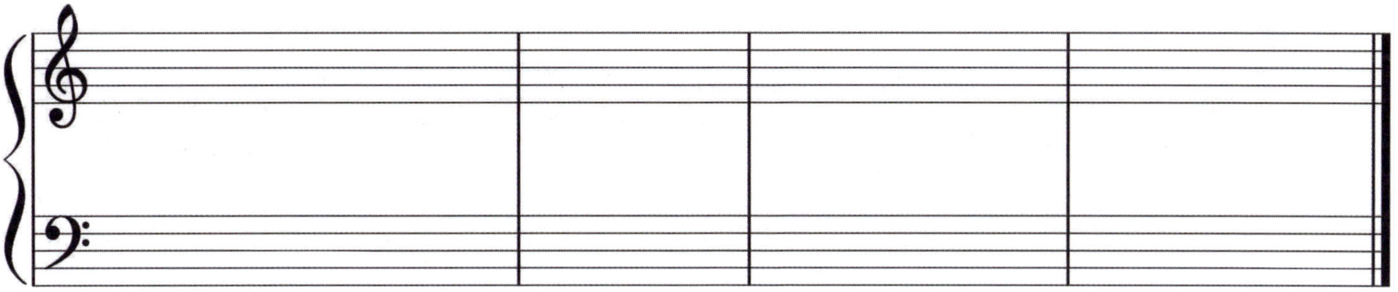

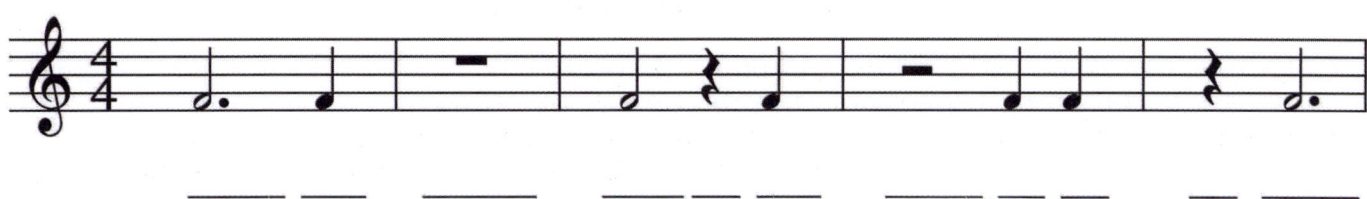 Write the count under the notes and rest on the following lines.

Ex: 1 2 3

Watkins Ale

Audio G122

Traditional Song

There was a maid this o- ther day, And she would needs go forth to play; And

as she walked, she sighed and said, I am a- fraid to die a maid.

When that be- heard a lad What talk this maid- en had There- of he was full glad

And did not spare To say "fair maid, I pray Whi- ther go you to play?"

"Good sir," then did she say "What do you care?" "For I will with- out fail Mai- den give you

Wat- kin's Ale" "Wat- kin's ale? Good sir," quoth she, "What is that I pray tell me."

D Major Scale 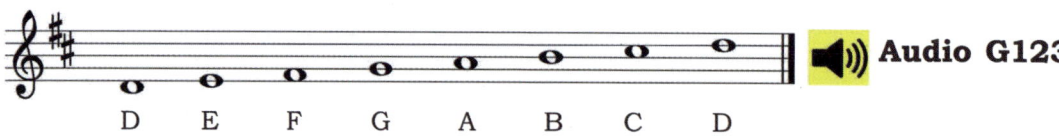 Audio G123

D E F G A B C D

- Practice singing the following song, "Watkins Ale."
- Since this song is written in D major, start by warming up your voices with D major scale. As you prepare to sing this song:
  - Use good breath support, vowels, and articulation.
- Sing musically.
- Slowly learn melody and words and pick-up speed.
- Play Audio G122 and have students echo phrase by phrase.
- Create or improvise a movement activity to accompany the song "Watkins Ale."
- Practice with a metronome and sing the song in andante, moderato, and allegro tempo.
- Perform rhythmic body movement, with accompaniment, in the appropriate tempo.

Brennan on the Moor

Traditional Song

It's of a fear- less high- way man, a sto- ry I will tell. His name was Wil- lie

Bren- nan in Ire- land he did dwell, And on the Li- me- rick Moun- tains he com-

menced his wild ca- reer, Where ma- ny a weal- thy gen- tle- man be- fore him shook with

fear And it's Bren- nan on the moor, Bren- nan on the moor, Oh,

bold and un- daun- ted stood Bren- nan on the moor.

A Major Scale   A B C# D E F# G# A    Audio G125

- Practice singing the following song, "Brennan on the Moor."
- Since this song is written in A major, start by warming up your voices with A major scale.
- Slowly learn melody and words and pick-up speed.
- Play Audio G124 and have students echo phrase by phrase.
- Practice with a metronome and sing the song in andante, moderato, and allegro tempo. Perform rhythmic body movement, with accompaniment, in the appropriate tempo.
- On this page, point out and circle the dotted quarter notes.

After you spend a few minutes analyzing the above song, grab a piece of paper and write about the following:
- Tempo
- Time signature
- Key signature
- Upbeat
- Note values / Rests
- Measures
- What do you feel while singing this song?

Fanny Mendelssohn

Fanny Mendelssohn was a Romantic-era German composer and pianist. She grew up in Berlin, Germany, and received a thorough musical education from teachers, including her mother, Ludwig Berger, and Carl Friedrich Zelter.

Fanny Mendelssohn Bartholdy was born on November 14th, 1805. Her mother taught her to play the piano. A J.S. Bach student had taught Fanny Mendelssohn's mother. By the age of 13, Fanny had mastered all 24 Preludes from Bach's *The Well-Tempered Clavier*.

Over their lives, Felix Mendelssohn and his older sister Fanny (1805-1847) developed a close relationship brought together by their common love of music and exceptional talents. While Fanny's gender prevented her from having the same social opportunities or receiving the same support in developing her musical abilities as her more famous brother, her abilities appeared to be nearly as formidable. From early in their lives until Fanny's death (she died only six months before her brother), Felix Mendelssohn Bartholdy would regularly submit his compositions to Fanny's discerning musical eye and ear, taking her critical advice to heart and never hesitating to modify or excise entirely material that she found questionable. Felix Mendelssohn Bartholdy began to refer to his older sister as "Minerva" for their highly developed musical and intellectual insights.

Fanny's piano virtuosity matched, if not exceeded, that of her brother Felix. But, if Fanny had musical ambitions of her own, to follow in her brother's footsteps as a performer and composer, those dreams were quickly dashed because women were not allowed to pursue musical careers at the time.

Fanny Mendelssohn married the painter Wilhelm Hensel in 1829 after a long courtship. Her only child, Sebastian Ludwig Felix Hensel, was born the following year, named after Fanny's favorite composer Johann Sebastian Bach. Her husband encouraged her to compose, and her works were soon being performed alongside those of her brother in a Sunday concert series at the family home in Berlin (Sonntagskonzerte). She made her public debut with her piano in 1838, when she performed her brother's *Piano Concerto No. 1* for the first time. Fanny Mendelssohn played with the grace and simplicity of someone who enjoys making music. She decided to publish a collection of her songs in 1846. With song-like qualities and striking juxtapositions of unrelated harmonies and chromatically colored progressions, Fanny Mendelssohn Helson's piano works show outstanding inspiration and originality. Many musicians find her compositions to be technically challenging, which reflects Fanny's brilliant style of virtuosity.

Fanny Mendelssohn wrote 466 pieces, including over 250 songs, 125 piano works, four cantatas, a large amount of instrumental chamber music, and choral works.

Fanny did not make her public performance debut until she was 33 years old when she performed her brother Felix's *Piano Concerto No. 1* at the age of 33.

Fanny published her first work under her name, *Opus 1*, in 1846, when she was 41 years old.

Fanny Mendelssohn died of complications following a stroke on May 14th, 1847, at 41. Felix, her brother, dedicated his *String Quartet No. 6* to her before passing away six months later.

Felix Mendelssohn with his sister, Fanny Mendelssohn

Fanny Mendelssohn

🔊 Audio G126

While coloring, you may listen *Vier Römische Klavierstücke* by Fanny Mendelssohn.

Fanny Mendelssohn Quiz

1. Which country was Fanny Mendelssohn born in?
a) France
b) Italy
c) Germany
d) the United States

2. Fanny Mendelssohn's works belong to _____ era.
a) Baroque
b) Romantic
c) Classical
d) Renaissance

3. Fanny and her brother, Felix, received their early piano instruction from their _____.
a) Aunt
b) Mother
c) Cousin

4. Fanny's favorite composer was _____.
a) Wolfgang Amadeus Mozart
b) Johann Sebastian Bach
c) Ludwig van Beethoven

5. Fanny Mendelssohn composed 466 pieces of music, including over 250 songs, 125 piano works, four cantatas, and much instrumental chamber music, as well as choral works.
a) True
b) False

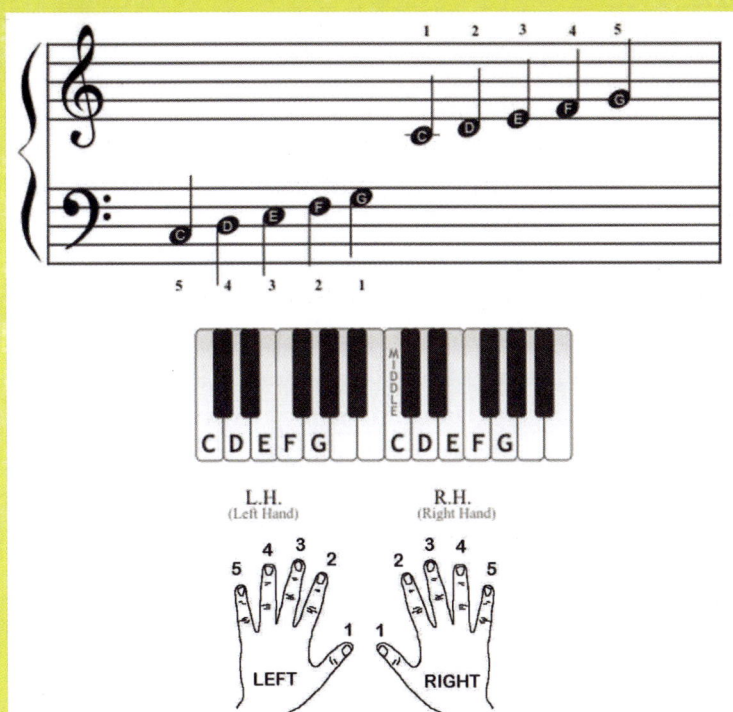

Position both hands on the piano in C position. Practice separate hands first and then hands together. Let us start with the right hand by pressing musical note G using finger number 5, hold it for one beat, and then as you lift a finger number 5, press finger number 3 on musical note E. Continue playing right hand (RH) a few times and then practice left hand (LH). To better understand how to practice "Step and Leap Piano Exercise," watch video L43.

Pay attention to note values, dynamics, and marks of expression. Encourage the student to attempt one line of the song and gradually build it up, phrase by phrase. Allow them to take their time and do not attempt the whole song if it seems too much.

Video L43

♩ = 80

Andante

Step and Leap Piano Exercise

What is tempo in music?

The tempo of a piece of music refers to how fast it is played. Since we traditionally use Italian for musical terms, we call "tempo," the Italian word for "time." It may be slow, fast, or in-between, but the tempo is one of the most important music ingredients. We would not play parade music very slowly or play a funeral dirge at an upbeat tempo. Musicians have developed a system of useful terms and tempo markings over time, allowing them to recognize a song's given tempo quickly and efficiently. Largo—very slow and wide (50-55bpm), Adagio—slow (60-72bpm), Andante—walking speed (84-90bpm), Moderate (96-108bpm), Allegro—fast, cheerful (120-128bpm), Presto—very fast. Originally, it consisted of several Italian terms. But with the advent of the metronome, a mechanical device used to keep time; musicians could calculate how many beats per minute were in music. Beats per minute is a measure of just that: the number of beats occurring in a minute, usually "b.p.m." A watch clicks once per second, 60 times a minute. Therefore, a 60bpm watch clicks. Eventually, each Italian term would be associated with a specific bpm, making the terms more accurate. Here are the most general terms, their translation, and approximate bpm:

Larghissimo	very, very slow	24 BPM and under
Grave	very slow	25–45 BPM
Lento	slowly	45–50 BPM
Largo	broadly	50–55 BPM
Larghetto	rather broadly	55–60 BPM
Adagio	slow and stately	60–72 BPM
Adagietto	slower than Andante	72–80 BPM
Andantino	slightly slower than Andante	80–84 BPM
Andante	at a walking pace	84–90 BPM
Andante moderato	between andante and moderato	90–96 BPM
Marcia moderato	moderately, in the manner of march	83–85 BPM
Moderato	moderately	96–108 BPM
Allegro moderato	moderately fast	108–112 BPM
Allegretto	close to but not quite allegro	112–120 BPM
Allegro	fast, quickly, and bright	120–128 BPM
Vivace	lively and fast	132–144 BPM
Vivacissimo	very fast and lively	144–160 BPM
Allegrissimo	very fast	145–167 BPM
Presto	extremely fast	168–200 BPM
Prestissimo	even faster than Presto	200 BPM and over

The tempo of a piece does not always remain constant. It may frequently change throughout work in order to pique the listener's interest or evoke specific feelings. Composers will use the Italian terms ritardando (meaning "slow down") or accelerando (meaning "speed up") to describe how music moves from one tempo to another. In music, these two terms are frequently abbreviated as "rit." or "accel."

 Johann Maelzel, a German inventor, invented the metronome in 1816. (though it was invented two years earlier by Dietrich Winkel).

The Italian tempo lexicon is rarely used by jazz and rock musicians. Instead, they use words like "fast," "slow," "lazily," "relaxed," and "moderate" from everyday English.

Tempo Crossword Puzzle

L A R G O

Fill in the crossword puzzle.

Across:
1 Broadly
6 Moderately
8 Extremely Fast

Down:
2 Slow
3 Slowly
4 Fast
5 Lively
7 Very Slow

Title:

Composer:
Lyrics:

• Students will improvise eight measures, melodic and rhythmic phrases, using various sound and notational sources.
 • Give your piece a proper title. Please put your name where it says the composer.
 • If you are using a poem for lyrics, write the poet's name where it says lyrics.
• Add treble clef, key signature, time signature, tempo markings.
• Your tune should be easy to play or sing. Upon finishing your composition, you may play it or sing it. You may partner with other students and work on this composition.
• Have fun composing the song.

Happy Birthday

🔊 **Audio G127**

Andante Moderato Bb   F7   **Traditional Song**

Hap-py birth-day to you! Hap-py

Bb

birth-day to you! Hap-py

Eb

rit..

birth-day dear (John-ny) A Tempo Hap-py

Bb/F   F7   Bb

birth-day to you!

🔊 **Audio G128**

Bb major

Bb C D Eb F G A Bb

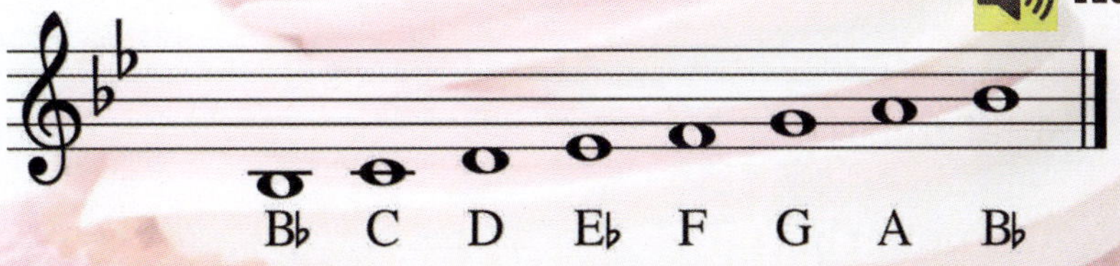

- Practice singing "Happy Birthday."
- Since this song is written in Bb major, start by warming up your voices with Bb major scale.

As you prepare to sing this song:
- Use good breath support, vowels, and articulation.
- Create or improvise a movement activity to accompany the song "Happy Birthday." You may also use a triangle instrument to accompany while singing the "Happy Birthday" song.
- On this page, point out and circle the dotted eighth notes.

After you spend a few minutes analyzing the above song, grab a piece of paper and write about the following:
- Tempo, time signature, key signature, upbeat, note values/rests, measures.
- What do you feel while singing this song?

-100-

Tempo Markings and Articulation Symbols

Tempo markings tell how slow or fast to play the music.
Grave – very slow
Largo – broadly
Lento – slowly
Adagio – slowly with great expression
Andante – at a walking pace
Andantino – slightly faster than andante
Moderato – at a moderate speed
Allegro – fast, quickly, and bright
Vivace – lively and fast
Allegrissimo or Allegro vivace – very fast
Presto – very, very fast
Accelerando - gradually get faster
Ritardando - gradually get slower

Articulation symbols guide the performer in interpreting the song.

⌒ **Fermata** - keep the musical note for a longer period of time than its face value.

> **Accent** - play a little louder on the musical note.

• **Staccato** - play the musical note short

— **Tenuto** - hold the musical note for its full value

1. Sing the following rhythm exercise on the syllable "tah," carefully observing the tempo markings and other musical symbols. 🔊 **Audio G129**

Moderato

accelerando

🔊 **Audio G130**

Lento

ritardando

2. Draw the symbol that means:

_____ play the note short
_____ hold the note longer than its normal value
_____ hold the musical note for its full value
_____ play the note a little louder

3. Write the tempo markings for the following speeds:

very slow _____
lively and fast _____
at a walking pace _____
gradually get faster_____
broadly _____

Dynamic Markings

Music has been a part of human culture since the dawn of time. On the other hand, music did not begin to be written until around 1000 A.D. Music writers had to invent their way of documenting how music was written at that time. The terms are still used today because the first people to try writing music were Italians.

When you look at music now, you will notice a lot of Italian terms and writing. When you read music, you are essentially learning a new language! It may seem confusing at first, but the more you are exposed to these terms, the easier it will become to remember them.

The term dynamics is used in music to describe the volume of the music.

One of the most important aspects of playing music is dynamics. They allow you to express a wide range of emotions.

Dynamic markings are traditionally based on Italian words, but there is nothing wrong with simply writing "quietly" or "louder" in the music. Piano means soft, and forte means loud.

Dynamic Markings
The main dynamic levels are:
- **p** or *piano*, which means soft
- **f** or *forte*, which means loud

More subtle degrees of loudness or softness are indicated by:
- **mp**, standing for mezzo-piano, which means moderately soft
- **mf**, standing for mezzo-forte, which means moderately loud

Beyond *f* and *p*, there are also:
- **pp**, which stands for *pianissimo* and means very soft
- **ff**, which stands for *fortissimo* and means very loud

Dynamic Changes
To gradually change the dynamics, composers use crescendo and diminuendo (also decrescendo).

- **crescendo** (**cresc.**): gradually play louder
- **diminuendo / decrescendo** (**dim.** or **decres.**): gradually play softer

Other dynamic markings
You probably will not see any of the following notations in a beginning-to-intermediate piece of music, but for more advanced pieces, you may find one or two:
- agitato: excitedly, agitated
- animato: with spirit
- grandioso: grandly
- con forza: forcefully, with strength
- dolce: sweetly
- sotto voce: barely audible

Practice the following examples using the syllables "ti" for eighth notes, "ta" for quarter notes, "ta-ah" for half notes, "ta-ah-ah" for dotted half notes, and "ta-ah-ah-ah" for whole notes. Observe all tempo markings, dynamics, and other musical symbols.

Sing "Darcy Farrow" and pay attention to the dynamic terms.

Musical dynamics demonstrate the loudness of the music. To explain the softness and loudness of a piece, we use the Italian words "piano" and "forte." They are generally abbreviated **p** and **f**. We can also add the word mezzo (**m**) to **p** and **f** to create **mp** (mezzo-piano) and **mf** (mezzo-forte). Mezzo-piano (**mp**) is moderately soft and mezzo-forte (**mf**) is moderately loud.

Can you find similarities/differences between rests and notes?

What influence do dynamics have on music?

G 5-Finger Position   G Major Scale

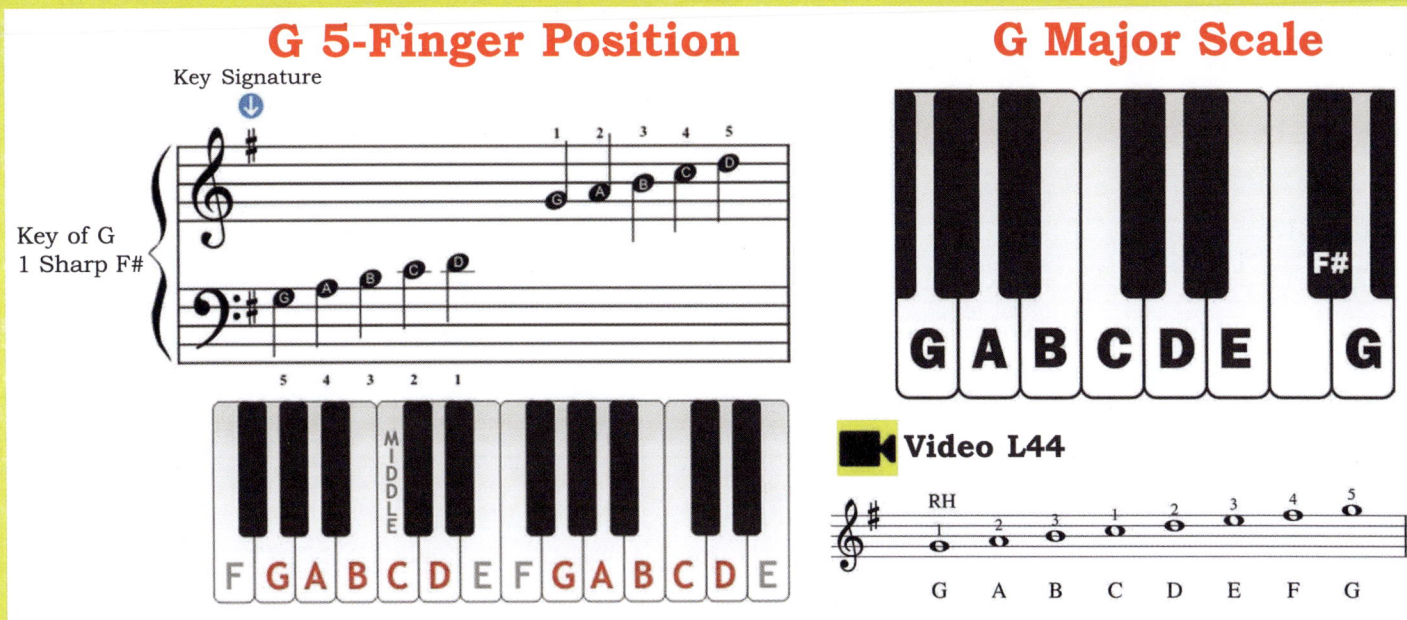

Raindrops

Piano Lesson
Watch Video L44 & L45 and learn to play G major scale and "Raindrops." Pay attention to tempo markings, dynamic markings, and other musical symbols.

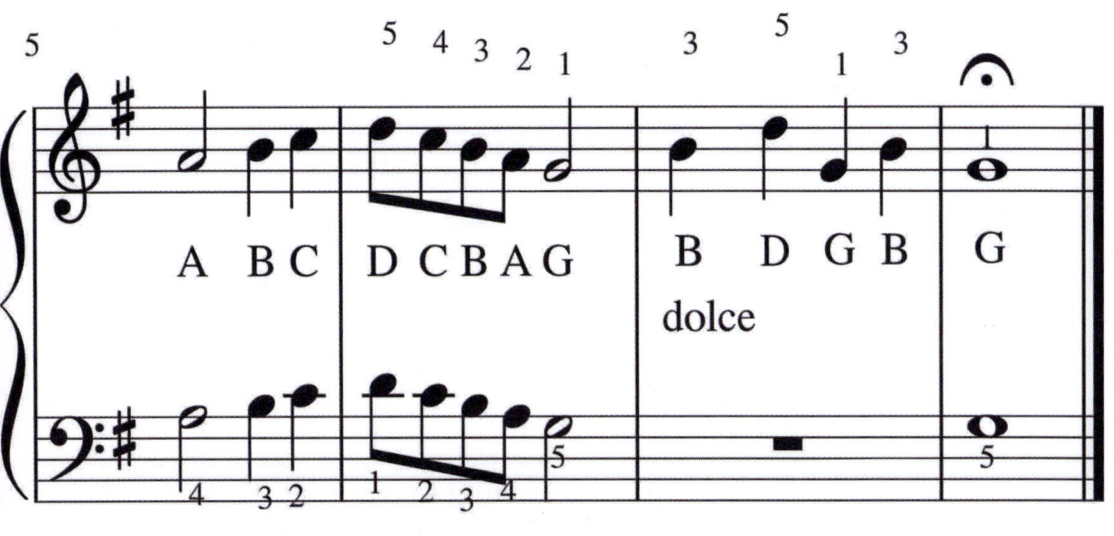

-104-

🔊 Audio G135

Solfege

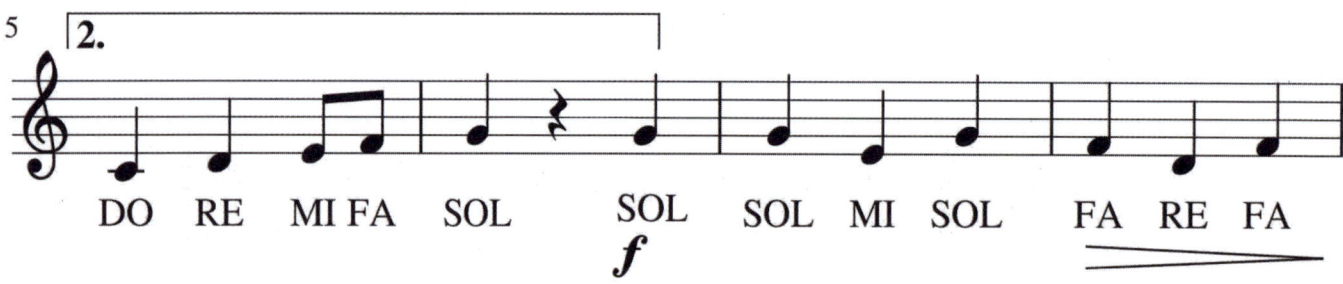

• Practice sight-singing this solfege.
• Review the beat's concept and have students clap the beat as they sing the solfege syllables.
• Discuss and describe how tempo portrays feelings and mood.
• Throughout their singing ranges, students sing correctly and with good breath control.
• Remember to sing dynamics in your performance.
• What do you do when you see a repeat sign and/or first and second ending?

Repeat Signs - D.C. al Coda - D.S. al Fine - D.S. al Coda

Repeat signs are used to repeat a specific section of music. They are made up of a thick bar line next to a thin bar line and two dots in the staff's center. The dots face towards the section to be repeated. A repeat sign can be either a "start repeat" or an "end repeat."

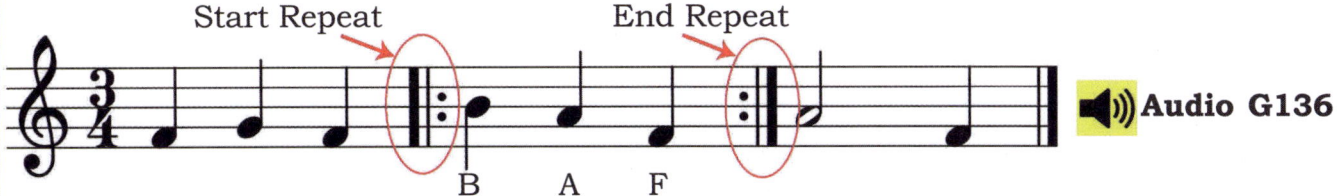

Multiple Endings/Variations

A bracket and numeral are used to mark alternate endings for a section. Here you should skip the first ending on the repeat and go on to the second ending. In this scenario, you would play the part bracketed as "1" the first time through the notes, and then instead of playing one, you would play the part bracketed as "2" the second time through. You will also find several different endings in a repeat "2, 3" or anything like "1, 3" in the first box and "2, 4" in the second.

D.C. al coda, or *da capo al coda*, simply means 'from beginning to coda.' D.C. al coda means that you should start at the beginning of the song and play until you find a coda, then skip to the next coda symbol to proceed.

D.S. al fine advises the musician to return to the sign and finish the piece at the measure marked fine.

D.S. al Coda

D.S. is an abbreviation for dal segno, meaning "from the sign," and tells the player to go back to the sign. D.S. is also followed by an instruction such as al fine or al coda. D.S. al Coda means to go back to the sign, play to the instruction "To Coda," and then jump forward in the music to the coda symbol.

Think of D.S. just like D.C., except instead of going back to the beginning; you go back to a specific point marked by the sign. The sign will always appear on top of the staff and at the beginning of a measure.

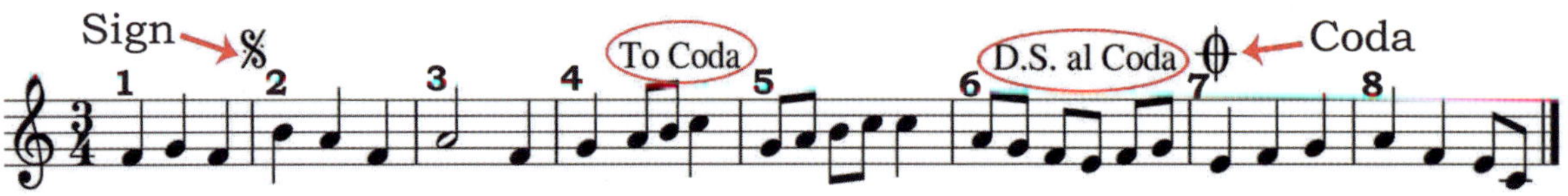

Let us talk through this example:
Play bars 1 through 6
Go back to the sign-in bar 2 (D.S.)
Play bars 2, 3, and 4, then take the coda.
Take the coda by skipping to bar 7 and continue.

Solfege No.1

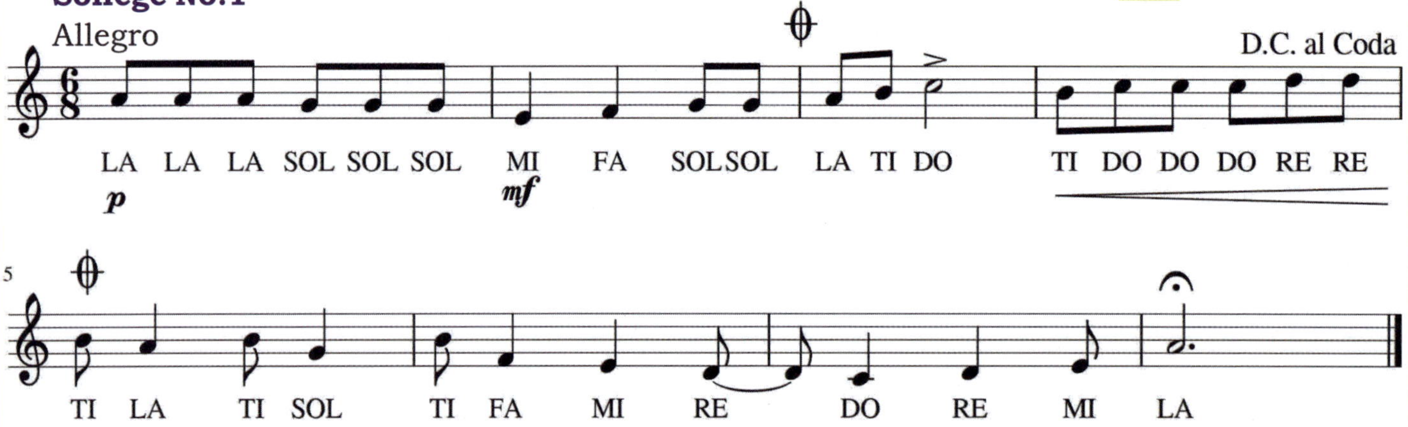

Solfege No.2

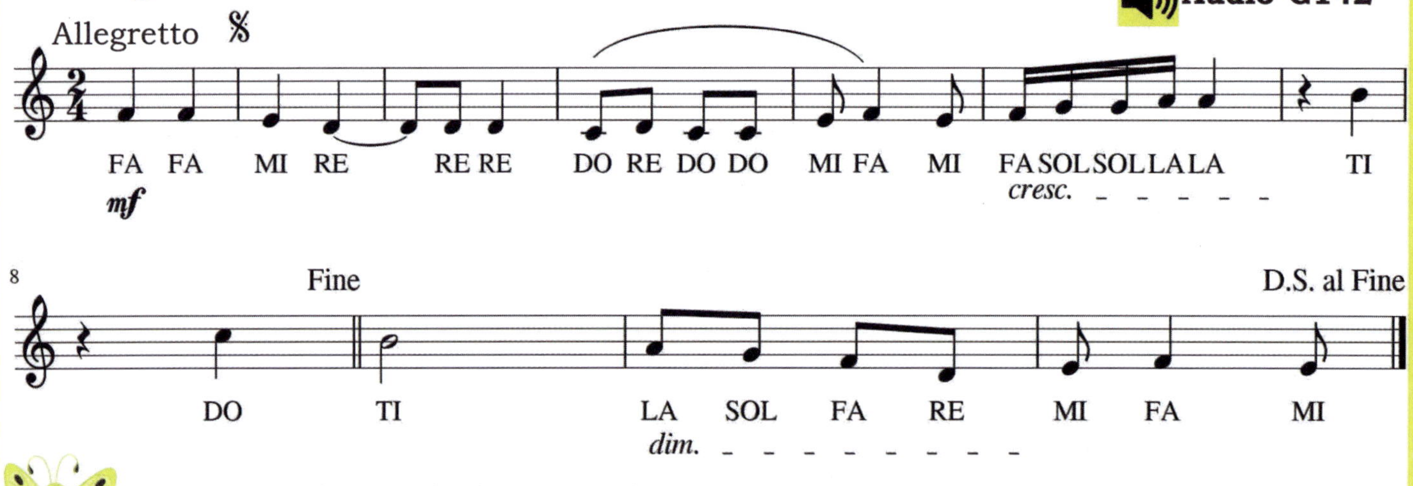

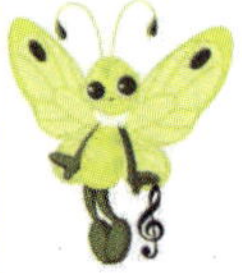

Let's talk through this example:
• As students experience solfege singing, they sing their way to musicianship;
• The world of music opens up to them as the student internalizes the syllables of solfege.
• When syllables are associated with musical notes, students can mentally hear pitches and sing them the first time they see a score as they develop their musicianship.
• Do a Think-Pair-Share activity in which students talk about tempo, dynamics, beat counting, rhythm, D.C al Coda, D.S. al Fine, time signature.
• The first skill we should develop is simply that of the matching pitch with our voice. Play Audio G141, G142 and sing along each pitch as you hear it.
• Practice sight-singing Solfege No.1 and Solfege No. 2 with a metronome.
• Respect tempo and dynamics.

Major and Minor Scale

A major scale is a diatonic scale. The intervals between the musical notes of a major scale are whole, whole, half, whole, whole, whole, half.

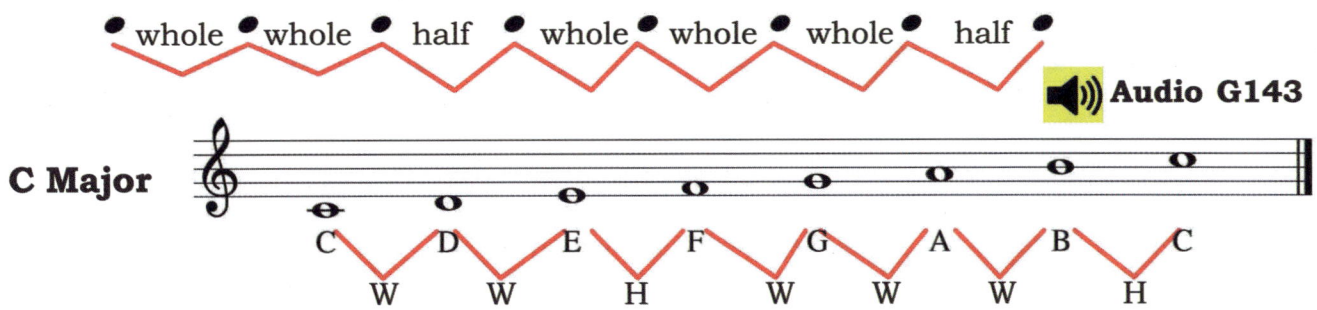

Start writing a major scale with the notes mentioned below. Write down the sharps and flats required to make the major scales. Then specify whether each note is separated by a half (H) or whole (W) move.

Inside an octave, a scale is a stepwise arrangement of notes/pitches. The major and minor scales are made up of seven notes or scale degrees. There are three forms of minor scales: natural, harmonic, and melodic. Natural Minor scale contains half-steps between 2-3 and 5-6 scale degrees (the natural form).

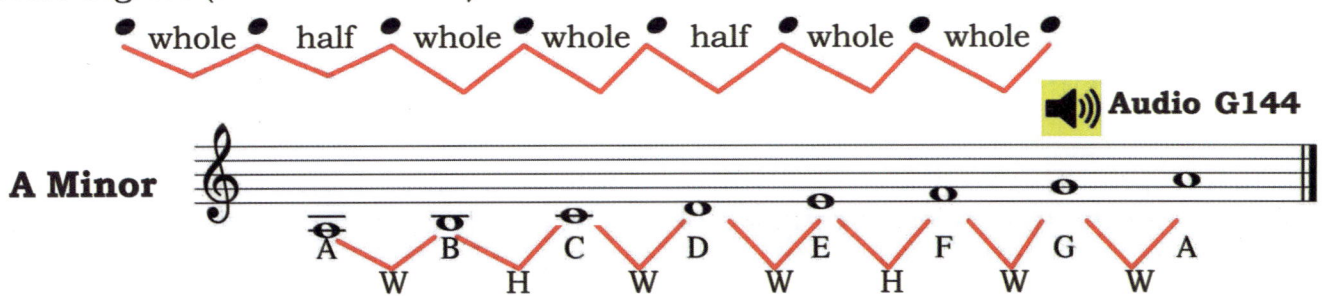

Start writing a natural minor scale with the notes below. Make natural minor scales by writing the sharps and flats required. Then specify whether each note is separated by a half (H) or whole (W) move.

Intervals Assignment

Example of intervals

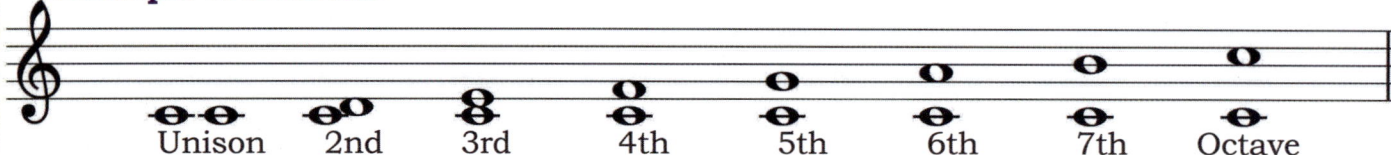

1. Recognize the musical intervals. Unison intervals receive a 'U,' octaves receive a 'O,' and all other intervals receive a numeric value (2nd, 3rd, 4th, 5th, 6th, 7th).

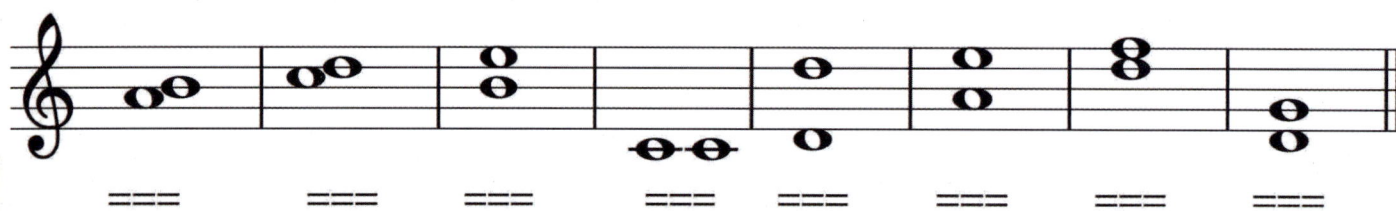

Example of intervals up and intervals down

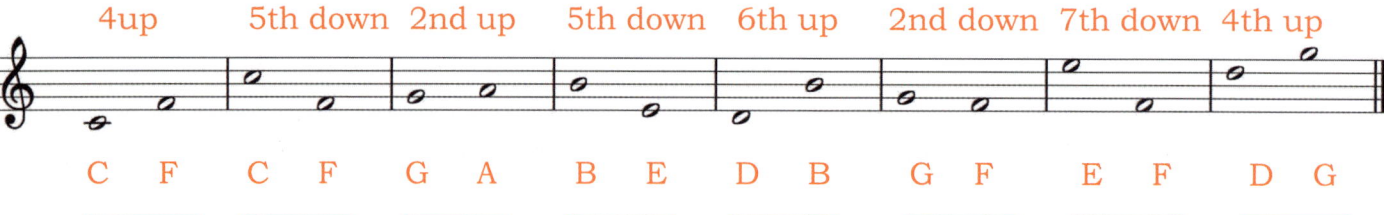

2. In the preceding exercise, you will write intervals up and intervals down from the printed note in the treble clef. Then label the two notes with their correct alphabet letter.

"Danny Boy" is a ballad written in 1913 by English songwriter Frederic Weatherly and put with "Londonderry Air." in traditional Irish melody. Weatherly changed the lyrics of "Danny Boy" to match the rhyme and meter of "Londonderry Air" after his Irish-born sister-in-law Margaret (known as Jess) sent him a copy in 1913 in the United States (an alternate version of the story has her singing the air to him in 1912 with different lyrics).

There are some theories about the true meaning of "Danny Boy." Some have interpreted the song as a letter from a parent to a son going to war or rebellion (as indicated by the reference to "pipes calling glen to glen") or leaving as part of the Irish diaspora.

Danny Boy

    Introduce the composition by singing it all the way through. Next, sing a two-measure phrase at a time when students are echoing short phrases. Then echo a four-measure phrase, and then finally the whole song. It allows students to discover and identify different pitches of the song. Add additional rhythm parts by first introducing them as chants with body percussion.

  Form a group of 2 students and describe the time signature, dynamics, marks of expression. Write the beats under each measure.
- is this song written in major or minor key signature
- what kind of feelings (happy/sad) does this song bring.
- describing what they like the most (rhythm, melody, lyrics, etc.) about this piece.
- identifying upbeat, legato, dotted notes, 1st, and 2nd ending.

Form   Theme And Variations

Theme and variation is a particular form of music. The form of a piece of music describes how it is structured. The piece starts with a theme, which is the main melody and is preceded by one or more variations of that melody. A variation is theme-like music, but it is also different enough not to precisely repeat the melody.

In theme and variations, the main theme is created in subsequent parts. The main theme is introduced in the first section. The first variation is added after that section is completed.

This variation and the rest would adopt the same harmonic progressions. Changes to the piece's pacing, articulations, and style are possible with each new variation. In certain cases, the key signature can also be modified. However, the relative harmonic structure in the new key will still be followed.

Beethoven's *32 C minor Variations* are a perfect example. Also, excellent examples are other piano works, such as Robert Schumann's *Variations on a Theme* and Mozart's variations *Twinkle, Twinkle Little Star*.

Analyze *32 Variations in C minor* discuss and describe changes in the theme with each variation.

32 Variations in C minor

🔊 Audio G146

Variations on a Theme by Robert Schumann, Op.9 (Brahms, Johannes)

Audio G147

There are 16 variations

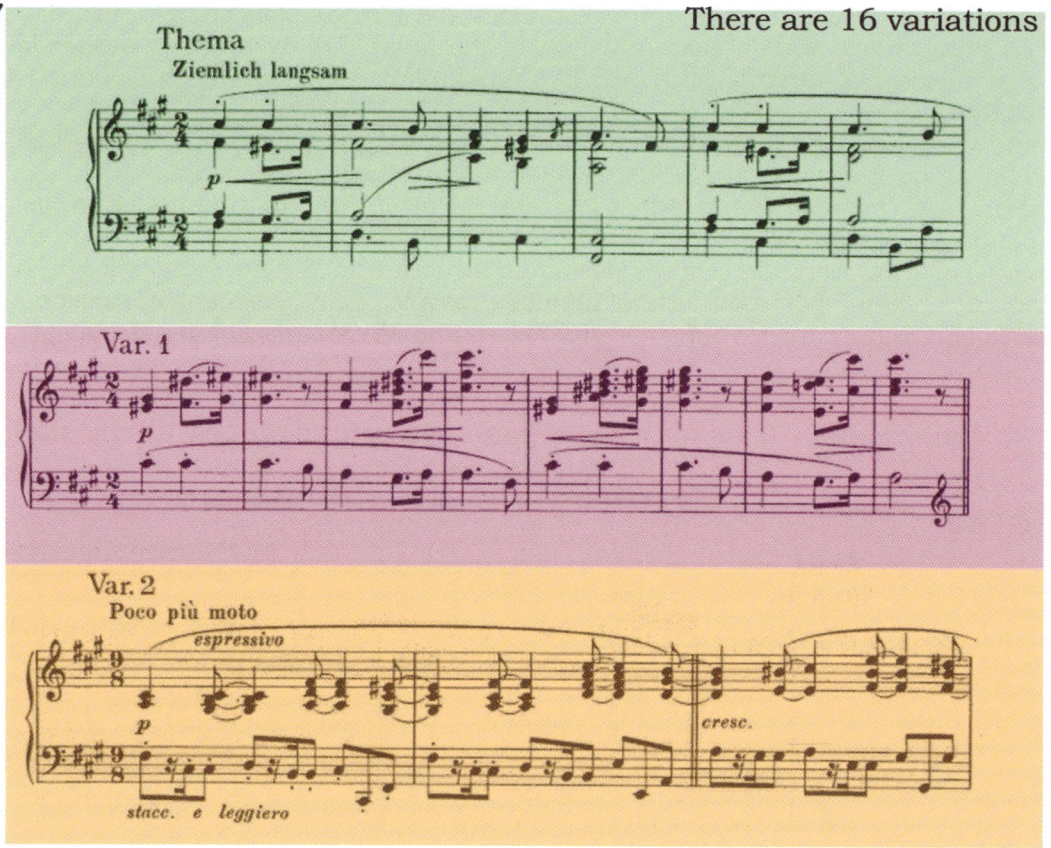

Have students determine if there are contrasting parts between the theme repeats. How many of them are there? Is there a difference between them, or are they the same? To explain the differences, use musical terms (e.g., the instrumentation is different, the dynamics are much louder, the tempo is slower, etc.).

Ah Vous Dirai-je Maman (Twinkle, Twinkle, Little Star)

Wolfgang Amadeus Mozart

Audio G148

-113-

Elephant Song

Traditional Song

1. One lit-tle el-e-phant went out to play, Out on a spi-der's web one day.

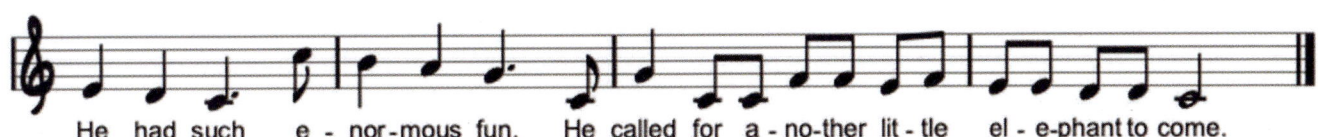

He had such e-nor-mous fun, He called for a-no-ther lit-tle el-e-phant to come.

Make your variation of "Elephant Song" by picking one of the song's themes and then changing the rest to make it your own. Once you finish composing your variations, try to practice playing or singing them.

Audio G149

Rondo Form

The term 'rondo' is a word in Italian that means round. A rondo form is characterized by a refrain that continually reappears throughout the piece. Unlike the song's verses, though, the music in a rondo changes between each repetition of the refrain.

The main theme or principal theme, also known as the refrain, is the basis for the Rondo form. The tonic key is used for this main theme or refrain because if the piece is in D major, the first theme is also in D major. Not only that, but the main theme is always in the tonic key or D major, in this case, "La Raspa." throughout the piece.

There are still some pieces that are in minor keys, of course, such as Mozart's "Turkish March." Whenever the main theme appears in that example, it is in the key of A minor. In addition to being in the A minor, the "Fur Elise" is in the rondo form A - B - A - C - A. The last movement of Beethoven's "Pathetique Sonata," "Sonata in C Minor Opus 13," is also in a minor key. However, Beethoven uses the 7-part rondo replacing D with another variant of B, common practice in rondo composition.

"La Raspa" is an example of a rondo. Listen to the song and analyze it.

Audio G150

1. What is the form of "La Raspa"
   • A B A B A
   • A B A C A
   • A B A C A B A
2. Which sections differs harmonically from the others?

Fur Elise by Ludwig van Beethoven

 Audio G151

- Write the letter for each section you hear it___ ___ ___ ___ ___
- Make different motions to the different sections
- Have them draw different scenes to depict what they hear in each section
- Show them different listening maps for each section and point to which they hear.
- Make it simpler by only focusing on Section A and require that they recognize when "A" comes back again.

You will respond to several true/false statements about the rondo form in music for this activity. If the statement is true, simply write 'T' or 'true' next to the respective statement. However, if the statement is false, write 'F' or 'false' next to the statement.
1. _____ A musical form refers to how a piece of music is organized and structured.
2. _____ The opening music is known as the theme or refrain.
3. _____ An episode refers to the parts of the piece that differ from the theme or refrain.
4. _____ In rondo form, the theme is never repeated in the piece of music.
5. _____ All music is written in the rondo form has five musical sections.
6. _____ "Fur Elise" by Beethoven is written in the rondo form.

Hear this piece or pick your piece in a rondo form. Students must find out if there is a recurring musical concept for each piece. For instance, does the instrument offer a clue to the refrain? Is there a dynamic?

Concentrate solely on the main, recurring theme.

Have students determine if there are contrasting parts between the theme repeats. How many are there? How are they different, or are they identical? To help you explain the differences, use musical terms (e.g., the instrumentation is different, the dynamics are much louder, the tempo is slower, etc.).

🔊 **Audio G152**   **Beethoven's *Pathetique Sonata, Sonata in C Minor Opus 13***

The last movement of Beethoven's *Pathetique Sonata, Sonata in C Minor Opus 13*, is also in A minor key. On the other hand, Beethoven uses the 7-part rondo in this piece, replacing D with a version of B, which was a common practice in rondo composition at the time.

Students must engage in group work. Have students work in pairs and write comments.

_____

_____

_____

_____

_____

_____

_____

_____

_____

_____

Opera, Operetta, Musical Theater, Concerto, and Oratorio

An **opera** is a form of theater in which the drama is primarily or entirely communicated through music and singing. Born in Italy more than 400 years ago during the Renaissance, opera—a blend of vocal and orchestral music, theater, visual arts, and dance—has been an inspiration to people for decades. The role of music in opera is to communicate an entire story/plot is interesting, special, and outstanding. It is focused on the feeling that music can express people's reactions and feelings better than words (read or spoken) or photographs. Opera takes some dramatic story and seeks to make it more thrilling and realistic with music. *Cinderella*, *Hansel* and *Gretel*, and *Romeo and Juliet* are only a few of the popular stories turned into operas. The opera terms are called the libretto (literally "little book"). Some composers, such as Richard Wagner, have written their libretti, while others, such as Mozart and Lorenzo da Ponte, have collaborated closely with their librettists.

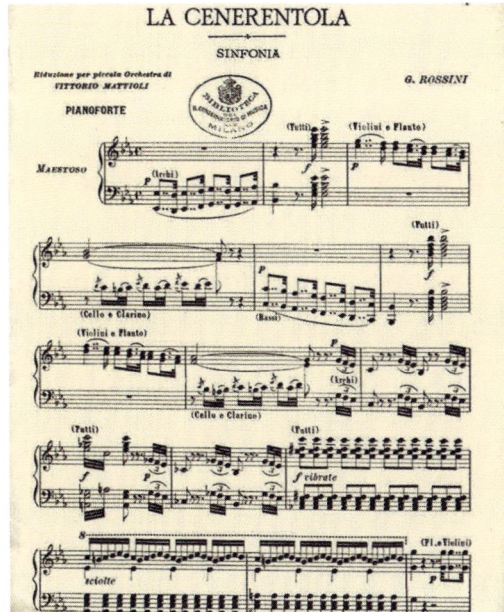

Are you ready to watch excerpts from a comic opera "Gianni Schicchi, A one-act Play of the Cenerentoli" by Giacomo Puccini and "The Match Girl" by Rossini? Rossini's version of *Cinderella* tells the story of an innocent girl, oppressed by her family, who ends up marrying a charming prince but encounters real dangers along the way.

▶ **Video L46, L47**

Operetta is a performing arts genre similar to opera, but it is lighter in music and subject matter. Because it is closely related to opera and musical theater, it is not easy to differentiate between them in many cases. In the seventeenth and eighteenth centuries, the term was used to describe stage works that were shorter or less ambitious than full-scale operas. Operetta became very popular in America in the nineteenth century, thanks in no small part to Gilbert and Sullivan and Johann Strauss's works. Operas typically emphasize an epic, grand style, with more focus on singing than on acting. Operettas, on the other hand, appears to have a conversation broken up by musical numbers. The operetta is almost relaxed in contrast, and the style of singing is quite different. Many operettas can be performed by average or fair singers, although most operas cannot be performed.

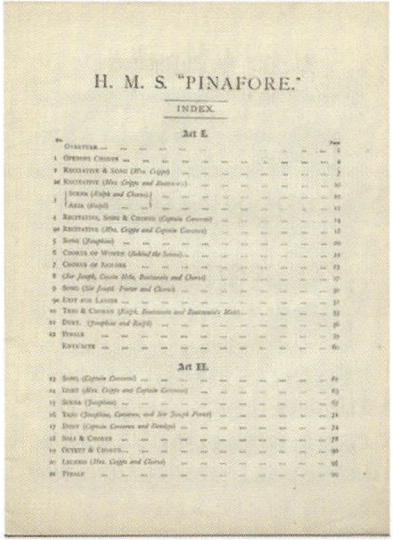

In England, Sir William S. Gilbert (1836-1911), a dramatist, and Arthur Sullivan (1842-1900), a composer and conductor, collaborated on 14 comic operettas. The Gilbert and Sullivan team created imaginative works featuring funny, rapid-fire lyrics and elaborate musical sequences.

Let us watch Gilbert & Sullivans HMS Pinafore, (A lowly sailor and his Captain's beautiful daughter find their love thwarted by their differences in rank, an evil shipmate, and an incompetent Lord.)

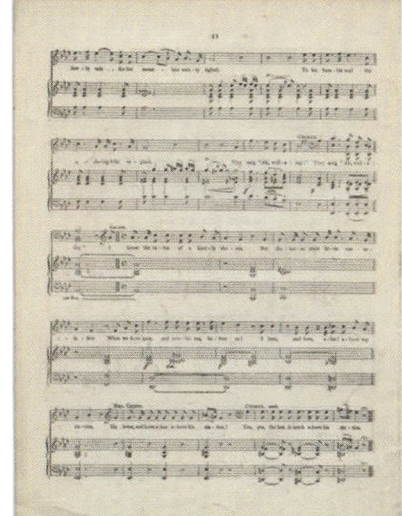

▶ **Video L48**

Musical theater is a type of theater that combines music, songs, spoken dialog, and dance. Today's musicals are typically seen in two acts with an intermission of 10 to 20 minutes. The first act is almost always a little longer than the second act and usually incorporates more of the music. A musical can be based on four to six theme tunes used several times in the show, or it may be made up of a collection of songs that are not musically related. With a few exceptions, the spoken dialogue is interspersed between musical numbers.

Types of the musical theater include

"comic opera" (or "light opera," which denotes a sung drama, usually with a happy ending);

"operetta" (a genre of light opera which is "light" in terms of both music and subject matter);

"musical play," "musical comedy," "burlesque" (theatrical entertainment usually consisting of comic skits);

"music hall" (a variety of entertainment involving a mixture of the populace) (multi-act theatrical entertainment that combines music, dance, and sketches).

Some works fit into more than one of the categories mentioned above.

The theater is still popular worldwide, but we almost always refer to the musical theater when discussing this concept in the United States. Musical theater is a form of dramatic production that tells a story by combining acting, singing, and dancing. We like to name these productions musicals, or often Broadway musicals, based on their prominent location. You will laugh, cry, cheer, and sing; it is an artistic experience unlike any other.

Let us watch Masquerade - *Phantom of the Opera*.

📹 **Video L49**

A **concerto** is a three-movement musical composition in which an orchestra or concert band accompanies either one solo instrument (such as the piano, violin, cello, or flute) or a group of soloists (concertino). In this modern context, the concerto emerged alongside the concerto grosso, which contrasted a small group of instruments with the rest of the orchestra during the Baroque era. Although the concerto grosso is a Baroque era, the solo concerto is still a vital musical force today. Before 1700, the term was applied to a broad range of pieces written for a wide range of performing media, including voices and instruments; it was often used in the sense of "ensemble" or "orchestra." It was not used regularly (though not exclusively) until the beginning of the 18th century for works in three movements (fast-slow-fast) for soloists and orchestra, two or more soloists, and orchestra (concerto grosso), or undivided orchestra.

Let us listen to Mozart's *Concerto for Flute, Harp, and Orchestra in C Major, K. 299/297c,* a concerto for flute, harp, and orchestra composed by Wolfgang Amadeus Mozart. It is one of only two true double concertos he composed and Mozart's only piece of harp music.

🔊 Audio G153

An **oratorio** is a large musical composition for orchestra, vocal soloists, and chorus, usually with narration to tie the dramatic story together. It is distinguished from an opera by the absence of theatrical scenery, costumes, or acting styles. In terms of musical style and type, the oratorio is somewhat similar to the opera, except that choruses are more common in oratorios than in operas. The use of choruses gave composers a distinct advantage in depicting Biblical tales. The *Messiah* by George Frideric Handel, a huge work focused on New Testament teachings, is one of the most well-known oratorios. The 17th and 18th centuries were the most active times for oratorio composition, as the Baroque era reached its pinnacle in terms of grandeur and splendor in its art forms.

Let's listen to *Messiah*, an English-language oratorio composed in 1741 by George Frideric Handel, with a scriptural text compiled by Charles Jennens from the *King James Bible* and the *Coverdale Psalter*, the version of the *Psalms* included with the *Book of Common Prayer*.

 Audio G154

Motive (Motif)

A motif is a musical unit that is small but recognizable. The motif could simply be a sequence of pitches or a distinct rhythm. It could be harmonically conceived; pitch and rhythm are often combined in motifs to produce separate melodic fragments. No matter its constituent elements, the motif needs to be repeated before it can be recognized as a unit.

Let us listen to the following:

The first movement of Ludwig van Beethoven's *Symphony No. 5* has the most famous motive in Western classical music.

Motive from Ravel's *String Quartet*, first movement.

Beethoven's Symphony No. 5

Ravel's String Quartet

 Audio G155, G156

Do a Think-Pair-Share activity in which students research examples of opera, operetta, musical theater, concerto, and oratorio. Identify the use of a motif in a listening selection and give examples. Identify and describe composite forms: opera, operetta, musical theater, concerto, and oratorio.

You may use the internet to do this research. Write all examples on the next page.

Ear Training Exercises

1. Listen to the example and place the following dynamic markings where applicable: p, mf, and f.

2. Circle the corresponding tempo marking in the above example: Largo, Allegro, Andante.

3. Listen to the example and notate where the ritardando (rit.) and accelerando (accel.) occur.

4. Circle the corresponding tempo marking in the above example: Largo, Allegro, Andante.

5. Listen to the example and highlight (>) under the accented notes.

6. Circle with blue color all quarter rests, green all sixteenth notes, red color for all the eighth notes.

7. Complete the notes by applying the stems to the first measure and the beamed notes to the second measure. Be sure the stems are pointed in the right direction.

Major Chords and Major Triads

The chord is a grouping of three or more notes played at the same time. A triad is a chord of three notes.

Major chords or triads are formed by taking root notes, say musical note C, and then going up to a major third, followed by a minor third (or a perfect 5th from the root). A perfect fifth interval is a major third plus a small third above the root note (or the 5th note in a major or minor scale). The major third interval is two whole steps, so if we were to create a C major chord, we would start with C and then move up two whole steps to our main third, E, for the chord's second note.

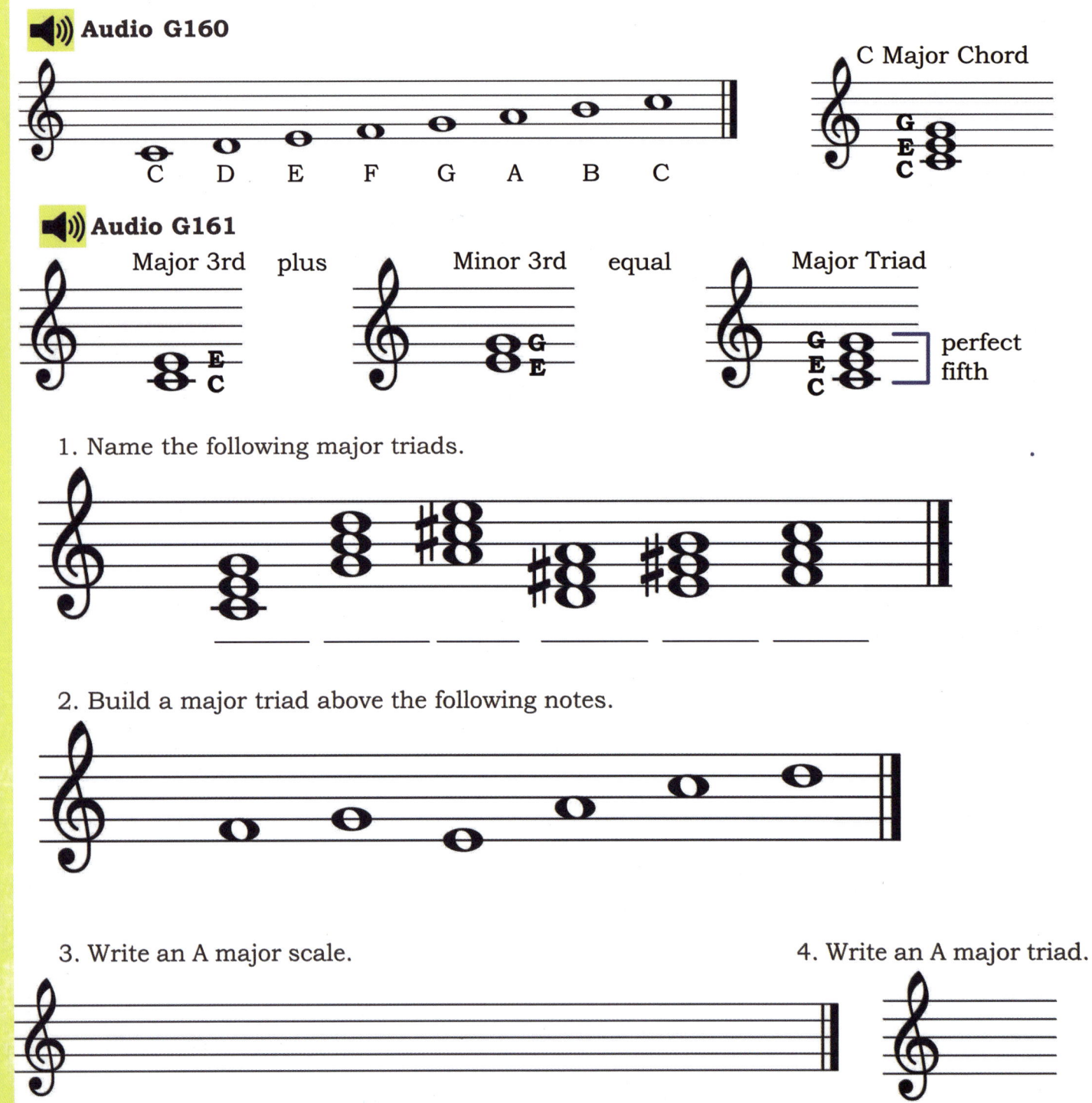

Minor Chords and Minor Triads

Minor chords are formed similarly to major chords, with the exception that the thirds are inverted. It means that instead of going up a major third from your root note (let us say C), we will go up a minor third first, then add a major third on top of that (or a perfect fifth above the root) to finish the chord. A minor third is a whole step plus a half step, so if we start on C, we can go up to E-flat instead of the E natural discussed earlier. From there, we would step up a major third to G, our final note.

When we compare the notes in a C major triad (C-E-G) to the notes in a C minor triad (C-E flat-G), we can see that the first third (second note in the triad) decides whether the triad is major or minor. You should also notice that the top note, G, does not shift. It is crucial to know and saves time when making chords.

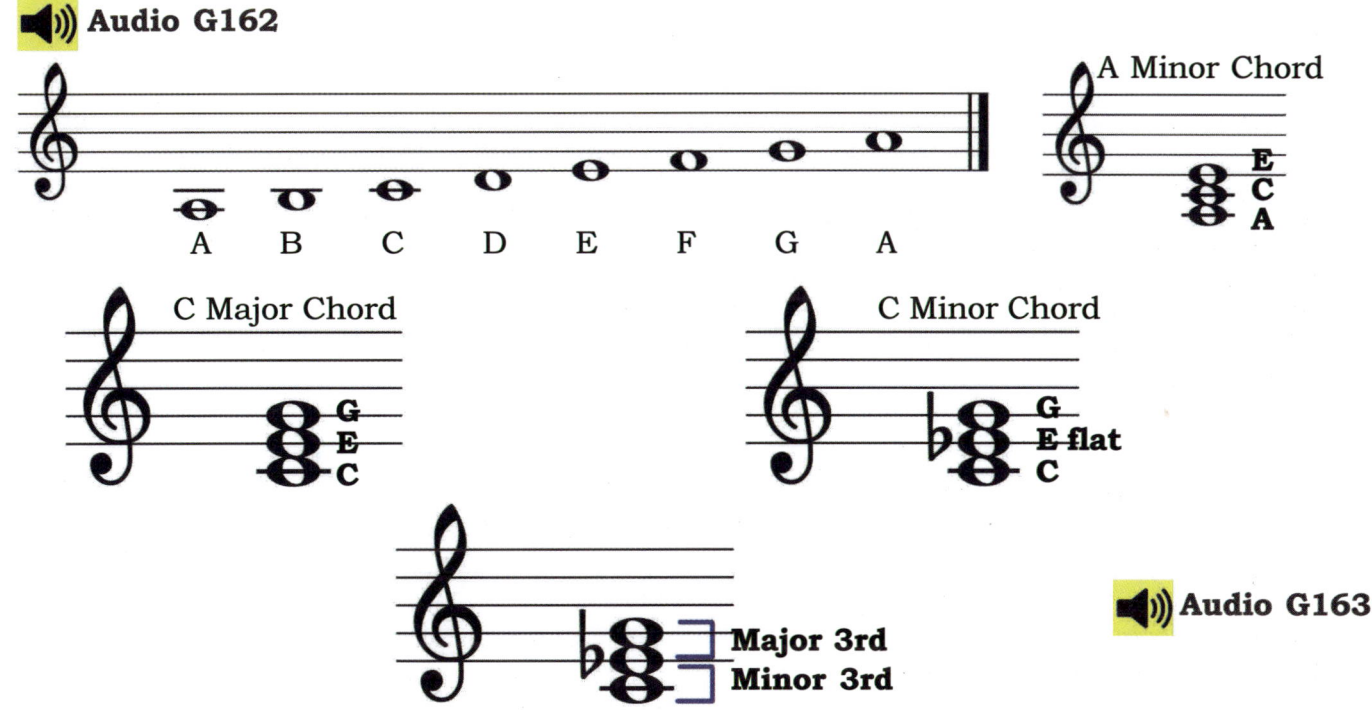

1. Write the chords indicated and then learn to play them on the piano. You may watch Video L50.

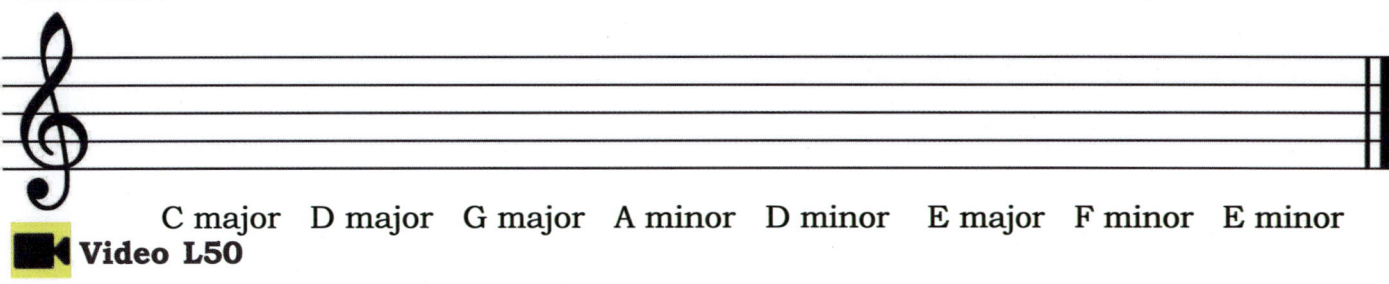

2. Learn to play the following chords on the piano. You may watch the Video L51.

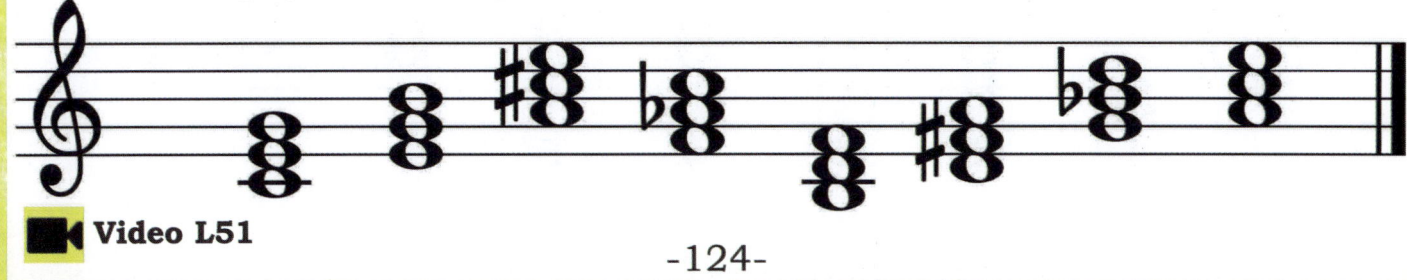

Scale Degree Names

A scale degree is a name given to each note in a scale. If the scale is A Natural Minor (Tonic Note: A) or D Major (Tonic Note: D), the Tonic note will always be Scale Degree 1 (or the first note in the scale) (Tonic Note: D). If the scale is A Natural Minor (Dominant note: E) or D Major (Tonic note: D), the Dominant Scale Degree will always be the 5th note in the scale (Dominant: A). Each Scale Degree has its name, which is mentioned in the table below. On a Minor (Natural) scale, the 7th Scale Degree is known as the Subtonic, while in a Major scale, it is known as the Leading Note.

Scale Degree	Scale Degree Name	A Minor scale
I	Tonic	A
II	Supertonic	B
III	Mediant	C
IV	Subdominant	D
V	Dominant	E
VI	Submediant	F
VII	Subtonic/Leading Note	G

The Roman numeral analysis is a musical analysis method in which Roman numerals (I, II, III, IV, etc.) are used to describe chords. In certain cases, Roman numerals are used to represent scale degrees. However, they typically refer to the chord whose root note is the scale degree. For example, the third scale degree or, more generally, the chord centered on it is denoted by the letter III. Major chords are usually represented by uppercase Roman numerals (such as I, IV, V). In contrast, minor chords are represented by lowercase Roman numerals (such as ii, iii, vi) (see Major and Minor below for alternative notations). On the other hand, some music theorists use upper-case Roman numerals for all chords, regardless of consistency.

Let us take a look at a C Major scale.

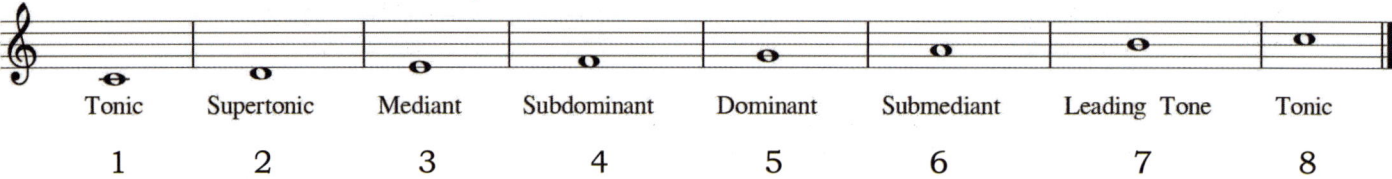

Every scale has the same scale degree numbers: scale degree 1 represents the first note, scale degree 2 represents the second, scale degree 3 represents the third, and so on.

Roman numerals refer to chords, while scale degrees refer to single notes. For example, you would not call an F Major chord in C Major a "scale degree four chord." You would call it a "four chord." Although some may opt to write the number "4," Roman numerals are used for more advanced music analysis. There are a few reasons why.

Identifying Major and Minor Chords

While numbers are not able to differentiate between major and minor chords, Roman numerals are. To demonstrate, let us go back to our C Major scale and build triads on each of the scale degrees.

Notice how certain Roman numerals are upper case, and others are lower case.
- Roman numerals in the upper case are major chords.
- Roman numerals in the lower case are minor chords.

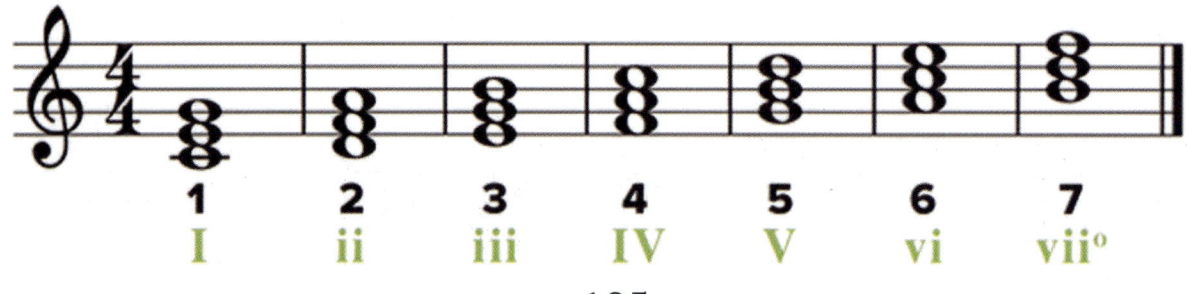

Chord Progression

The movement from one chord to another is called chord progression.

A chord progression is a set of chords that are played one after the other. The main challenge when finding chords within the progression is to find their harmonic functions within the key, which means comparing the chord to the tonic of the key. The harmonic functions are written in Roman numerals I, II, III, IV, etc. Each number stands for its corresponding degree within a scale. Therefore, identifying the degree of progression of the chord requires your ability to correctly distinguish the intervals.

All seven degrees of the major and minor scales can serve as the root of the triad. In Western music, the triads on the scale degrees of C, F, and G are of utmost importance for establishing a piece's tonality.

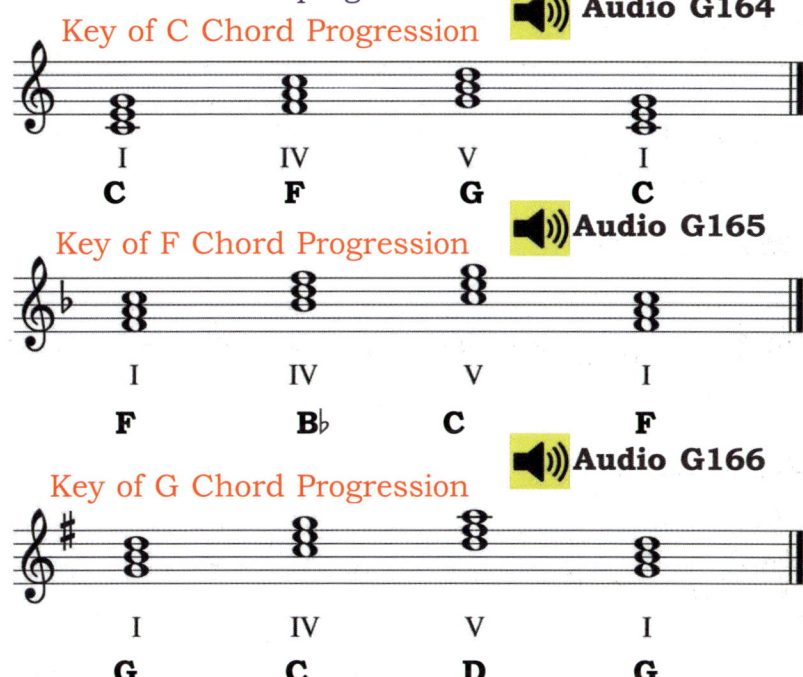

Below is shown the seven degrees of a C major scale:

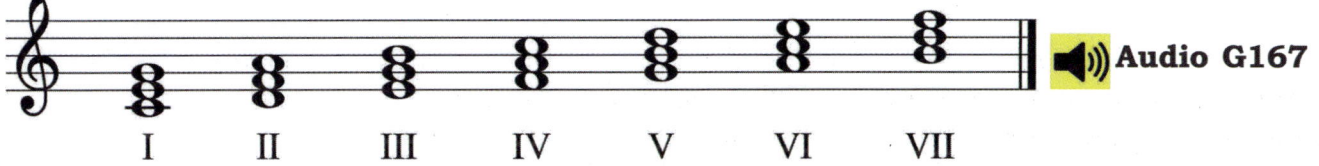

1. Write the A scale.

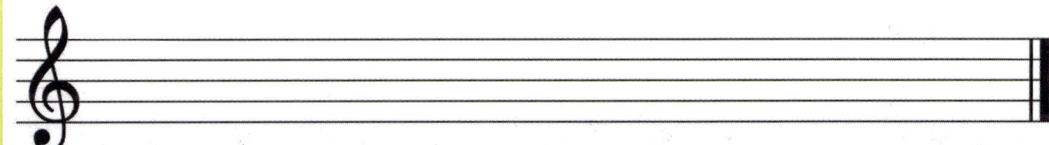

2. Write the I IV V I progression in the key of A. Then give each chord's letter name.

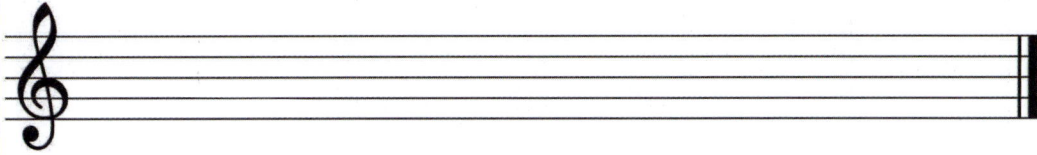

3. Write the E scale.

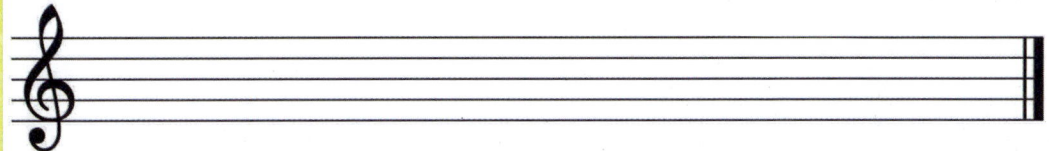

4. Write the I IV V I progression in the key of E. Then give the letter name of each chord.

Harmonizing A Melody & Composing A Melody

Harmonization in music is the chordal accompaniment to a line or melody: "Using chords and melodies together, creating harmony by stacking scale tones as triads." Harmonizing melodies is a lot like playing chess in that there are many rules and countless possibilities and variations thereof for any given position. Since you know the chords' notes, you can analyze the melody to see if the notes outline a chord you know. Usually, chords change in each measure.

In measure 1 the notes C E E G G are all found in the C chord.
In measure 2 the notes F F A A are all found in the F chord.
In measure 3 the notes G B D D are all found in the G chord.
In measure 4 the notes G E C C are all found in the C chord.

1. Harmonize the following melody.

2. Compose a melody over the existing harmony.

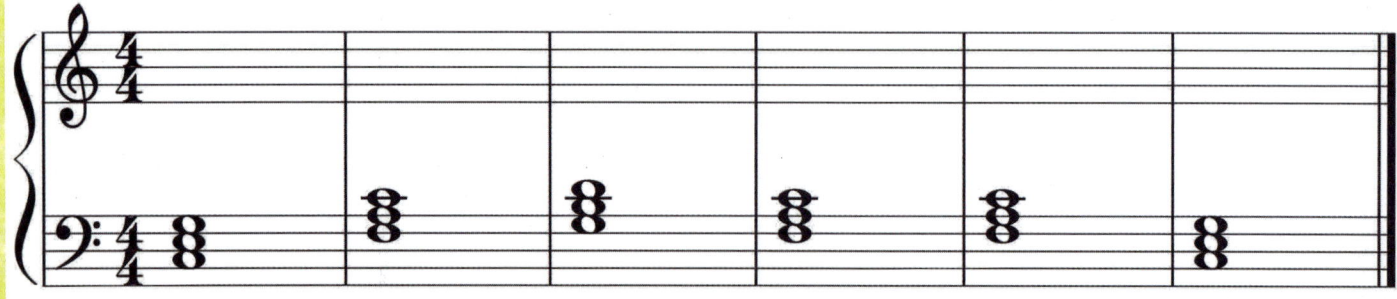

Down by the Sally Gardens

Audio G171

Traditional Song

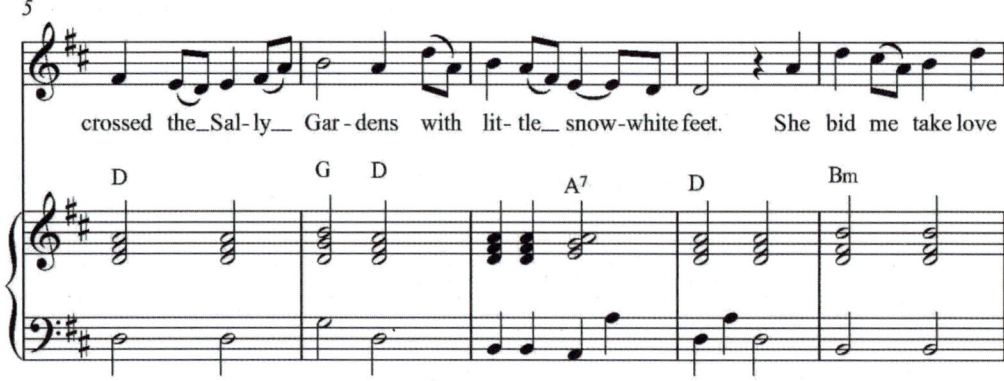
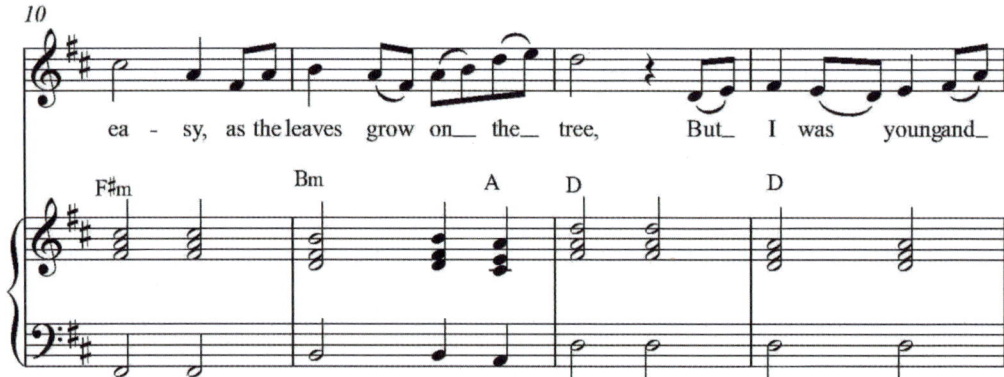

continue next page

Down by the Sally Gardens

• Form groups of four students and analyze how the melody is harmonized in each measure.
• Analyze the harmony and write the Roman numerals below the staff, then circle the chord symbols.
• Identify major/minor chords. Point to the voice line and piano lines.
• Identify and comment on 4/4 time signature, key signature, note values.

• Play Audio G171 and have students echo phrase by phrase.
• Add movement. This can be simultaneous or while echoing.
• Practice singing with the metronome.

1. Compose a melody over the existing harmony. Write the Roman numerals below the bass staff and the key-chord above the treble staff.

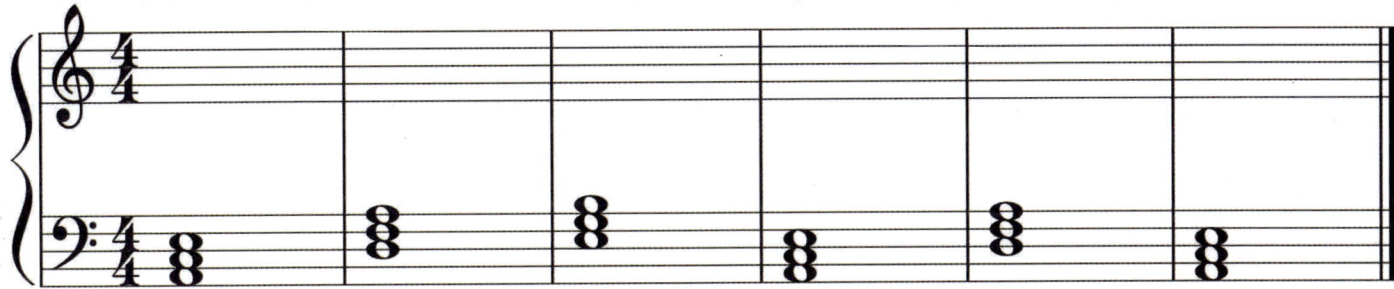

2. What is the first scale degree?
a) Dominant
b) Tonic
c) Mediant
d) Leading Tone

3. On what scale degree is F in the key of C?
a) Tonic
b) Subdominant
c) Dominant
d) Mediant

4. What is the 5th scale degree?
a) Submediant
b) Subdominant
c) Dominant
d) Mediant

5. What is the 2nd scale degree?
a) Submediant
b) Leading Tone
c) Supertonic
d) Mediant

What is Ostinato?

Ostinato is a repetitive pattern of short notes. It can be quite simple, played on a single note repeatedly, or very complicated, using different notes from a scale or even from beyond the scale of your music. It may have a basic rhythm, or a very complex rhythm, even with some syncopation.

Ostinato patterns may be simple or complex. Here is an example of ostinato. The first measure on the bass line is an ostinato. As you may notice, this is a repeating pattern.

 **Audio G172**

Form groups of 2 students and compose an ostinato song.

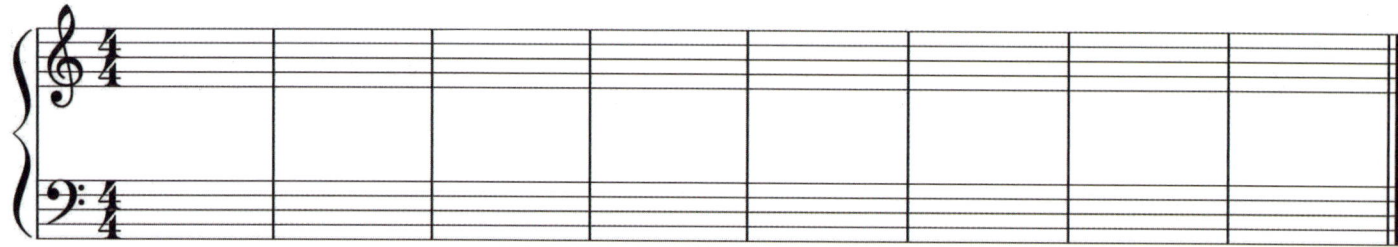

You may listen to some other ostinato examples.
- Frédéric Chopin - B*erceuse Op 57 D Flat Major*
- Johann Sebastian Bach - *Passacaglia in C minor for organ*

Audio G173, G174

- Sight-sing the solfege (in cut time) while the students perform the ostinato.
- Divide the class in half. Half sings. Half performs the ostinato. Trade jobs.
- Divide students into classes of two or four. Each group creates the 4-beat ostinato that they can perform as a group while singing the song.
- Sing with proper pitch and tuning.
- Can you recognize the ostinato?

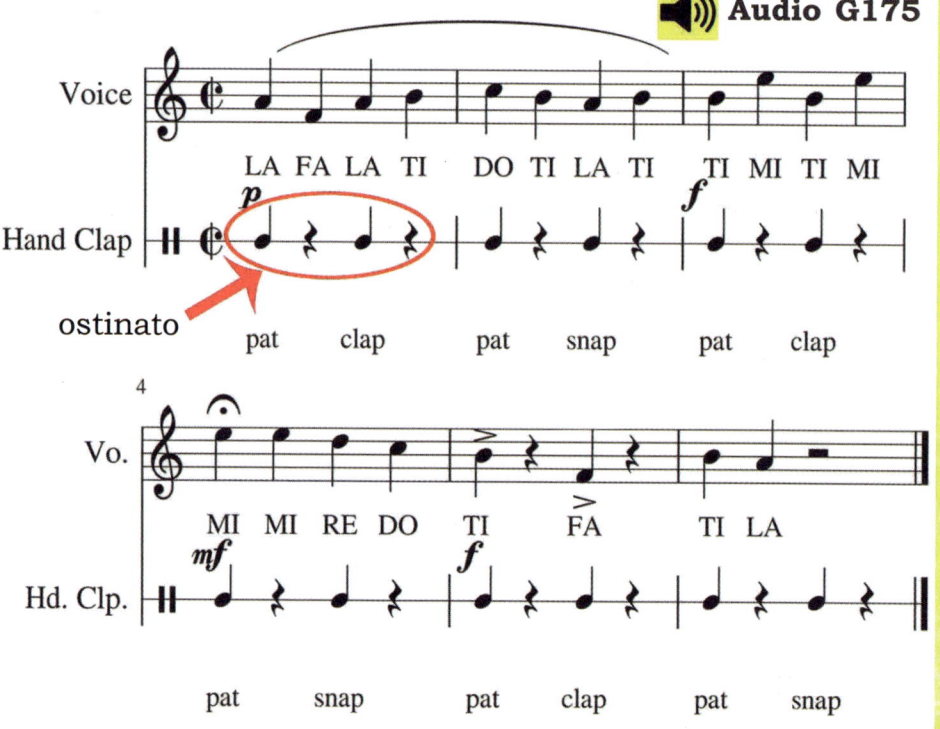

What is a Round?

Rounds are when two (or more) groups sing the *same song* at different times to create harmony.

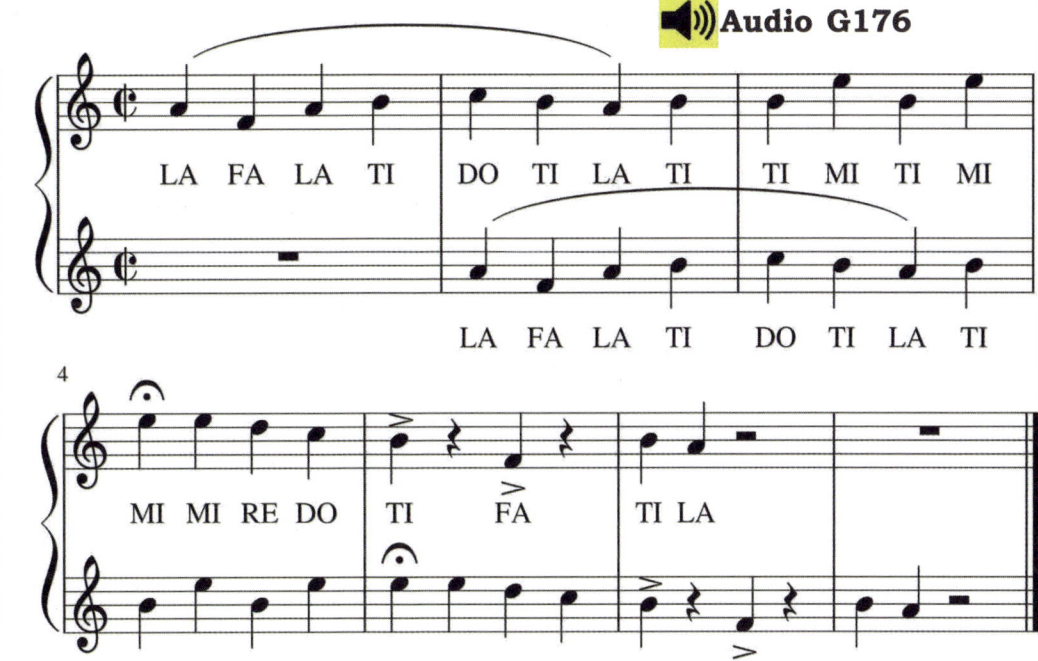

- Students should be divided into two groups for round sight-singing the following solfege.
- The first group starts ahead, while the second group follows the first measure.
- Students can demonstrate concept of texture in music by singing a two-part round.
- Students can sing in correct rhythm.

Remember!
We have a single melodic line when we sing songs in unison; and multiple melodic lines when we sing in round. A single melodic line produces a thin sound and multiple melodic lines produce thick sounds.

Form groups of 2 students and compose a round song.

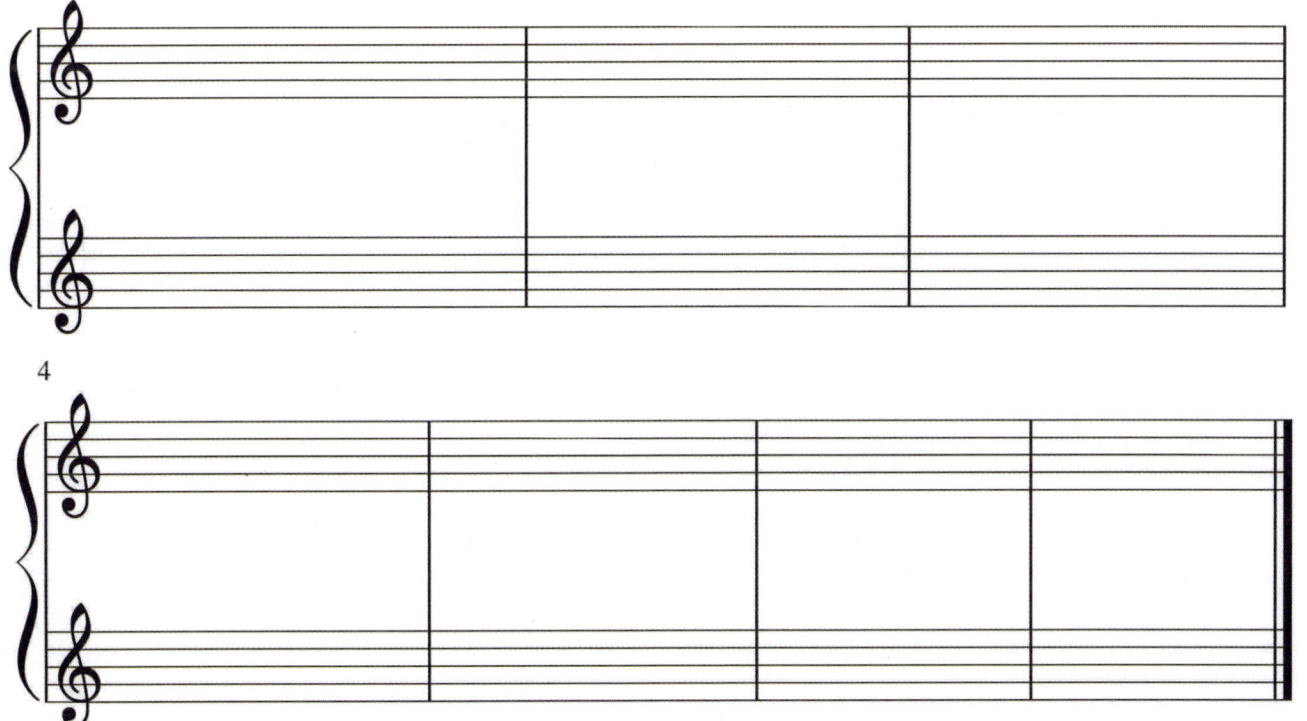

-132-

What are Partner Songs?

Partner songs are when two separate songs are sung together to achieve harmony.

Partner Songs

Silver Birch: Land of the sil-ver birch, home of the bea-ver, Where still the migh-ty moose wan-ders at will. Blue lake and rock-y shore, I will re-turn once more. Boom-de-de boom boom Boom-de-de boom boom Boom-de-de boom boom boom.

My Paddle: My pad-dle's keen and bright, flash-ing with sil-ver. Fol-low the wild goose flight; dip dip and swing. Dip dip and swing her back, flash-ing with sil-ver. Swift as the wild goose flies, dip dip and swing.

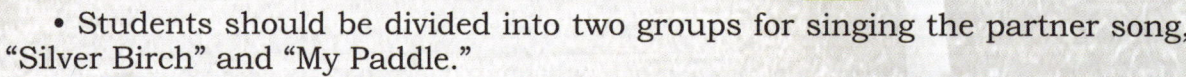
Audio G177, G178

- Students should be divided into two groups for singing the partner song, "Silver Birch" and "My Paddle."
- Maintain a good singing posture. Activate the articulators (lips, teeth, tongue).
- After both groups learn very well to sing their part, you can have them sing together.
- Produce good tone by concentrating on vowel formation and vertical space inside the mouth.
- Sing with expression.

Descant

A descant is a medieval music genre in which one singer sings a fixed melody, and others accompany with improvisations. Descant is an additional melody played or sung in a voice higher than the existing music.

🔊 **Audio G179**

- One student sings the "descant." The other classmates sing the "melody."
- Divide the class in half and sing in two parts.

Counter-melody

A counter-melody gives the listener two melodies at once and considerably boosts melodic interest. A counter-melody is a second melody that is sung or played simultaneously as the main one. It's not a commonly used compositional device but can be an extremely effective way of boosting song energy. A counter-melody will provide harmonic support for the main melody, but it differs from a simple harmony line because it can and should stand on its own as a viable melody.

🔊 **Audio G180**

- Repeat the melody line and rhythm multiple times. Practice with a metronome.
- Divide the class in half. Half sings the counter-melody using solfege syllables. The other half sings the melody with solfege syllables. Trade parts.
- Pay attention to dynamics, 1st, and 2nd ending.

What is a two-part harmony?

The first person performs the melody and the second person sings above or below it, the melody within the chord structure in basic two-part harmony. In rock or pop music, the backup singer harmonizes with the lead singer by changing the pitch of their note depending on the lead singer's pitch so that they are in tune.

- Form groups of four students and analyze how the melody is harmonized in each measure.
- Separate students into two groups. One group will sing "soprano," and the other group will sing "alto."
- Teacher will play Audio G181 for "soprano group" or Audio G181a for "alto group" and sing the starting pitches of Happy Birthday. Listen, tune, and blend your voice with other voices around you.
- First, practice the rhythms. Next, sing the melody.
- Maintain a good singing posture. Activate the articulators (lips, teeth, tongue).
- After both groups learn very well to sing their part, you can have them sing together.

Old Folks At Home

🔊 Audio G182

Stephen Foster (1851)

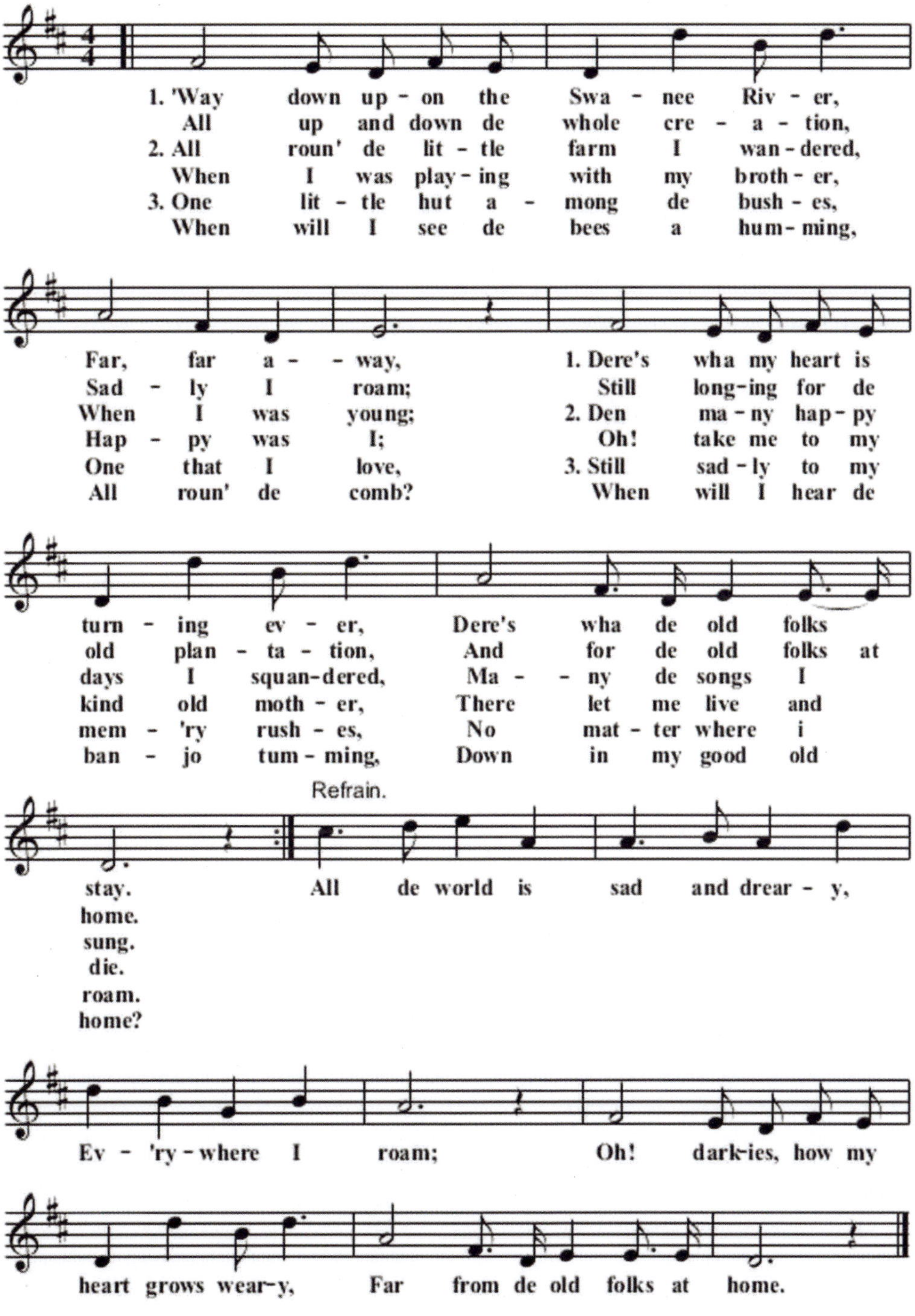

[Sheet music with lyrics:]

1. 'Way down up-on the Swa-nee Riv-er,
   All up and down de whole cre-a-tion,
2. All roun' de lit-tle farm I wan-dered,
   When I was play-ing with my broth-er,
3. One lit-tle hut a-mong de bush-es,
   When will I see de bees a hum-ming,

Far, far a-way, 1. Dere's wha my heart is
Sad-ly I roam; Still long-ing for de
When I was young; 2. Den ma-ny hap-py
Hap-py was I; Oh! take me to my
One that I love, 3. Still sad-ly to my
All roun' de comb? When will I hear de

turn-ing ev-er, Dere's wha de old folks
old plan-ta-tion, And for de old folks at
days I squan-dered, Ma-ny de songs I
kind old moth-er, There let me live and
mem-'ry rush-es, No mat-ter where i
ban-jo tum-ming, Down in my good old

Refrain.

stay. All de world is sad and drear-y,
home.
sung.
die.
roam.
home?

Ev-'ry-where I roam; Oh! dark-ies, how my

heart grows wear-y, Far from de old folks at home.

• Sing the song correctly, be expressive, keep your lips slightly rounded, have a clean emission, and a loose body position. Sing the song and play the rhythm of the musical toy you have created (drum, shakers, etc.)

Do a Think-Pair-Share activity in which students talk about:
• meaning of the song
• what kind of feelings (happy/sad) this song brings
• major or minor key (there is a common assumption about music that major is happy, and minor is sad)
• describing what they like the most (rhythm, melody, lyrics, etc.) about this piece.

Popular music styles

Popular music is a general term that encompasses several various types and genres of music from the late 18th century onwards, which are considered part of the current day-to-day culture.

A music genre is a conventional category that defines such pieces of music as belonging to a shared tradition or collection of conventions.

In several ways, music can be divided into various genres. Music's artistic nature means that these classifications are often subjective and controversial, and some genres may overlap.

Rock Music:

Originated as "Rock & Roll" in the United States, Rock music has shaken the world since the 1950s. It is a music genre that began around string instruments but now uses other modern instruments, making it difficult to give it a definite meaning. Its loud and powerful beats make it famous among the youth. Little Richard, Bill Haley, and Chuck Berry are some of the rock stars who popularized the culture, while modern bands like Pink Floyd, The Doors, Metallica, Nirvana, and Megadeth have taken the culture by storm.

Country Music:

Another popular genre of American music originated in the 1920s; Country music has its roots in American folk and western music. Simple instruments such as electric and steel guitars, drums, and mandolin or mouth organ are used to create it. Some of the most famous country music singers include Shania Twain, Johnny Cash, Taylor Swift, and Kenny Rogers.

Pop Music:

The roots of pop music can be found in various musical forms, including ragtime jazz piano melodies, a musical genre associated with the late 19th and early 20th centuries. It has origins in improvised rhythms from the jazz age of the 1920s and 1930s and orchestras from the big band era of the 1940s.

A new genre of music originated in the 1950s and 1960s. Quick rhythms, heavy beats, and soulful lyrics defined this emerging music genre, dubbed rock and roll. Elvis Presley, regarded as the "King of Rock and Roll," was one of the first performers to popularize the new genre. Presley's influence was matched by The Beatles, a British rock and roll band that was part of the British music invasion. The Beach Boys surfed into the mix with their musical representation of Southern California.

In popular music, "pop music" is often distinguished from other subgenres by stylistic traits such as a danceable rhythm or beat, simple melodies, and a repeating structure reminiscent of vocalists' songs Karen Carpenter and Roberta Flack. Pop song lyrics are often emotional, relating to love or dancing.

The Beatles' rhythms and harmonies inspired a generation, actually - and this was evident in the 1970s, when pop drifted between styles, from T. Rex's Glam Rock to punk's raw fire. Arguably, the biggest pop star to emerge from the period was a singer and pianist, Elton John, whose popularity has remained constant.

Jazz:

Jazz, associated with swing and blue notes, has origins in West African and European cultures. Jazz is known as "One of America's original art forms" with a rare mix of imagination, collaboration, and interactivity. Jazz, which dates from the late 1800s to the early 1900s, was influential in introducing the world to various female artists, including Ella Fitzgerald, Betty Carter, Abbey Lincoln, and Ethel Waters.

Popular music styles

Research Project:
Each student can write about his/her music style or genre and give examples of his/her favorite songs. Some questions that can help with your project.

1. What is the name of the genre you have chosen?
2. When was this genre at its peak (dates and times)?
3. Is this a sub-genre of another genre? If that is the case, what separates it?
4. What are the main characteristics of this genre (and how can I know if I am listening to it)?
5. Who were the founders (creators/developers) of this fashion trend?
6. How has it evolved? Have you made any changes?
7. Describe the context or environment in which this genre will be performed.
8. What are the typical outfits worn by performers in this genre?
9. Describe various artists or groups that work in this genre (at least 5).
10. What is the meaning of the music? (Parties, dancing, sharing thoughts, and so on.)
11. Identify the target audience for this genre (young, old, conservative, etc.) Discuss how elements and expressive qualities define the music's style.
12. What kind of education (or preparation) is needed to succeed in this genre?
13. How does this genre compare to or differ from those you have heard?
14. Why did you choose this genre, and what do you think makes it "good"?
15. In this category, who is your favorite artist or group?
16. Offer a brief history of your favorite musician or group (please be detailed).
17. Describe why you choose 1-2 of this group's or artist's songs as your favorites.
18. Any additional material you want to provide (which could be worth "extra credit points"), such as a poster board to visually improve the presentation, audio samples, etc.

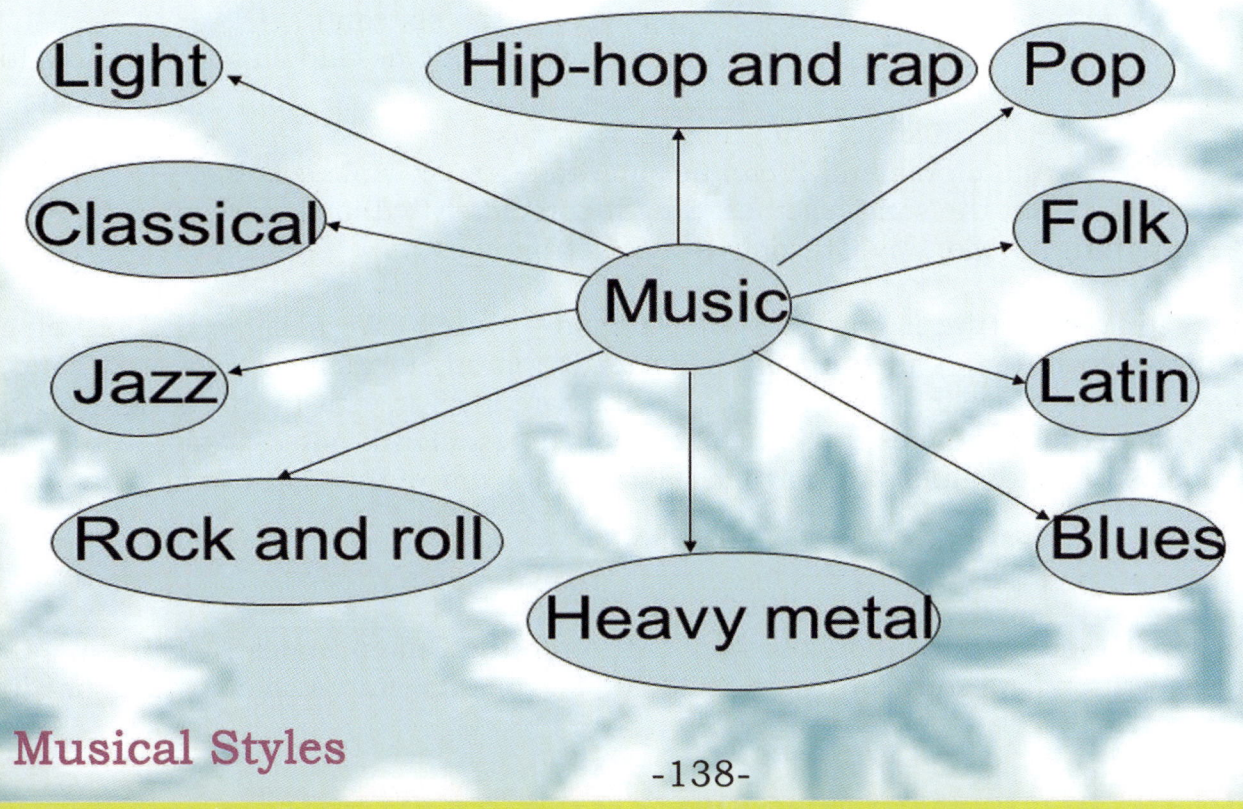

Musical Styles

Oregon My Oregon

Audio G183　　　　　　　　　　　　　　　　　　　　Henry B. Murtagh 1920

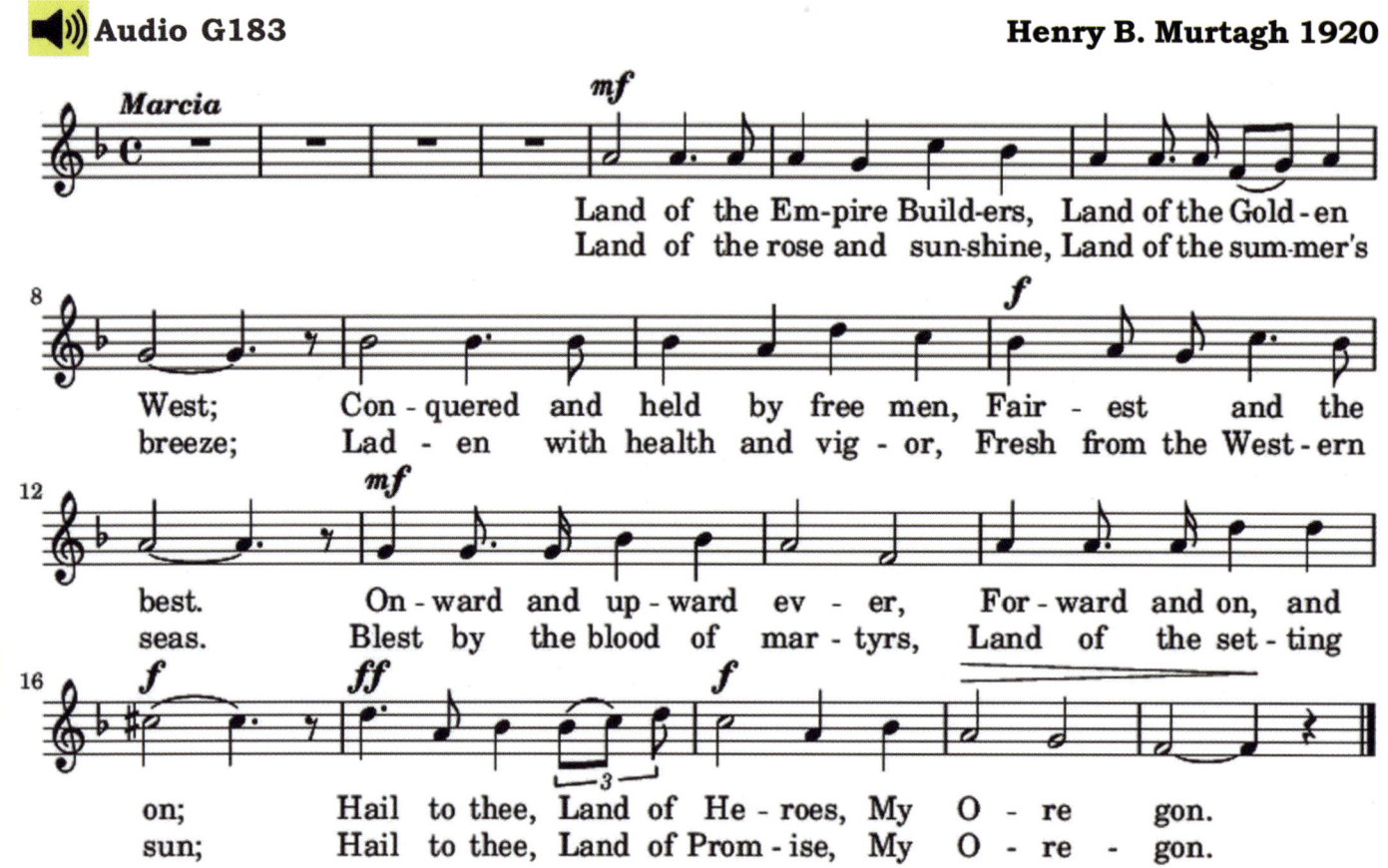

• "Oregon My Oregon" is a good song for preparing, making conscious, or practicing the rhythmic element dotted quarter note followed by an eighth note and dotted eighth note followed by the sixteenth.
• Sing to children alone, rocking your body or clapping or stomping to the beat.
• Have children echo, phrase by phrase.
• Add movement. It can be simultaneous or while echoing.
• Put the song together. Sing it completely without echoing.
• Practice chanting "Oregon My Oregon" with a metronome.

This song's time signature is common time, tempo - Marcia. We observe the following dynamics: mezzo-forte (mf) – medium loud, forte (f) – loud, fortissimo (ff) – very loud, decrescendo – gradually playing softer. Ties and slurs are also present in this song. Dotted quarter notes, dotted eighth notes, half notes, quarter notes, eighth notes, triplet. Circle all musical symbols and note values. Choose one color for each one of them. Count all measures and beats.

"Oregon, My Oregon" is the national song of Oregon in the United States. The 16-line, 2-verse song was written for a song contest in 1920 and became the state's official state song in 1927.

Brazilian Music Styles

Although Brazil is the world's fifth-largest country with a total land area greater than the United States, most people only know two of its musical forms: samba and bossa nova. However, there is a lot more to it than that. Music is an important part of Brazilian culture, and the country's music is as diverse as its people.

Map of Brazil

Brazil is located in eastern and central South America. Encompassing around half of the continent's landmass with a population of over 200 million, it is the fifth-largest country by area and by population in the world.

Native Americans followed their religious ceremonies with exotic rattlers, shakers, and panpipes, which gave Brazilian music its rhythmic vitality. Beginning in the 17th century, slaves from Africa brought their candomble rituals along with the hot, impassioned drumming. The first Portuguese colonists introduced slow, heartbreaking ballads, accompanied by cavaquinhos (similar to the ukulele), bandolim (mandolin), bagpipes, and the Portuguese guitar.

Samba (Audio G184)

19th century painting of Afro Brazilian music and dancing

The term "samba" is thought to have originated from the Kimbundu (Angolan) term semba, which meant "invitation to dance," as well as a popular name for dance parties organized by slaves and former slaves in Rio's rural areas. These dances featured gyrating hip movements (called umbigada) and had origins in Congolese and Angolan circle dances from the colonial era. Brazilian popular music began with the samba in the late 19th century. Choro was the forerunner to samba, and by 1928, samba schools were founded to provide training in the samba, not the least for Carnaval. By the 1930s, radio was available to most people, and samba popularity spread throughout the country. Since that time, various forms of popular music have all been influenced by the samba, including Brazil's earlier traditional song and dance forms. Let us listen to "A Voz do Morro" by Ze Keti.

Bossa Nova (Audio G185)

In the late 1950s, a small group of mostly middle-class students, artists, and musicians came together on Rio de Janeiro's tropical beaches to create a new sound. Bossa Nova was a light samba inspired by traditional Brazilian music and rhythms and American jazz, and a modern Portuguese lyrical form. It was a youthful celebration of romance and beach culture.

Antônio Carlos Jobim, a talented composer, and Joo Gilberto, a guitarist and singer from the poorer Bahia region, are the twin figureheads of Bossa Nova. A larger Bossa Nova family surrounds these key figures. It features lyricist Vincius de Moraes, jazz pianist Sérgio Mendes, composer/guitarist Roberto Menescal, and Nara Leo, the muse of the Bossa Nova. Let us listen to "Girl from Ipanema," a Brazilian bossa nova and jazz song.

🔊 Audio G184, G185

Samba Rhythm

Audio G186

Bossa Nova Rhythm

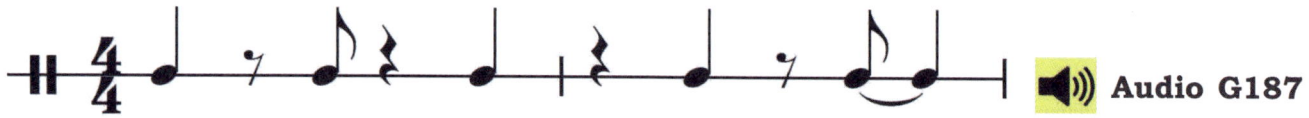
Audio G187

Samba, a traditional Brazilian dance with many variants, has African roots. It has been performed as a street dance at the carnival, the pre-Lenten festival, for nearly a century. At Rio's local carnival, several different Samba variations (from Baion to Marcha) are performed. Samba, also known as Carioca, is a Brazilian ballroom. Samba has been around for a long time and is derived from the rural "Rocking Samba." (The Carioca is a small river that flows through Rio de Janeiro; the word Carioca refers to Rio's residents.) Samba is still popular in Rio today. During the carnival, there are thousands of elaborately costumed dancers performing a national theme based on Brazil and Rio's music characteristics in particular.

Samba has a distinct rhythm, which is intensified by traditional Brazilian musical instruments such as the tamborim, chocalho, reco-reco, and cabaca.

Boomba

Audio G188

Brazilian Folk Song

Have fun learning to sing this song.

I Love You California

Audio G189

A.F. Frankenstein (1913)

Have the students sing the tune. Once everyone is singing with confidence, try breaking them into two groups and sing the song. Have group one sing the entire song while group two claps the rhythm.

Do a Think-Pair-Share activity in which students talk about:
- meaning of the song.
- major or minor key (there is a common assumption about music that major is happy, and minor is sad).
- what they like the most about this piece describing rhythm, melody, lyrics, etc.
- change of time signature, key signature, note values.
- improvising an accompaniment rhythm for this song and performing it while your classmates sing "I Love You California."

Word Search

 Circle the words from the word list in the puzzle below.

```
T N Y Q P G G H S O T E T F V
A E B A S S O O N T T E U L S
M T R O M B O N E I D T B U A
B S I V I O L A Q M O C A T X
O F V M T T N C C P U L A E O
U G R P F M O E T A B A B C P
R O M E M X B L D N L R G Y H
I N W R N R U L X I E I H M O
N G J D D C P O W O B N V B N
E H K R O A H I V M A E I A E
J I W U Q Q N H C E S T O L S
T R U M P E T B O C S J L E H
C M T P E W X D X R O E I L A
S N Z O B O E C B V N L N V R
W D Z Z D H P D W P R S O T P
```

French horn	double-bass	trombone	saxophone
clarinet	tambourine	bassoon	trumpet
piccolo	cymbal	violin	viola
oboe	drum	timpani	flute
cello	tuba	harp	gong

-143-

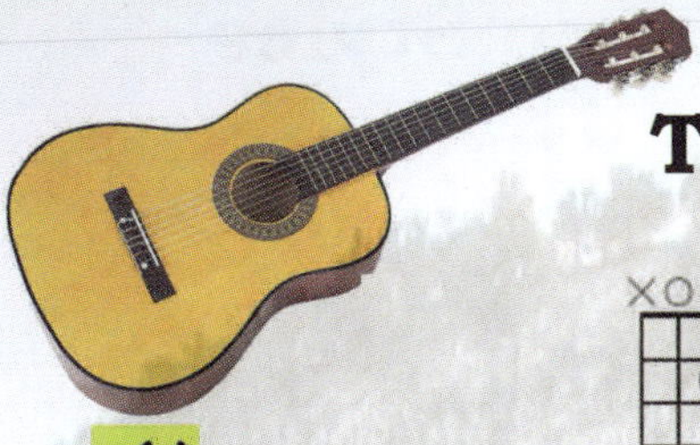

The Yellow Rose Of Texas

J.K. (1858)

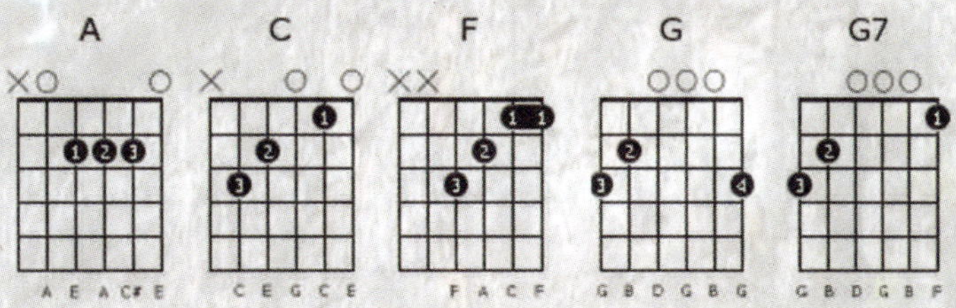
A
C
F
G
G7
A E A C# E
C E G C E
F A C F
G B D G B G
G B D G B F

Audio G190

Video L53

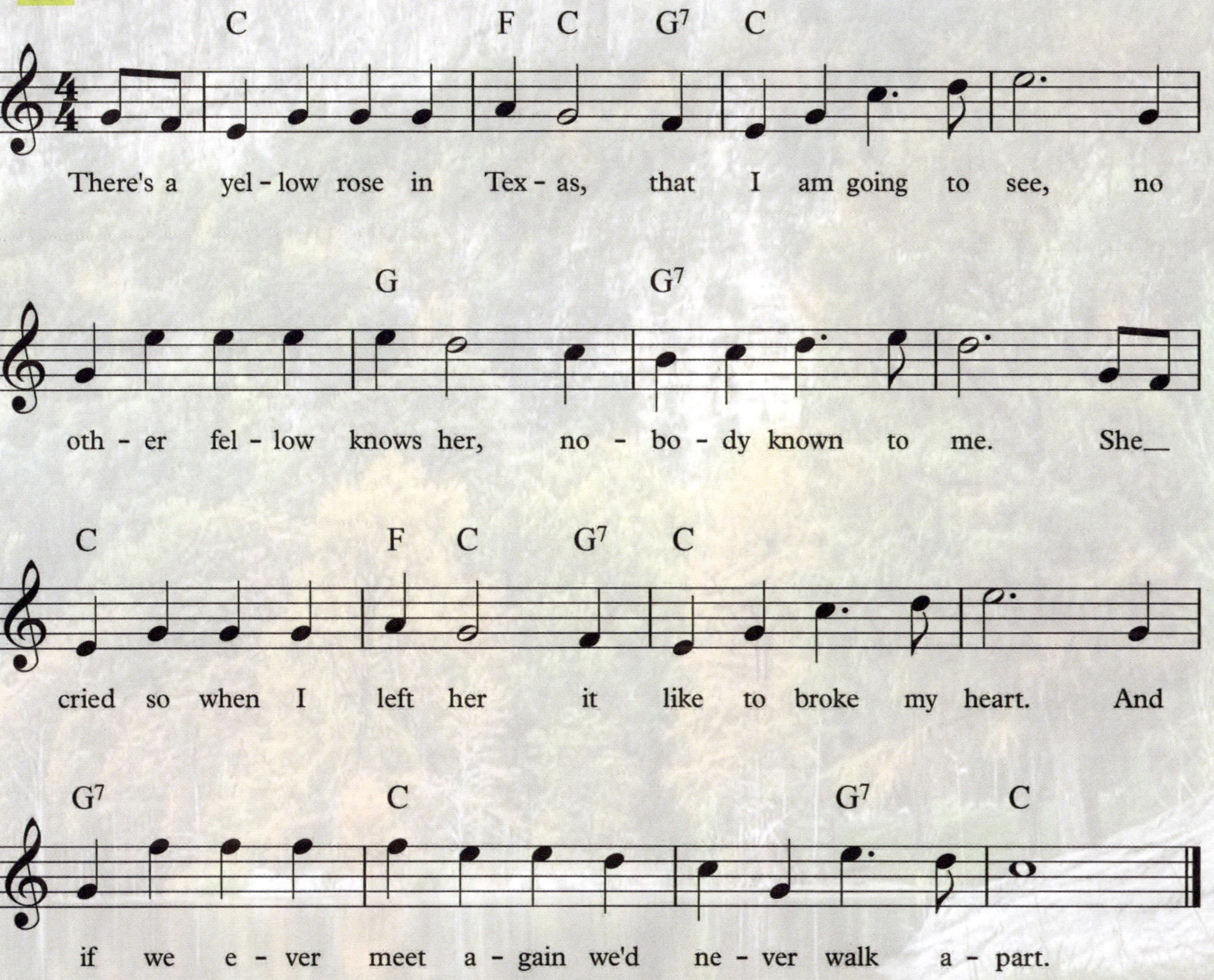
C
F C
G7
C
There's a yel - low rose in Tex - as, that I am going to see, no
G
G7
oth - er fel - low knows her, no - bo - dy known to me. She__
C
F C
G7
C
cried so when I left her it like to broke my heart. And
G7
C
G7
C
if we e - ver meet a - gain we'd ne - ver walk a - part.

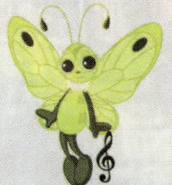

• Sing the song correctly, be expressive, keep your lips slightly rounded, have a clean emission, and a loose body position.

• Play Audio G186 and have students echo phrase by phrase.

• Create or improvise a movement activity to accompany the song "The Yellow Rose of Texas."

• Your teacher can help you learn to play on the guitar the chords for this song.

• Play Audio G186 and have the students work in pairs to guess what kind of song it is, for example — fast, slow, happy, sad, etc.

• Analyze the song and discuss if it was written in a major or minor key?

• What is the key signature? Point to the dotted notes and upbeat. Count the beats under each measure.

Japanese Music Styles

Traditional music in Japan has a long and varied history. Many musical forms were introduced from China over a thousand years ago, but they were reshaped into uniquely Japanese expression styles over time. The shamisen, shakuhachi, and Koto were among the most important instruments adapted and developed to meet local needs.

J-Rock is short for "Japanese rock." The genre dates to the '60s and has been continually evolving. At first, J-Rock was heavily influenced by British and American rock bands, but now, the genre has become one-of-a-kind.

J-Rock is another diverse genre that encompasses a sound close to the West's alternative/rock sound. Guitar and/or drums power the majority of the bands. Many rock bands, especially in the United States and Europe, rise through the ranks of "indies," bands or bands signed to smaller labels. They would probably be signed to a major label if they were renowned by Japanese teenagers.

Visual Rock is a subgenre of J-Rock that focuses on visuals as well as music. Visual Rock stars often wear bright costumes and flamboyant hair and makeup, allowing their appearances and gestures to be as relevant as the music they produce. Male Visual Rock artists can dress androgynously or in drag. Famous Visual Rock bands include Dir En Grey and Malice Mizer. The distinction between Visual Rock and J-Rock is often hazy, with common bands such as GLAY and L'Arc-en-Ciel arguing whether they are Visual Rock or merely a J-Rock subset.

J-Ska

Ska music has a strong presence in Japan, despite being much less popular than J-pop, J-rock, or J-Synth (Electronica). The Japanese ska scene, which began about a decade ago with forerunner bands Ska-Flames and Tokyo Ska Paradise Orchestra, experienced a huge popularity surge in 1997 (similar to the popularity surge in the United States) that faded quickly. Despite the lack of mainstream support, many Japanese ska bands continue to exist. The Determinations, The Side Burns, and Blue Beat Players are three well-known Japanese ska bands.

The **shakuhachi** is a bamboo flute that is played by blowing on one end of the instrument. Since it has four front holes and one back hole, it is often referred to as a "five-holed bamboo flute" in English. The shakuhachi's limited number of holes allows it to generate a wide variety of sounds; in reality, the shakuhachi's poignant tone is due to the small number of holes.

The Japanese **Koto** is a horizontal harp zither similar to the East Asian horizontal harp zither. The Koto is Japan's national instrument. Koto is made of Kiri wood and measures 180 centimeters (71 inches) in length (Paulownia tomentosa). They have 13 strings that run the length of the instrument and are strung over 13 movable bridges. Before playing, players can change the string pitches by shifting these bridges and plucking the strings with three finger picks (on the thumb, index finger, and middle finger). There are also contemporary versions of 17, 21, or 25 strings.

Shakuhachi Flute

Koto Japanese Harp

🔊 Audio G191 (J-Rock), Audio G192 (J-Ska)

🔊 Audio G193 (Shakuhachi)

🔊 Audio G194 (Koto)

Musical Repertoire

Practice singing the following songs.
Do a Think-Pair-Share activity in which students talk about:
• meaning of each song.
• major or minor key (there is a common assumption about music that major is happy, and minor is sad).
• what they like the most about each piece describing rhythm, melody, lyrics, etc.
• time signature, key signature, note values.
• clapping or playing the rhythm of each song on instruments like drums, shakers, or tambourine.
• creating or improvising a movement activity to accompany each song.
Your teacher can help you learn to play each song on the xylophone, guitar, recorder, or piano.

Alabama

Audio G195

Edna Gockel-Gussen (1917)

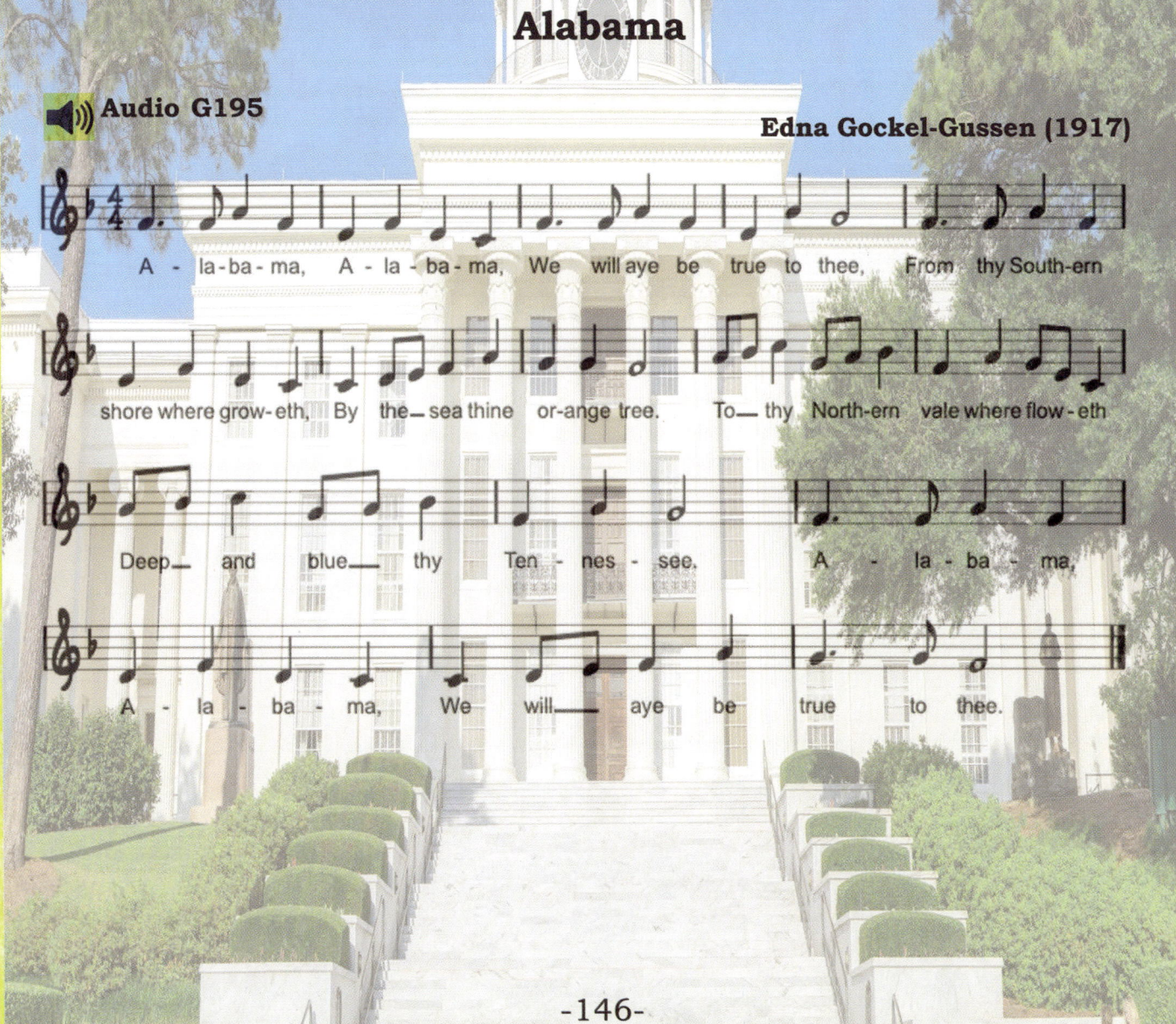

A - la - ba - ma, A - la - ba - ma, We will aye be true to thee, From thy South-ern shore where grow-eth, By the sea thine or-ange tree. To thy North-ern vale where flow-eth Deep and blue thy Ten-nes-see. A - la - ba - ma, A - la - ba - ma, We will aye be true to thee.

Here We Have Idaho

Sallie Hume-Douglas

Go, Mississippi

Audio G197

Houston Davis

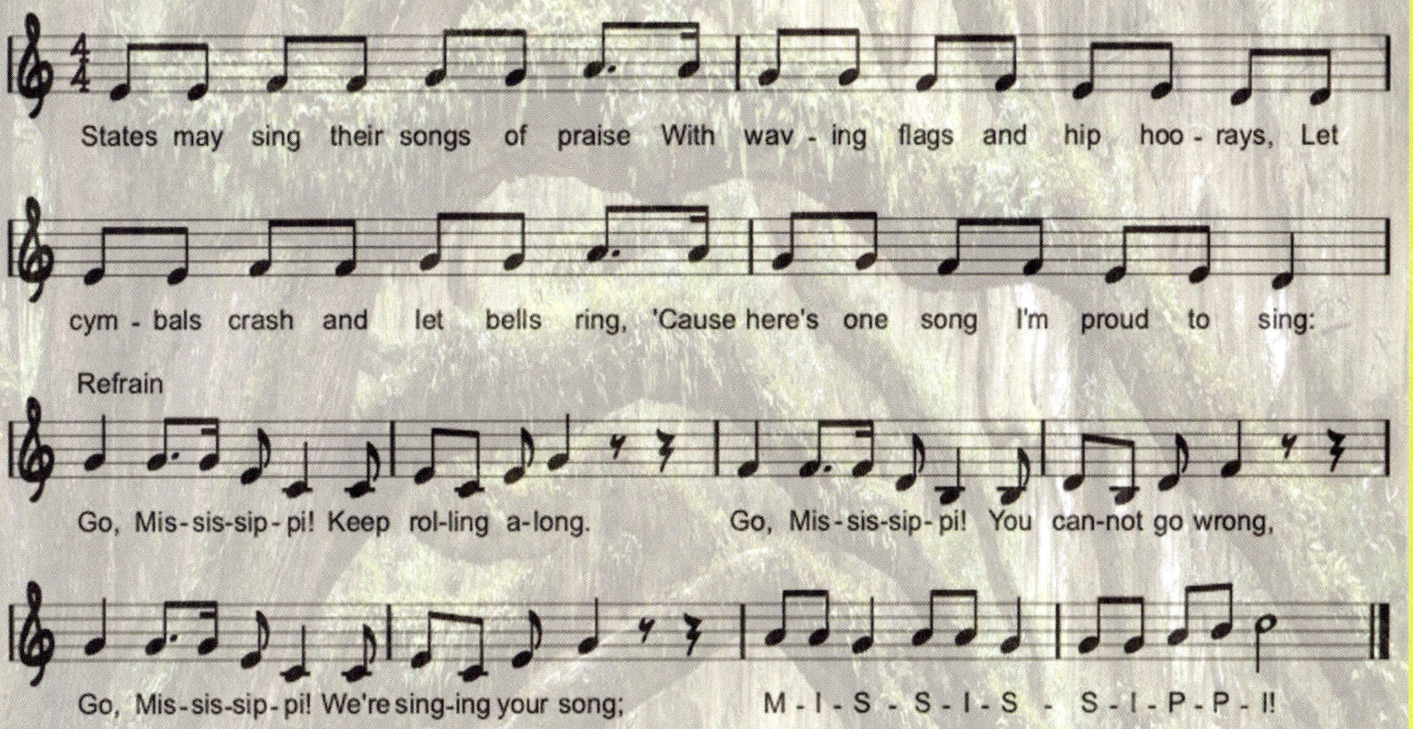
States may sing their songs of praise With wav - ing flags and hip hoo - rays, Let
cym - bals crash and let bells ring, 'Cause here's one song I'm proud to sing:
Refrain
Go, Mis-sis-sip-pi! Keep rol-ling a-long. Go, Mis-sis-sip-pi! You can-not go wrong,
Go, Mis-sis-sip-pi! We're sing-ing your song; M - I - S - S - I - S - S - I - P - P - I!

Carolina

Audio G198

Anne Custis Burgess (1874-1910)

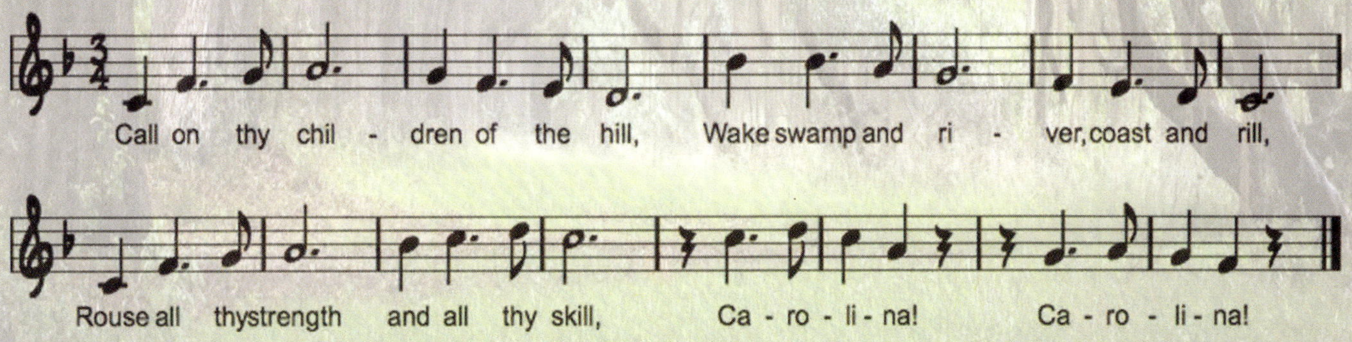
Call on thy chil - dren of the hill, Wake swamp and ri - ver, coast and rill,
Rouse all thystrength and all thy skill, Ca - ro - li - na! Ca - ro - li - na!

O, Fair New Mexico

Audio G199

Elizabeth Garrett (1915)

My Oklahoma Home, It Blowed Away

Audio G200

Traditional Song

When they o-pened up the strip, I was young and full of zip, I wan-ted a place to call my own. And so I made the race, and staked me out a place, And set-tled down a-long the Cim-ma-ron. It blowed a-way, It blowed a-way, My Ok-la-ho-ma home, blowed a-way, It looked so green and fair when I built my shan-ty there, But my Ok-la-ho-ma home it blowed a-way.

Going to Kentucky

🔊 Audio G203

Traditional Song

We're go-ing to Ken-tuck-y, We're go-ing to the fair To see the se-ño-ri-ta with flo-wers in her hair. So shake it, shake it, shake it, Shake it if you dare, Shake it like a milk-shake and shake it here to there. Roll it to the bot-tom and roll it to the top, And turn a-round and turn a-round and turn a-round and stop!

The Old North State

🔊 Audio G204

Traditional Song

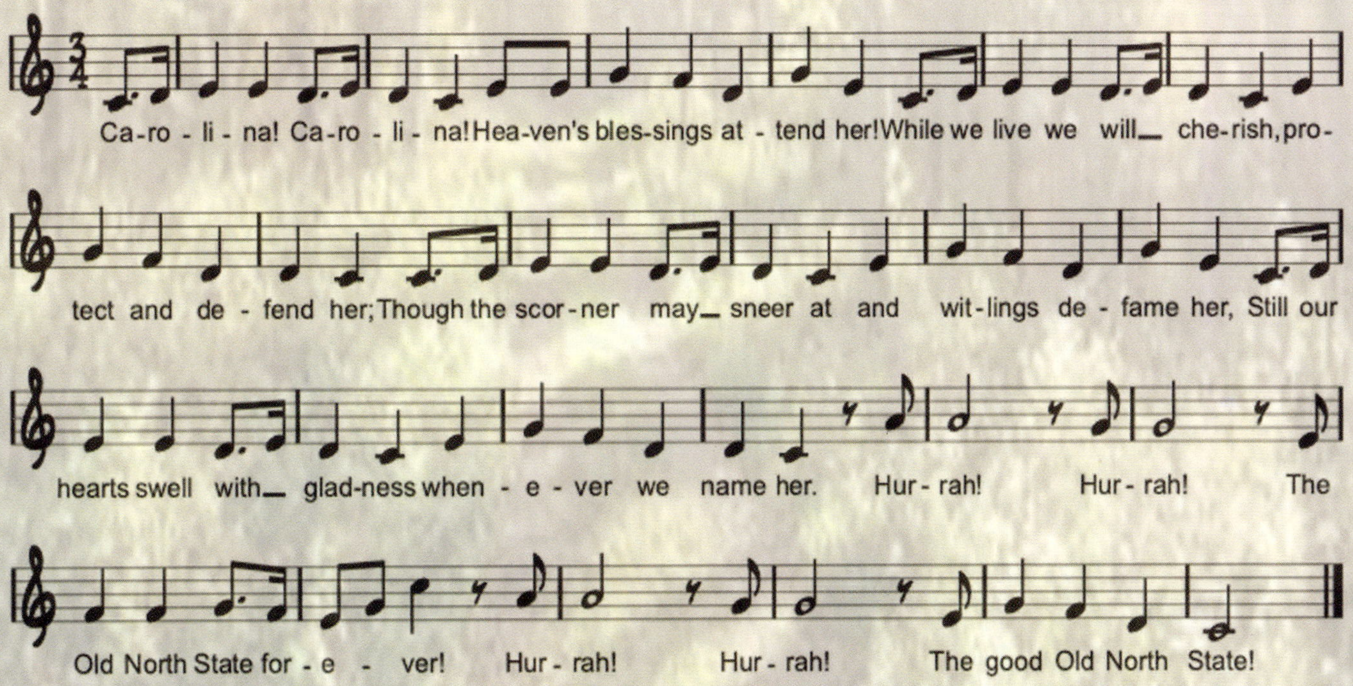

Ca-ro-li-na! Ca-ro-li-na! Hea-ven's bles-sings at-tend her! While we live we will che-rish, pro-tect and de-fend her; Though the scor-ner may sneer at and wit-lings de-fame her, Still our hearts swell with glad-ness when-e-ver we name her. Hur-rah! Hur-rah! The Old North State for-e-ver! Hur-rah! Hur-rah! The good Old North State!

Old Folks at Home

Audio G205

Stephen Foster

Moderately

1. Way down up-on the Swan-ee riv-er, Far, far a-way,
2. All 'round the lit-tle farm I wan-dered, When I was young,
3. One lit-tle hut a-mong the bush-es, One that I love,

That's where my heart is turn-ing ev-er, That's where the old folks stay;
Then man-y hap-py days I squan-dered, Man-y the songs I sung;
Still sad-ly to my mem-'ry rush-es, No mat-ter where I rove;

All up and down the whole cre-a-tion, Sad-ly I roam,
When I was play-ing with my broth-er, Hap-py was I,
When will I see the bees a-hum-ming, All 'round the comb,

Still long-ing for the old plan-ta-tion, And for the old folks at home.
Oh! take me to my kind old moth-er, There let me live and die.
When will I hear the ban-jo strum-ming, Down in my good old home.

All the world is sad and drea-ry, Eve-ry-where I roam,

Oh! broth-er, how my heart grows wea-ry, Far from the old folks at home.

Meet Me in St. Louis

Kerry Mills (1904)
Andrew B. Sterling

1. Now Louis came home to the flat, He hung up his coat and his hat, He gazed all around but no wifey he found So he said, "Where can Flossie be at?" A note on the table he spied He read it just once, then he cried, It ran, "Louis dear, it's too slow for me here So I think I will go for a ride."

Refrain
Meet me in St. Louis, Louis, Meet me at the fair. Don't tell me the lights are shining Any place but there. We will dance the hoochee koochee. I will be your tootsie wootsie. Won't you meet me in St. Louis, Louis, Meet me at the fair."

Home Means Nevada

Audio G207

Cameron R. Tolbert

-155-

Utah, We Love Thee

Audio G208

Evan Stephens (1895)

Utah's official state hymn is "Utah, We Love Thee" Evan Stephens, a Utah native, wrote the song in 1895. It was first performed at Utah's 45th statehood celebrations in 1896. From 1890 to 1916, Evan Stephens was the conductor of the Mormon Tabernacle Choir. In 1937, the Utah State Legislature declared "Utah, We Love Thee" to be the official state song.

1. Land of the mountains high, U-tah, we love thee!
2. Co-lum-bia's new-est star, U-tah, we love thee!
3. Land of the Pi-o-neers, U-tah, we love thee!

Land of the sun-ny sky, U-tah, we love thee!
Thy lus-tre shines a-far, U-tah, we love thee!
Grow with the com-ing years, U-tah, we love thee!

Far in the glo-rious west, Throned on the moun-tain's crest,
Bright in our ban-ner's blue, A-mong her sis-ter's true,
With wealth and peace in store, To fame and glo-ry soar,

In robes of state-hood dressed, U-tah, we love thee!
She proud-ly comes to view, U-tah, we love thee!
God-guard-ed ev-er-more, U-tah, we love thee!

Slowly learn these words and melody and gradually pick up the speed. Learn to sing the song with good intonation, rhythm, interpretation, and good pronunciation of each word. Pay attention to the accents, fermata, dynamics, note values, as well as silent beats (rest). Repeat a few times until you feel comfortable singing the entire song. Practice clapping the rhythm while singing.

Glossary of Musical Terms

accelerando: steadily increasing the rhythmic beat's pace.
accent: accent, emphasis
adagio: a slow tempo
allegro: a fast tempo
alto: a low-ranged female voice; the second-lowest instrumental range.
baritone: a moderately low male voice; in the range between a tenor and a bass.
Baroque Era: c1600-1750; a musical age characterized by highly ornate and intricate approaches to the arts. The growth of instrumental music, the invention of the modern violin family, and the founding of the first orchestras occurred during this period (Vivaldi, Handel, JS Bach).
bass: the lowest male voice
beat: a musical pulse
blues: Afro-American secular music in a melancholy style focused on a basic musical/poetic structure.
chord: a harmonic combination in which three or more pitches sound at the same time
chromaticism: harmonic or melodic movement by half-step intervals
counter-melody: a secondary melodic idea that accompanies and opposes a main thematic idea
da capo: a written indication telling a performer to go back to the start of a piece.
diatonic: a melody or harmony built on one of the Western seven-tone major or minor scales.
ensemble: a group of musical performers.
form: an elemental category that defines the shape/design of a musical work or movement.
genre: a form of musical composition that falls into one of several categories (the specific classification of a musical work).
improvisation: the term used to describe the "on-the-spot" creation of music (while it is being performed).
interval: the calculated distance between two musical pitches.
jazz: a style of American modern popular music combining African and Western musical traits
key signature: sharps and flats immediately following the clef sign. These sharps and flats (accidentals) affect every note on the line or space they represent throughout the composition.
Koto: a 13-stringed Japanese plucked instrument with movable bridges.
leitmotif: is a "short, recurring musical phrase" associated with a particular person, place, or idea.
major key: music based on a major scale (traditionally considered "happy" sounding).
major scale: a family of seven alphabetically ordered pitches within the distance of an octave, following an intervallic pattern matching the white keys from "C" to "C" on a piano).
minor key: music based on a minor scale (traditionally considered "sad" sounding).
minor scale: a family of seven alphabetically ordered pitches within the distance of an octave, following an intervallic pattern matching the white keys from "A" to "A" on a piano).
musikdrama: (genre) a form of ultra-dramatic German operatic theatre created by Richard Wagner in the mid/late Romantic era.
notation: a method of writing down the music so that crucial aspects of its performance can be correctly recreated.
ostinato: a brief rhythmic/melodic concept that is repeated over and over in a musical section or work.
pentatonic scale: a folk or non-western scale with five distinct notes within an octave.
phrase: a musical "sentence" often 4-8 measures long.
progression: a series of chords that functions similarly to a sentence or phrase in written language
rondo form: a musical form made up of three or more contrasting parts, one of which is repeated, such as ABACA.
scale: a family of pitches arranged in an ascending/descending order
syncopation: an "off-the-beat" accent
tonality: the tonic or key tone that a piece of music is based around.
tonic: the very first note on any scale. If the key is C major, the tonic is C.
unison: both singers or musicians sing or play the same notes, either at the same pitch or in a different octave.
upbeat: the weak beat that comes before the strong downbeat of a musical measure
whole step: an interval twice the size of a half-step (Ex.: the distance between C and D on the piano).